Nature in
Its Greatest
Extent

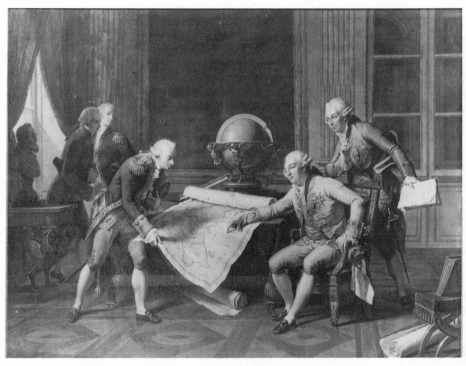

Louis XVI giving final instructions to the Comte de la Pérouse, 1785,
by N. A. Monsiau (Musées Nationaux)

Nature in Its Greatest Extent

Western Science in the Pacific

EDITED BY

Roy MacLeod

AND

Philip F. Rehbock

UNIVERSITY OF HAWAII PRESS
HONOLULU, HAWAII

Library of Congress Cataloging-in-Publication Data

International Congress on the History of Sciences (17th: 1985:
   University of California, Berkeley)
   Nature in its greatest extent: Western science in the Pacific/
edited by Roy MacLeod and Philip F. Rehbock.
      p.   cm.
   "Papers in this volume were presented at the XVIIth International
Congress of History of Science, University of California, Berkeley,
31 July–8 August 1985"—T.p. verso.
   Includes index.
   ISBN 0-8248-1120-8
   1.   Science—Pacific Area—History—Congresses.   2.   Scientists-
-Pacific Area—Biography—Congresses.   3.   Science—Europe—History-
-Congresses.   I.   MacLeod, Roy M.   II.   Rehbock, Philip F., 1942–
III.   Title.
Q127.P23I56   1985   87–30069
509.182'3—dc19   CIP

Early versions of most of the
papers in this volume were presented at the
XVIIth International Congress of History of Science
University of California, Berkeley
31 July–8 August 1985

Acts, Volume VII

My object was nature in its greatest extent: the Earth, the Sea, the Air, the Organic and Animated Creation, and more particularly that class of Beings to which we ourselves belong.
—Johann Reinhold Forster, *Observations made during a Voyage round the World . . .*

Contents

Part III. Pacific Science in the Making

Figures

Preface

The Pacific century, we are often told, is upon us, or will be by the end of the next decade. Within the space of one generation, we have seen a rapid shift in the world's economic center of gravity from the Atlantic to the Asia-Pacific region, with vast potential political and military consequences. With this shift is emerging a new sense of shared experience among nations bordering the Pacific rim, quickened by the dynamics of modern economic production, resource management, and international trade. The role of Japan in the world economy has already become one of the most significant factors of our time. But today the newly industrializing countries of South Korea, Taiwan, Hong Kong, and Malaysia are also of rising importance, already supplying over half the Third World's total exports. Their dynamism will set dramatic challenges to those concerned with the destiny of the Pacific. So too will new developments in ocean-floor survey, minerals and fisheries, and the politics of nuclear testing.

While the factors underlying these developments are demonstrably political and economic, there are also important cultural dimensions. With a sense of "Pacific destiny" has come a sense of partnership and a new recognition of the importance of improving Pan-Pacific communication. The last decade has seen many attempts to encourage a more Pacific view of the art, literature, anthropology, and ethnology of the region. The enormity of the task is sufficient to explain the slow progress so far achieved in finding common cause among cultures that are neighbors in ways almost too complex to imagine. Yet, certain factors have united the region. And among these has been the history of European exploration, acquisition, and science. Long after Asian voyagers first traversed the ocean, and migrations formed island communities, European interests came to stay. In this process, the Pacific became, by the late eighteenth century, the scene of some of the most important work in European science.

The impact of the Pacific on the modern European mind has filled countless volumes of romance and scholarship. But despite the effects of two world wars, the influence of European (and its offspring, American) science on the Pacific is still largely unexplored. Historians of science await a literary *Endeavour* to survey the world and report on those sciences that sailed with the "expansion of Europe," beyond the Tasman and around the Horn, from the Bering Straits to the Beagle Channel, from the China Sea to the Antarctic ice fields.

This ambitious task awaits collective enterprise. We offer in this volume a collection of essays arising from a symposium on Western science in the Pacific, held at the XVIIth International Congress of History of Science at Berkeley, California, in August 1985. At a time when our profession is still predominantly Eurocentric in its traditions, it does us no harm to look at the "new" Pacific. There we find the material and intellectual products of both European enterprise and native sagacity, sometimes juxtaposed, occasionally interacting, and inevitably fascinating.

In every sense, the symposium—like this book—was Western in focus; the natural knowledge possessed by Pacific peoples remains a subject for symposia yet to come. To encourage this expanding program, a "Pacific Circle" of interested scholars has been formed, and a newsletter is now issued from the History Department of the University of Hawaii.

In the organization of the Berkeley symposium and the later compilation of this book, we have accumulated many debts. We must particularly acknowledge the assistance of Bruce Wheaton of the University of California, Berkeley, Judith Diment of the British Museum (Natural History, London), and David Stoddart in Cambridge; and the cooperation of several symposium participants who were unable to contribute essays—including Michele Aldrich, Rod Home, Alan Leviton, Peter Lingwood, Beth Newland, Elaine Shaughnessy, Garry Tee, and Masao Watanabe. We would also like to record our thanks to Karen Rehbock in Honolulu; and to Ruth Bennett, Diane O'Donovan, Jeanette Neeson, and Melanie Oppenheimer in Sydney. Sailing in unfamiliar currents is usually hazardous, and during a period that has seen the America's Cup return from Australia to America, we are particularly glad to report cordial teamwork from both American and Australian crews.

Roy MacLeod   Philip F. Rehbock
Sydney   Honolulu

Introduction

*I*T has been over a quarter-century since Bernard Smith in his *European Vision and the South Pacific* taught us to look at the Pacific with the eyes of an artist, controlled in the service of science.[1] Even then it was clear that the opening of the Pacific to the Western world represented to a high degree the victory of an empirical appeal to nature, born of the scientific revolution of the seventeenth century, clothed in Baconian precept, and employed in expeditions and discoveries over the next two hundred years.

Scholars now have no difficulty in seeing the Pacific as a historical laboratory for scientific methods and mentalities, as well as an atelier for European art and anthropology. From the abundant diversity of the Pacific, early explorers, surviving great hardships and loneliness, amassed an incalculable legacy: from their travels and collections, their descriptions and narrations, came discoveries that transformed European ideas of evolution and change. The Pacific, while opening new realms for European acquisition, also challenged European views of man's place in nature, presenting evidence that ultimately broke the great "chain of being," unravelled the neoclassical fabric of the fixity of species, undermined the argument from design, and expanded European conceptions of geological time.

But if in the hundred years after Cook the Pacific became a veritable school for science, and a vast classroom for educating the European mind, so it also became a great oceanic stage for the deployment of Western political, military, economic, and religious

I

interests. By steps that appear sometimes deliberate, but more often inadvertent, the European presence in the Pacific saw a convergence of focus: the "swing to the East" met the voyagers from the West. The motives guiding Pacific expeditions from Europe were usually mixed. International prestige, the promise of strategic sites, sources of tropical products and customers for manufactured goods, converts to Christianity—all these and many other objectives appear in Europe's rendering of Pacific history.

For some time, the history of Western science has had at best a peripheral relationship with Pacific history. Research on Pacific subjects has been a limited, localized activity, pursued by a handful of scholars, often working from traditional disciplines and national perspectives. The "new Pacific" must continue to reflect the history of individual disciplines and the rivalries between European nation-states. But if we are on the threshold of a new era, one in which the Pacific, having once been peripheral to European scholars, is now becoming central, then a special significance attaches to our understanding of science and its usages in the region as a whole. Such an understanding must embrace not only the role of the Pacific in shaping Western views of nature, but also the role of the sciences in influencing relationships among "Pacific peoples"—including those nations which, in addition to the islands of Oceania, have become represented as Pacific powers.

In this volume, we take the term "Pacific" to have geographical, historical, and political meanings. Geographically, it encompasses the island chains of the Pacific and the coastlines of the Pacific "rim"; thus, Melanesia, Micronesia, and Polynesia are Pacific by definition, as are the coastlines of Australasia, Antarctica, and the Aleutians, and so the Americas, China, and Japan. At times, even this broad definition can hardly be considered adequate, as areas reached by Europeans through or en route to the Pacific—including South Korea, the Philippines, and the East Indies—can also be considered part of the Pacific region.[2] Politically and historically, the Pacific includes the activities of European powers whose interests led them into the region. A useful image may be that of three concentric circles: the island groups of Polynesia, Micronesia, and Melanesia occupying the center; the Pacific rim surrounding these island groups constituting a second ring; and the Euro-Pacific nations, a third.

Within this context, the following essays form contributions to what might be called the history of Pacific science. We take "Pacific science" to include the sciences of the island and oceanic circle; the scientific endeavors of rim nations that relate specifically to the Pacific, both historically and geographically; and the practices of European (or Atlantic) nations insofar as they refer to Pacific questions. To date, the history of Pacific science may be said to have a tradition without a literature. The *ISIS Cumulative Bibliography*[3] has no separate category for science relating to the Pacific as such. Its index refers the reader to the Asian-Pacific region, to Australia and New Zealand, or (perhaps following anthropological conventions) to Southeast Asia. Other sources, including S. A. Jayawardene's recent *Reference Books for the Historian of Science,*[4] fail to mention the Pacific in their indexes; and bibliographies of the history of particular sciences, like Roy Porter's *The Earth Sciences: An Annotated Bibliography,* neglect the Pacific when organizing titles by geographic region or national tradition.[5]

These omissions reflect the nature of our predominantly Eurocentric scholarship. Perhaps they also mirror a belief of at least some historians of the physical sciences, that, viewed in a narrow sense (and until our own time), the Pacific has neither been a significant site for international science nor produced scientific institutions of more than local importance. But if this is so, it is not wholly so; and the bias of historical geographers and historians of exploration has leaned far in the other direction. One need mention only J. C. Beaglehole's classic, *The Exploration of the Pacific,* and Spate's multivolume *The Pacific since Magellan.*[6] Moreover, the scientific contributions of specific voyages, from Cook through Wilkes to HMS *Challenger,*[7] are now well-known, and although many lesser expeditions still await scholarly attention, their cumulative effect on European scholarship has been well recognized. Nevertheless, the history of science has yet to accept the Pacific and embrace newcomers in the history of Pacific science.

There are signs that this pattern is changing. Individual countries along the rim—including the United States, Canada, Mexico, and Chile—are looking more to the Pacific. Australia's active cadre of historians of science include some who are looking to Pacific questions,[8] and New Zealand and Japanese scholars have shown evidence of expanding into "regional" questions. In addition, scholars in the disciplines of Pacific science are continuing to contribute essential materials. Thus, New Guinea's botanical history has been examined by J. R. Croft, while that of Tahiti has been chronicled by Howard M. Smith; Polynesian ornithology has been well described by D. T. Holyoak and J. C. Thibault; and the work of naturalists in Hawaii has been brilliantly surveyed by E. Alison Kay.[9] There are clear opportunities, however, awaiting historians of Pacific anthropology and oceanography, for example, and social historians interested in science. We have as yet no work for the island groups comparable to that of Ann Moyal, Michael Hoare, C. A. Fleming, and F. R. Callaghan for Australia and New Zealand, or that of Pieter Honig and Frans Verdoorn for the Netherlands Indies.[10]

Possibly the single most abundant literature in the history of Pacific science is biographical, ranging from the numerous accounts of Cook and other members of his expeditions,[11] to careful studies of lesser figures, such as John Bastin's study of Joseph Arnold.[12] Anthropologists, especially Margaret Mead and Ruth Benedict, have received considerable biographical attention,[13] but less thoroughly treated and certainly ripe for investigation are the many naturalists and geologists who visited the Pacific in the wake of Joseph Banks and J. R. Forster.[14]

An important place in the recent history of science in the Pacific must be given to the influence of European imperialism. "Science follows the flag" is a respectable if overused catchphrase, and no one who recalls accounts of the "Spanish lake," or rediscovers the eponymy of Botany Bay can overlook the historical relationships that have long inspired motives for scientific discovery, geographical exploration, territorial conquest, colonial settlement, and trade. Equally, no one familiar with the history of scientific expeditions can overlook the history of conflict between the interests of science and the expectations of scientists; or the tensions between metropolis and periphery—between the "deep leather" strategists of South Kensington and the Académie des sciences, Whitehall and the Quay d'Orsay, and those who met the extremities of life in isolated, frequently hostile, and always alien regions of the earth. No one familiar with the history of imperialism and its contemporary consequences can ignore the problematic implications of European and American science and technology for colonial and postcolonial economic development. Nor can one overlook the powerful impetus given to scientific internationalism by the competitive spirit of Pacific exploration.

Within the overall framework of European contact, there arise many such themes of great importance. The work of Lewis Pyenson, among others,[15] has provided structures for further analysis.[16] But much remains to be said about the influence of explorers, missionaries, and medical men in discovering and transmitting knowledge about the Pacific to a wider world. Just as the history of Spanish and Portuguese science can scarcely be separated from Pacific sciences between 1500 and 1900, so historians of China, India, and Japan will remind us that the Pacific and its science was in many ways "known" to the world before it was known to Europe. The role of Asian nations in Pacific scientific expeditions during this century is already attracting attention.[17] Above all, perhaps, Western historians of science are recognizing the complex relationships that have arisen between European knowledge and indigenous "systems of belief." We have need to explore precontact, "Pacific" ways of perceiving nature, categorizing and cultivating plants and animals, treating disease, measuring time, observing the heavens, and following the movements of wind and sea.

With this expanding agenda before us, it is premature to do more than outline certain routes others may follow. The present volume has been limited to a small number of studies on questions that have classically interested Western scholars. Part I, "Europe in the Pacific," addresses the development of the region, the literature it generates, the knowledge it quickened, and the reputations it made for Europeans in the eighteenth and early nineteenth centuries. O. H. K. Spate illuminates the elusive quality of "new knowledge" in the Pacific in the century between Dampier and Vancouver—and discusses a species of description and accounting that reflects the mores and manners, as much as the philosophical methods, of Europe. He touches, too, upon the rivalry of European powers in their zeal to "know," thence to acquire and control positions of strategic usefulness. This point is also central to Alan Frost's analysis of Anglo-French intrigues, both before and after the Seven Years' War. Imperial interests, in his view, ultimately overshadowed scientific motives.

Against the rhetorical endorsement of "scientific internationalism," so widely advertised by Banks and Franklin,[18] emerges a picture of struggle transferred and contests renewed, from the New World that was already known, to the great "southern continent" that lay unknown. Meanwhile, Isabel Ollivier and Miranda

Hughes consider the impact of the Pacific on several key navigators—notably Pierre Lesson, Nicolas Baudin, and François Péron
—who mediated the Pacific message that Europeans eventually
received. The distance that separated their instructions from their
actual observations reveals both the triumphal hopes and the
tragic conclusions that European art, science, and literature were
to draw from Pacific nature and natural man.

In Part II, our authors examine certain constructions of imperial
science, principally as viewed from Britain and Australia, with the
political connotations these acquired. David Frodin charts the
contributions of New Guinea to Western scientific knowledge and,
moving south, Barry Butcher and Roy MacLeod explore the imperial relations of science in colonial Australia. From the general to
the particular, these studies reveal aspects of the imperial relationship, and the complexity of factors that actuated scientific life on
the "moving frontier." In this section, the absence of New Zealand
material is sorely missed, for from trans-Tasman comparisons
there is much to learn; as no doubt there is from the imperial styles
of other major European powers, whose naval presence, especially
after the 1880s, presaged the political divisions of the Pacific
today.

Finally, Part III considers three examples of Pacific enterprise,
reflecting the collective efforts of Pacific nations and the politics of
the United States and the Soviet Union. Both dimensions are likely
to make the region one of more, rather than less, active interest to
historians of science in the years ahead. Philip Rehbock assesses
the internationalist spirit that inspired a generation of Americans
after 1918 to encourage intellectual cooperation in the Pacific, just
as the victorious Allies conceived a new framework for postwar
scientific union in Europe. That the idealism of Pan-Pacific cooperation still endures is underscored by Harry Scheiber's account of
American enthusiasm for Pacific exploration after the Second
World War. In the meantime, "scientific entrepreneurship," linked
with understanding the ocean environment, has become an important objective of the Soviet Union, whose activities in Pacific
marine biology are discussed by Robert Randolph and John Bardach.

The interplay of science and strategy, familiar to the Pacific
since Magellan, appears no less evident today. Historians will one
day write of Pacific nuclear testing and of Asian "scientific imperi-

alism" in the Pacific region. If such subjects lie beyond the scope of this book, they cannot remain absent from the wider frame of reference we seek to encourage. Since the war, we have seen many attempts to make "peace in the Pacific" an enduring tautology. The hour of a "Pacific community," in the phrase of Gough Whitlam, has yet to come. But we look to the hope, as we maintain the principle.

Notes

1. Bernard Smith, *European Vision and the South Pacific, 1768–1850; A Study in the History of Art and Ideas* (Oxford: Oxford University Press, 1960).

2. D. Alsmeyer and A. G. Atkins, *Guide to Science and Technology in the Asia Pacific Area: A Reference Guide* (Harlow, England: Francis Hodgson, 1979); *Pacific Research Centres: A Directory of Organizations in Science, Technology, Agriculture and Medicine* (Harlow, England: Longman Group, 1986). The latter contains descriptions of thirty-five hundred institutions it regards as belonging to the Western Pacific, principally in Australia, Brunei, the People's Republic of China, Hong Kong, Indonesia, Japan, Korea, Malaysia, New Zealand, Papua New Guinea, the Philippines, Singapore, Taiwan, Thailand, and Vietnam. The only Pacific basin countries included are Fiji, Kiribati, New Caledonia, Samoa, Solomon Islands, and Vanuatu.

3. Magda Whitrow, ed., *ISIS Cumulative Bibliography 1913–65,* vol. 3 (London: Mansell, 1976).

4. S. A. Jayawardene, *Reference Books for the Historian of Science* (London: Science Museum, 1982).

5. Roy Porter, *The Earth Sciences: An Annotated Bibliography* (New York, London: Garland Publishing, 1983).

6. J. C. Beaglehole, *The Exploration of the Pacific,* 3d ed. (London: Stanford University Press, 1966); O. H. K. Spate, *The Pacific since Magellan,* vol. 1: *The Spanish Lake,* vol. 2: *Monopolists and Freebooters* (Canberra: Australian National University Press, 1979, 1983). See also Ernest S. Dodge, *Beyond the Capes: Pacific Exploration from Captain Cook to the 'Challenger,' 1776–1877* (Boston: Little Brown, 1971); Christopher Lloyd, *Pacific Horizons: The Exploration of the Pacific before Captain Cook* (London: Allen and Unwin, 1946); A. Grenfell Price, *The Western Invasions of the Pacific and Its Continents: A Study of Moving Frontiers and Changing Landscapes, 1513–1958* (Oxford: Clarendon Press, 1963); Andrew Sharp, *The Discovery of the Pacific Islands* (Oxford: Clarendon Press, 1960); Herman R. Friis, *The Pacific Basin: A History of Its Geographical Exploration* (New York: American Geographical Society, 1967); John C. Dunmore, *French Explorers in the Pacific,* 2 vols. (Oxford: Clarendon Press, 1965).

7. The literature on Cook's voyages is considerable and still growing, especially since the 1978 bicentenary of Cook's death. A selection of papers given at the Cook conference in British Columbia appears in Robin Fisher and Hugh

Johnston, eds., *Captain James Cook and His Times* (Vancouver: Douglas and McIntyre, 1979). See also T. C. Mitchell, ed., *Captain Cook and the South Pacific* (London: British Museum Publications, 1979). On the natural history of Cook's voyages, see P. J. P. Whitehead, "Zoological Specimens from Captain Cook's Voyages," *Journal of the Society for the Bibliography of Natural History* 5 (1969): 161–201; William T. Stearn, "The Botanical Results of the *Endeavour* Voyage," *Endeavour* 27 (1968): 3–10. The European background for the first voyage is described in H. Woolf, *The Transits of Venus: A Study of Eighteenth-Century Science* (Princeton: Princeton University Press, 1959). For the Wilkes expedition, see W. R. Stanton, *The Great United States Exploring Expedition of 1838–42* (Berkeley and Los Angeles: University of California Press, 1975); and H. J. Viola and C. Margolis, eds., *Magnificent Voyagers: The U.S. Exploring Expedition, 1838–1842* (Washington, D.C.: Smithsonian Institution Press, 1986). Of the substantial literature on the *Challenger* expedition, Eric Linklater's *The Voyage of the Challenger* (London: John Murray, 1972) is the most recent and best illustrated account. J. Sinclair, *Wings of Gold* (Sydney: Pacific Publications, 1980), describes the Brandes and Archbold expeditions in New Guinea. And Peter Lingwood has investigated the natural history of the voyage of HMS *Blossom* in "Admiral Sir Edward Belcher (1790–1877): Natural History Catalyst or Catastrophe?" in *From Linnaeus to Darwin: Commentaries on the History of Biology and Geology* (London: Society for the History of Natural History, 1985), 195–203.

8. See Ann Mozley Moyal, Elizabeth Newland, and Irene Davey, *Science, Technology, and Society in Australia: A Bibliography* (Brisbane: Griffith University, 1978); Colin M. Finney, *To Sail Beyond the Sunset: Natural History in Australia, 1699–1829* (Adelaide: Rigby, 1984); Winston G. McMinn, "Botany and Geography in Early Australia: A Case Study," *Records of the Australian Academy of Science* 2 (1970): 1–9; T. G. Vallance, "Origins of Australian Geology," *Proceedings of the Linnean Society of New South Wales* 100 (1975): 13–14; David F. Brannagan and K. A. Townley, "The Geological Sciences in Australia—A Brief Historical Review," *Earth Science Review* 12 (1976): 323–346; R. W. Home and Masao Watanabe, "Physics in Australia and Japan to 1914: A Comparison," *Annals of Science* 44 (1987): 215–235.

9. J. R. Croft, "An Historical Survey of Botanical Exploration in the Admiralty Islands, Manus Province, Papua New Guinea," *Science in New Guinea* 10 (1983): 1–15; Howard M. Smith, "History of the Botanical Exploration of the Society Islands," in Martin Lawrence Grant et al., *Partial Flora of the Society Islands: Ericaceae to Apocynaceae*, Smithsonian Contributions to Botany, No. 17 (Washington: Smithsonian Institution Press, 1974), 54–69; D. T. Holyoak and J. C. Thibault, "L'Exploration ornithologique de la Polynesie Orientale," *Journal de la Société des Oceanistes* 38, nos. 75, 76 (1982): 259–273; E. Alison Kay, "Hawaiian Natural History: 1778–1900," in *A Natural History of the Hawaiian Islands: Selected Readings* (Honolulu: University of Hawaii Press, 1972), 604–653.

10. Ann Moyal, *Bright and Savage Land* (Sydney: William Collins, 1986); M. E. Hoare and L. E. Bell, eds., "In Search of New Zealand's Scientific Heritage," *Royal Society of New Zealand, Bulletin* 21 (1984); C. A. Fleming, "Sci-

ence, Settlers and Scholars," *Royal Society of New Zealand, Bulletin* 25 (1987); F. R. Callaghan, ed., *Science in New Zealand* (Wellington: A. H. and A. W. Reed, 1957); Pieter Honig and Frans Verdoorn, eds., *Science and Scientists in the Netherlands Indies* (New York: Board for the Netherlands Indies, Surinam and Curacao, 1945).

11. Alan Villier, *Captain Cook, the Seaman's Seaman: A Study of the Great Discoverer* (London: Hodder and Stoughton, 1978); Daniel Conner and Lorraine Miller, *Master Mariner: Capt. James Cook and the Peoples of the Pacific* (Seattle: University of Washington Press for the Vancouver Museums and Planetarium Association, 1978); Tom Stamp and Cordelia Stamp, *James Cook, Maritime Scientist* (Whitby: Caedmon of Whitby Press, 1978). A massive Cook bibliography, including manuscript sources, is M. K. Beddie, ed., *Bibliography of Captain James Cook,* 2d ed. (Sydney: State Library of New South Wales, 1970). For the lives of some of Cook's fellow voyagers, see H. C. Cameron, *Sir Joseph Banks* (London: Batchworth Press, 1952); Charles Lyte, *Sir Joseph Banks* (Newton Abbot: David and Charles, 1980); Michael E. Hoare, *The Tactless Philosopher, Johann Reinhold Forster, 1729–98* (Melbourne: Hawthorne Press, 1976); D. J. Carr, ed., *Sydney Parkinson, Artist of Cook's Endeavour Voyage* (London: British Museum [Natural History] in association with Australian National University Press, 1983); Roy A. Rauschenberg, "Daniel Carl Solander: Naturalist on the *Endeavour*," *Transactions of the American Philosophical Society* 58, no. 8 (1968): 1–66.

12. John Bastin, "Dr. Joseph Arnold and the Discovery of *Rafflesia arnoldi* in West Sumatra in 1818," *Journal of the Society for the Bibliography of Natural History* 6 (1973): 305–372.

13. Derek Freeman, *Margaret Mead and Samoa: The Making and Unmaking of an Anthropological Myth* (Cambridge, Mass.: Harvard University Press, 1983); Jane Howard, *Margaret Mead: A Life* (London: Harvill, 1984); Judith Modell, *Ruth Benedict: Patterns of a Life* (Philadelphia: University of Pennsylvania Press, 1983); James Clifford, *Person and Myth: Maurice Leenhardt in the Melanesian World* (Berkeley and Los Angeles: University of California Press, 1982). See also Michael C. Howard, "Social Scientists in Paradise," *Journal of Pacific Studies* 9 (1983): 1–8; idem, "A Preliminary Survey of Anthropology and Sociology in the South Pacific," *Journal of Pacific Studies* 9 (1983): 70–132.

14. Elena Grainger, *The Remarkable Reverend Clarke: The Life and Times of the Father of Australian Geology* (Melbourne: Oxford University Press, 1982); M. Jacobs, *Herman Johannes Lam* (Amsterdam: Rhodopi, 1983); A. Webster, *The Moon Man* (Melbourne: Melbourne University Press, 1985), a biography of Nicholas Miklouhou-Maclay. There have been some useful autobiographical accounts by scientist themselves, which, for the historian, can never be too abundant. See, for example, Lee Saunders Crandall, *Paradise Quest: A Naturalist's Experiences in New Guinea* (New York: Charles Scribner's Sons, 1931); and David Fairchild, *Garden Islands of the Great East: Collecting Seeds from the Philippines and Netherlands India in the Junk 'Cheng Ho'* (New York: Charles Scribner's Sons, 1943).

15. Lewis Pyenson, "Cultural Imperialism and Exact Sciences: German Expansion Overseas, 1900–1930," *History of Science* 20 (1982): 1–43; idem, "Astron-

omy and Imperialism: J. A. C. Oudemans, the Topography of the East Indies, and the Rise of the Utrecht Observatory, 1850–1900," *Historia Scientiarum* 26 (1984): 39–81; idem, "Functionaries and Seekers in Latin America: Missionary Diffusion of the Exact Sciences, 1850–1930," *Quipu* 2 (1985): 387–420. See also Roy MacLeod, "On Visiting the 'Moving Metropolis': Reflections on the Architecture of Imperial Science," *Historical Records of Australian Science* 5 (1982): 1–16; D. R. Headrick, *The Tools of Empire: Technology and European Imperialism in the Nineteenth Century* (New York: Oxford University Press, 1981).

16. Lucile H. Brockway, *Science and Colonial Expansion: The Role of the British Royal Botanic Gardens* (London: Academic Press, 1979); A. P. Elkin, *Pacific Science Association: Its History and Role in International Cooperation* (Honolulu: Bishop Museum Press, 1961); Sir George Currie and J. Grahame, *The Origins of CSIRO: Science and the Commonwealth Government, 1901–1926* (Melbourne: CSIRO, 1966); R. Strahan, *Rare and Curious Specimens: An Illustrated History of the Australian Museum, 1827–1979* (Sydney: The Australian Museum, 1979). Joanneke de Bruin and Lewis Pyenson have examined the early development of the Royal Magnetical and Meteorological Observatory in Jakarta, in " 'Gentleman-Scientist': Elie van Rijckevorsel and the Dutch Overseas Effort in Exact Sciences at the End of the Nineteenth Century," *Annals of Science* 43 (1986): 447–473.

17. Tōru Yano, *Nihon No Nanyōshikan* (A Japanese View of the History of the Southern Seas) (Tokyo: Chūōkōron Sha, 1979); cf. also Taeko Stubbs, "Japanese Scientific Exploration in the Pacific Region, 1900–39" (M.A. thesis, University of Sydney, in preparation.)

18. Gavin de Beer, *The Sciences Were Never at War* (London: Thomas Nelson and Sons, 1960).

PART I
EUROPE IN THE PACIFIC

1

Seamen and Scientists:
The Literature of the Pacific,
1697–1798

O. H. K. SPATE

CURIOUSLY enough, despite the fact that a ship launched for Charles I's ship-money navy in 1637 was named *Sovereign of the Seas,* in the seventeenth century the nation that made that immodest claim produced singularly little literature on maritime travel. Richard Hakluyt of course was a host in himself, but he was too old-fashioned to be admitted into the world of polite literature, and there was no reprint of his *Principal Navigations* between 1600 and 1809, and no great collection of voyages between *Purchas His Pilgrimes* in 1625 and the next century.[1] The only notable works with a Pacific bearing before 1697 are *The Observations of Sir Richard Hawkins* (1622), *Sir Francis Drake Revived* (1626), *The World Encompassed by Sir Francis Drake* (1628), and then a long gap until the account of John Narborough's voyage (1694), the first and last dealing with abortive raids on Chile and Peru.

Then in 1697 William Dampier preluded a century in which voyage accounts streamed from the presses until those of Jean-François de la Pérouse and George Vancouver, both published in 1798. And there were the great collections of voyages such as those compiled by John Harris and John Campbell, Charles de Brosses and his impudent plagiarist John Callender, and David Henry, all but the last more or less tied up with Terra Australis Incognita.[2]

It was this span of 101 years that revealed the Pacific Islanders to Europe and gave them a place in the history of ideas, a place they lost with the rise of evangelical missions and commercial enterprise in the South Pacific, which regarded them as benighted heathen or mere suppliers of goods and services. This place was not regained until the advent of modern anthropology. This chapter will not deal with fiction—there was none based on firsthand experience—except to note that the South Seas became a preferred locus, perhaps *the* preferred locus, for highly subversive Utopias (including a most sentimental and conventionally moral one by the Marquis de Sade), a fascinating chapter in the history of European thought.[3] The influence of the islands on Romanticism far exceeded their negligible economic significance. Europe could do without coconuts, and it was not until the nineteenth century that the Pacific's whales became the great suppliers of lamps and corsets; but the Tahitian Venus and the noble savage fired the imaginations of poets and philosophers, most of the poets, at least, poor ones. The impact of the islands was overwhelming in the Age of Feeling, which was also the age of the great circumnavigations.

In 1697 Dampier's *New Voyage round the World* added a new dimension to British publishing. It was an instant best-seller, five editions in six years, and his publisher, James Knapton, became a specialist in the genre. Dampier was one of those great artless artists, a born writer, a serious and acute observer of the natural and human worlds, curiously aloof from his ribald companions, keeping his notes safely in a bamboo through the tropical jungles of Panama. He took "savages" as he found them, like his comrade Lionel Wafer,[4] not as pegs for sensationalism but as natural men and women: he had none of Defoe's grisly fixation on cannibalism (that superb journalist knew his market). And there was no one like Dampier for vividness until George Forster.

Of course Dampier claimed to be no more than an unlettered seaman, anxious that the polite and educated reader should make allowance for his inelegant writing. This was expected of him; he was followed by James Cook in the famous passage on his ascent from prentice boy on a collier to Post Captain RN, and a hundred years after Dampier, Vancouver echoes the modest protestation.[5] But Dampier influenced more sophisticated professionals. Defoe draws on him in eight of his fictions;[6] Swift's genius took him into regions beyond Dampier's ken, but the travels of Gulliver are inspired parodies of the South Sea voyage genre—all are set in the Pacific, and the book begins with Captain Lemuel Gulliver referring to "my cousin Dampier." And Coleridge found the right word for him: "a rough sailor, but a man of exquisite mind."[7]

Dampier had also less literary followers, buccaneers and privateers—Funnell, Betagh, Shelvocke, Woodes Rogers—all with axes to grind, producing tales of derring-do padded with ill-digested history and geography of the Spanish empire, pointing out the weaknesses and extolling the riches of that constant magnet for Britain's predatory instincts. They also used the unlettered-seaman ploy, with more reason than did Dampier, and their books are loaded with useful but tedious nauticalities.

In 1726 Dampier himself was introduced into William Chetwood's *Voyages and Adventures of Captain Robert Boyle,* which married the buccaneer voyage with the picaresque novel. Buccaneer narratives were the progenitors of three centuries of popular fiction, down to the subliterature of the airport bookstalls of our own day. But one of the best-loved poems in the English language, *The Rime of the Ancient Mariner,* reproduces the pattern of a buccaneer voyage to the South Seas, and Coleridge took the Albatross direct from the privateer Shelvocke.[8] Cowper's "monarch of all I survey" also comes directly from another privateer, Woodes Rogers.

The first breach with the apologetic tradition of the uncouth sailor-writer came with George Anson's *Voyage;* published in 1748, this was another best-seller with over eighteen hundred prepublication subscribers and five editions in seven months. It was not overloaded with the technical detail of positions fixed and courses set (though these were not neglected); it was organized chronologically but was not just a chronological outpouring, rather a carefully structured work, a patriotic epic, ghosted by competent writers; in short, a great contrast to "the slipshod literary efforts of Anson's privateering predecessors."[9] It also had its literary heritage: it gave a hint to Montesquieu and shocked Voltaire; Rousseau's Saint-Preux in *La Nouvelle Héloïse* endeavors to forget his sorrows by sailing with Anson; and one of the harrowing passages on disease and tempest on the real voyage inspired Cowper's incomparably plangent poem *The Castaway.*[10]

Anson's *Voyage* became to some extent a model for the narratives of the great explorations after 1764, which however had a new element in detailed descriptions of the manners of the South Sea Islanders; Anson had met none of them. Of course, manners and customs had always been a part of travel literature, but they were now to be observed with a new detachment and deliberation, as an essential, not just a curious or sensational ingredient. These voyages coincide with the rise of "sentiment" in literature; it is highly appropriate and symbolic that two diploma-pieces of the movement, Laurence Sterne's *Sentimental Journey* and Henry Mackenzie's *Man of Feeling,* its every chapter bathed in tears, should have been published in 1768 and 1771, the opening and closing years of Cook's first voyage. And "feeling" then meant what "caring" means today, only more so.

It was the age of the cult of Rousseau's "noble savage," who incidentally had nothing to do with Jean-Jacques; the man had enough real bastards without having this fictitious one fathered on him, but then clichés are stubborn things. It is surprising that good writers can go on repeating this time-dishonored phrase fifty years after Fairchild and Lovejoy. In fact, what Rousseau is talking about in the discourse on inequality is an amoral isolate, an ape or at best a missing link, not really a human being.[11] But his rhetoric suited an age given to self-righteous moralizing and "elevation of style" that often topped over into pomposity. So, would a public used to such a grandiloquence have accepted a simple sailor's tale?

Yes, if it contained something more exciting than new geography. Anson's voyage with its dangers and distresses produced a good crop; the wreck and mutiny of his ship the *Wager* and the astonishing boat voyage of the mutineers from Chile to Brazil spawned half-a-dozen "ripping yarns."[12] And later on, of course, the mutiny of the *Bounty*—what an ocean of ink would have been saved if she had sunk with all hands before reaching Tahiti! A bit of sex did not come amiss, witness the lascivious "poems" about Omai, and Joseph Banks's alleged amours with Queen Purea; hence what the French aptly call the mirage of Tahiti, beautifully expressed by Erasmus Darwin:

> So where pleased VENUS, in the southern main,
> Sheds all her smiles on Otaheite's plain,
> Wide o'er the isle her silken net she draws,
> And the Loves laugh at all but Nature's laws.[13]

Bougainville's naturalist Philibert Commerson, a Rousseauist in excelsis, puts it perfectly: he says bluntly that he will not deal with trivial details of navigation, clearly the province of inferior minds;

he much prefers raptures about the Tahitian Venus.[14] Note also the common attitudes of Horace Walpole and Samuel Johnson, men poles apart in their understanding of life and its conduct, but both seeing no point whatsoever in going to the other side of the world to find new plants and meet poor Indians with untutored minds—at best "an account of the fishermen of forty islands."[15] The sailor's tale needed varnish.

The great expeditions, for all their ostensibly disinterested devotion to the advancement of knowledge, were quite as much devoted to the finding and preempting of potential economic and strategic openings; they were calculated moves in imperial rivalry. They used science as both a tool and a cover in the sparring of the then superpowers, Britain and France, for strategic positions of strength in the new world of the Pacific, as do the superpowers of today in the new world of space.

Hence the admiralities had a vested interest in checking or at least controlling the flow of information; they impounded the journals kept on board. This could be counterproductive. The public wanted to know, and there was a crop of free-lance "quickies" of varying authenticity after each of Cook's voyages. There was no immediate official publication from those of John Byron or Samuel Wallis or George Cartaret, only a great fuss in the press over Byron's meeting with the alleged Patagonian giants, a fuss probably fostered by the authorities with the political motive of throwing dust in Spanish eyes as to the first object of the expedition, the strategically placed Falkland Islands.[16]

However, Cook's first voyage fostered a more positive attitude. Its first objective was to observe the transit of Venus across the sun's disk, needed to establish the earth's distance from the sun. There had been a transit in 1761, when for one reason or another —partly bad luck—Britain had made a poor showing in comparison with some other countries. For the 1769 transit there was to be a great effort, with 270 astronomers from many countries observing from places as far apart as Hudson's Bay, Lower California, Norway, and the South Seas—what J. P. Faivre called the "International Venusian Year."[17] Hence Tahiti, discovered by Samuel Wallis only two years earlier and of course named for King George III, would be a very appropriate locale for a British effort, and after 1761 publicity was needed for the British share: a matter of national prestige.

And so John Hawkesworth was commissioned to write *An*

Account of the Voyages undertaken by the order of his present Majesty for making Discoveries in the Southern Hemisphere, published in June 1773. The work began with Byron's expedition and ended with Cook's first voyage, which initially was often regarded as Banks's and Daniel Solander's, and for some time remained so on the Continent, partly because of Banks's scientific reputation—he became a Fellow of the Royal Society at age twenty-three, ten years before Cook did so at forty-eight—partly because of the novelty of a young man of wealth and social position going to sea round the world as a botanist.

Hawkesworth, well-known as a good generalist man of letters in Johnson's vein, must have seemed a very suitable choice for the task; the age had no pedantic prejudices about previous experience as a necessary qualification. But he made mistakes that fatally damaged his contemporary reputation. As Helen Wallis says, that reputation, almost on a par with Johnson's, was "destroyed by a book which also preserved his name for posterity."[18] This was despite its immediate and long-lasting success. By the end of 1774 there had been a second authorized issue and editions in Dublin and New York, four editions of a French version, and translations into Dutch and German; by the end of the century there were four more English editions, two more French, two German, one Italian; and of course it was a liberally ransacked quarry for biographers of Cook and compilers of voyages. Between 1773 and 1784 it was borrowed more often—201 times—than any other book in the Bristol Library.[19]

Hawkesworth was criticized for dwelling unduly on the amorous abandon of the Tahitians, in licentious detail: "our Libertines may throw aside the *Woman of Pleasure* and gratify their impure Minds with the Perusal of infinitely more lascivious Recitals than are to be found in that scandalous Performance!"[20] This was extreme; but Hawkesworth was not altogether innocent, though perhaps more sinned against than sinning: "It was not Hawkesworth but Banks who was ultimately responsible for many of the features unacceptable to contemporary readers."[21] Hawkesworth did somewhat heighten Cook, in whose account one would not expect to find "lascivious Recitals."

There was a graver charge. It was a teleological age; for all but the unmentionable materialist infidels, the world had to show a guiding providential purpose: under the Almighty at the top, a Great Chain of Being governed everything down to the humblest worm. Yet Hawkesworth rashly edited out references to a particular providence preserving the lives of mariners—notably Cook's on the Great Barrier Reef—and as John Wesley said, anything but a particular providence was no providence at all. But as Wesley spoke of an island known apparently to Tupaia of Tahiti and distant from that island by eleven hundred degrees of latitude, he cannot have read the book very carefully.[22]

In the long run Hawkesworth's main significance may be that he created the image of the explorer as hero—specifically a British hero—an image that would remain popular some two centuries. He cast his accounts into first person narration, where "I," whether representing Byron, Wallis, Cartaret, or Cook, is an upright man, with humane instincts but capable of stern action, firm in adversity and ever ready in resource. The individual captains are subsumed into a potently symbolic figure, almost a mythos. To quote William H. Pearson, "Hawkesworth is creating the prototype of that hero of Victorian boys' fiction, the magnanimous British commander. . . . It is this heroic figure who is Hawkesworths's creation. . . ."[23]

This is a monumental, an inspirational achievement; but there are flaws. Today, Hawkesworth's "immorality" lies not in libertine writing but in the editorial liberties he took with his texts, to the extent of transposing Cook's remarks on the Tierra del Fuegians and the Australian Aborigines.[24] This, in modern eyes, is his real sin against the light. Cook himself seems to have thought so; he took good care to write the published account of his second voyage himself, with the able assistance of the Reverend Dr. John Douglas, canon of Windsor and later doubly a bishop, and presumably above suspicion of infidelity or immorality.[25]

Nevertheless, after Hawkesworth and the Forsters, voyage narratives ranked, temporarily at least, as "literature," not just as entertainment for the populace. There was a tendency to separate out the technical detail from the story, well exemplified in William Wales's supplement to the second voyage, *The Original Astronomical Observations*. According to J. C. Beaglehole, "This, and not Forster's *Observations* is the true appendix to Cook." This remark seems singularly absurd, but it does point up the tension between the necessities of captains and the desires of their scientists. Cook's explosion, "Curse the scientists, and all science into the bargain!" hardly deserves the weight that has been put on it, but there was a real problem.[26]

No voyage in the South Seas before that of Bougainville carried any official scientists; in the North Pacific the Russians, with Georg Steller and Delisle de la Croyère (who however drank himself to death) on Vitus Bering's 1741 voyage, were well ahead. Till Bougainville any natural history observations were made by surgeons—botany was still part of medical training as supplying *materia medica,* herbal drugs; and some surgeons were able and acute observers.

Bougainville had the ineffable Commerson as official botanist; Cook had fifteen scientists and artists on his three voyages, some of high standing indeed; La Pérouse's ships were floating laboratories, even with small hot-air balloons to gauge upper-air winds and a large one used to amuse the Chileans at Concepción.[27] At the end of the century the unfortunate Nicolas Baudin, himself a cantankerous man, was burdened with twenty-three scientists, artists, and hangers-on, most of them also cantankerous.

Housing these supernumeraries and their gear was an eternally messy problem, the source of frictions rising to hatreds. On the whole commanders found the "scientific gentlemen" interesting and instructive, but nuisances reluctantly submissive to ship discipline, often obstructive, sometimes infuriating. Captains had to keep a watchful eye on wind and weather and tide; they wanted to see what lay around the next headland and were ever anxious to avoid getting shut in a bay by adverse winds. The naturalists were ever anxious to linger botanizing in the bay.

The term "scientist" had not been invented (though the French had "savant")—we do not know what word Cook actually used in his outburst, since he is quoted by Johann Reinhold Forster at secondhand and in German. But by Cook's time there was a recognizable species of man skilled in the observation of natural phenomena, even if the test of mastery was breadth rather than depth of knowledge in a given branch.[28] There was thus a profession of what we call science, and its practitioners were jealous of their recent dignity; they seem in general to have had a high degree of prickliness. Much tact was needed from both parties, cooped up in cramped little ships for two or three years, and tact was often wanting on both sides. J. R. Forster's *Journal* is often horrifying in its outbursts of frustration and despair—he had toothache and rheumatism in Antarctic waters—and his attacks on the inhuman Cook can be bitter. Yet the relations between the two men were amiability itself compared with those between Baudin and his naturalist François Péron, whose official account of the expedition constantly and obsessively denigrates his commander but never by name—always "le Commandant."[29]

There are other examples of this syndrome—Bering and Steller, Vancouver and Menzies, d'Entrecasteaux and La Billardière. Of course there were exceptions. Cook got on very well with the cheerful Banks, but then he owed Banks the deference due superior social position, while Banks owed him the deference due a man sixteen years older. Johann Reinhold Forster was anything but a cheerful man; in fact, he was exceedingly cranky—his sympathetic biographer finds him sometimes infuriating—and he and Cook were of an age.[30]

The two Forsters hold a unique position in Pacific literature. They were in part men of the philosophical Enlightenment, in part inheritors of a German moralizing pietistic tradition, in part avant-garde Romantics. They ministered to both the scientific demands of the Enlightenment and to the emotional demands of the Age of Feeling. Science was then not so separate from humanism and the arts as it became in the nineteenth century; moralizing and elevated "fine writing" were not considered incompatible with sober scientific observation and analysis. Johann Reinhold Forster "combined a passion for empirical observation with a delight in general philosophical observation."[31]

There is thus a good deal of moral edification and stilted, high-flown humanitarianism in the Forsters' work, though one wonders if they were at heart much more humane than some of the seamen they condemned for brutality. Certainly they called for tough measures when their own property or persons were at risk—in which they were probably not very different, the case arising, from any of us. But George Robertson, Master of Wallis's *Dolphin,* took part in the murderous firing on the Tahitians, and yet he seems to regard them much more as *persons*—not just types of the noble or ignoble savage—than do the Forsters, who again had nothing like the genial rapport that the Spanish marine Maxímo Rodríguez had with the Tahitians.[32]

It is true that now and then the Forsters do unbend, in an elephantine manner. The penis-cases of the Vanuatans (to be anachronistic) are compared, with cumbersome humor, to sixteenth-century European codpieces; but even here there had to be a moral, and it must be rammed home.[33] By and large the Forsters are more interested in Man and Woman than in women and men.

Nevertheless, Johann Reinhold's *Observations made during a Voyage round the World, on Physical Geography, Natural History and Ethnic Philosophy* is a landmark—his "Ethnic Philosophy" is the first attempt at an anthropology of Pacific Islanders. Forster's accounts of Tahitian and Tongan society are not so detailed as those of Cook and his surgeon William Anderson, but they are more systematic and analytical, taking much more of a comparative view and forming much more of a sociology, even if some of his guesses today seem weird.

On the physical side, do the *Observations* mark a real advance, or simply the application of current ideas in a novel setting? Johann Reinhold was certainly very well versed in the natural sciences of his time; he was not afraid to take on the great French naturalist Georges Buffon, whose authority was almost sacrosanct; and he could change his mind—indeed, he had to in the diverting case of the Araucarias on the Isle of Pines, which he took to be basalt columns, against the uncultured seamen who thought they were trees. But he was very sound in his views on Antarctic ice formation, and this in opposition not to the sailors but to Buffon and the conventional scientific wisdom of the day.[34] Yet there is still a moralistic teleology: Forster has a good account and explanation of the formation of atoll islets, but "the animalcules forming these reefs *want* to shelter their inhabitants [apparently "the finest fishes"] from the impetuosity of the winds, and the power and rage of the ocean. . . ."[35]

Notwithstanding such lapses, this is the first survey, in both physical and human aspects, of the area—or of any oceanic area— by a trained and versatile scientist. And what an area, from Easter Island via the Marquesas, Tahiti, Tonga, the New Hebrides (Vanuatu), and New Caledonia, to New Zealand, and right round Antarctica! Despite Beaglehole's contemptuous dismissal, the *Observations* hold a firm place in the foundations of modern geography, recognized as such by one of the leading theoreticians of the discipline, Richard Hartshorne.[36]

Johann Reinhold's son George is a much more sympathetic character, even if he did at times take up too much coloration from his father. His *Voyage round the World* (1777) has as much moralizing and teleology as his father's book; indeed, it is very closely linked with Johann Reinhold's *Journal,* as can be seen in Michael Hoare's excellent edition of the latter. But it has qualities of its own. As writing, it is better than anything since Dampier, and English was not George's mother tongue. It is very vivid, at its best perhaps in the lyrical description of Tahiti first seen, or the relaxed account of alfresco meals at Dusky Bay, with good words even for the rough sailors.[37] Indeed, from his references to "natural passions" one wonders whether George would not have enjoyed himself more without Johann Reinhold leaning over his shoulder.

It is no small thing to have been cited by Alexander von Humboldt, probably the greatest scientific traveler the world has seen, as one of the three sources "whence sprang my early and fixed desire to visit the land of the tropics." (The others were the paintings of William Hodges—but of India not the Pacific—and a great dragon tree in the Berlin Botanical Gardens.)[38]

The end of the century, like its beginning, saw a great outburst of maritime publishing, with John Stockdale inheriting the mantle of James Knapton, and Aaron Arrowsmith issuing his delicate maps. The genre had become rather stereotyped in form, and after the great Russian circumnavigations of the first quarter of the new century, there was in fact little left to explore, in the spatial sense, on the surface of the Pacific. The whalers picked up a few new islands, but exploration in depth—literally in depth in the *Challenger*'s voyage—was taken over by strictly scientific governmental efforts such as Charles Wilkes's United States Exploring Expedition of 1838–1842.

Neither the whalers' logs nor the voluminous scientific reports were "literature" in the generally accepted sense. Some whalers had literary inclinations and published narratives that provided raw material to Herman Melville for *Moby Dick;*[39] the Yankee sealer and trader Amasa Delano captured some faint echo of Dampier's quality.[40] But the first fine rapture of the opening of the Pacific was over, though there was one notable contribution yet to come: Charles Darwin's *Voyage of the Beagle.*

Notes

1. W. H. Bonner, *Captain William Dampier: Buccaneer-Author* (Palo Alto, 1934), 3; G. R. Crone and R. A. Skelton, "English Collections of Voyages and

Travels, 1625–1846," in E. Lynam, ed., *Richard Hakluyt and His Successors,* Hakluyt Society, 2d Ser., 113 (London, 1946), 63–140, esp. 67, 83, 133.

2. John Harris, *Navigantium atque Itinerantium Bibliotheca* (London, 1705; revised and enlarged by J. Campbell, London, 1744–1748); Charles de Brosses, *Histoire des Navigations aux Terres Australes* (Paris, 1756); John Callender, *Terra Australis Cognita, or Voyages to the Terra Australis* (Edinburgh, 1766–1768); [David Henry], *An Historical Account of all the Voyages round the World Performed by English Navigators* (London, 1774).

3. O. H. K. Spate, "The Pacific: Home of Utopias," in E. Kamenka, ed., *Utopias* (Melbourne: Oxford University Press, in press). Sade's Utopia is *Aline et Valcour* (Paris, 1793).

4. *A New Voyage and Description of the Isthmus of America* (1699), Hakluyt Society, 2d Ser., 73 (Oxford, 1934).

5. William Dampier, *New Voyage* (Dover ed., New York, 1968), 4; O. H. K. Spate, *The Pacific since Magellan,* vol. 2: *Monopolists and Freebooters* (Canberra: Australian National University Press, 1983), 157, 373 n. 63; James Cook, *A Voyage towards the South Pole* (London, 1777; Adelaide: Library Board of South Australia, 1970), xxxvi; George Vancouver, *A Voyage of Discovery to the North Pacific Ocean* (1798; Hakluyt Society, 2d Ser., 163–166, London, 1984), 1:290–291.

6. Bonner, *William Dampier,* chap. 9, passim; Spate, *Monopolists and Freebooters,* 373 n. 65.

7. Cited in J. L. Lowes, *The Road to Xanadu* (Cambridge, Mass., 1927), 49.

8. J. Shelvocke, *A Voyage round by the Way of the Great South Sea* (London, 1726; Amsterdam: N. Israel, 1971), 72–73; J. Burney, *A Chronological History of Discoveries in the South Sea or Pacific Ocean* (London, 1803–1817; Amsterdam: N. Israel, 1967), 4:526–529; Lowes, *Road to Xanadu,* 222–228, 529–532 —with no reference to Burney!

9. G. Williams, ed., *A Voyage round the World . . . by George Anson* (London: Oxford University Press, 1974), x, xxi–xxv. The ghosting has usually been attributed to Richard Walters, but Benjamin Roberts seems more likely; see Williams's introduction.

10. Montesquieu, *De l'esprit des lois* (1748; Paris: Gallimard, 1949–1951), book 7, chap. 21; Voltaire, *Le Siècle de Louis XIV* (1755–1769; Paris: Gallimard, 1957), chap. 27; Rousseau, *Julie, ou la nouvelle Héloïse* (1761; Paris: Gallimard, 1961), part 3, letters 25–26, part 4, letter 3.

11. H. N. Fairchild, *The Noble Savage: A Study in Romantic Naturalism* (New York: Russell and Russell, 1928), chap. 4, passim; A. O. Lovejoy, "The Supposed Primitivism of Rousseau's *Discourse on Inequality*" (1923), reprinted in his *Essays in the History of Ideas* (Baltimore: Johns Hopkins University Press, 1948), 14–37; cf. M. Duchet, *Anthropologie et histoire au siècle des lumières* (Paris: F. Maspero, 1971), 329–346; and R. Mauzi, "Représentations du paradis terrestre sous les tropiques," in E. Taillemitte, ed., *L'Importance de l'exploration maritime au siècle des lumières* (Paris: Centre Nationale de la Recherche Scientifique, 1982), 169–175.

12. Detailed references in Spate, *Monopolists and Freebooters,* 393 nn. 8, 12.

13. E. H. McCormick, *Omai: Pacific Envoy* (Auckland: Oxford University

Press, 1977), 300–308; C. Lyte, *Sir Joseph Banks* (Newton Abbot, England: David and Charles, 1980), 207–212; quotation from *The Loves of the Plants* (London, 1789), 4:487–490, in D. King-Hele, *The Essential Writings of Erasmus Darwin* (London: MacGibbon and Kee, 1968), 151.

14. E. Taillemitte, ed., *Bougainville et ses compagnons autour du monde, 1766–1769* (Paris: Imprimerie Nationale, 1977), 2:411, 506–510.

15. J. C. Beaglehole, ed., *The Journals of Captain James Cook* (Cambridge: Hakluyt Society Extra Series 34, 1966–1969), 1:ccxlix; J. Boswell, *The Life of Samuel Johnson* (London, 1791; Everyman ed., 1905), 1:409, 2:9; Helen Wallis, "Publication of Cook's Journals: Some New Sources and Assessments," *Pacific Studies* 1 (1978): 163–194, 167 (quotation).

16. H. Wallis, "The Patagonian Giants," in R. E. Gallagher, ed., *Byron's Journal of His Circumnavigation, 1764–1766,* Hakluyt Society, 2d Ser., 122 (Cambridge, 1964), 186–188; Abbé [G. F.] Coyer, *A Letter to Dr. Maty* (London, 1767), 22, 65.

17. J. P. Faivre, "Savants et navigateurs: Un Aspect de la cooperation mondiale entre 1750 et 1840," *Cahiers d'histoire mondiale (Journal of World History)* 10 (1966): 98–124.

18. Wallis, "Cook's Journals," 173.

19. William H. Pearson, "Hawkesworth's *Voyages,*" in R. F. Brissenden, ed., *Studies in the Eighteenth Century* (Canberra: Australian National University Press, 1973), 2:239–258, esp. 239.

20. "A Christian," in *Public Advertiser,* 3 July 1773, quoted in J. L. Abbott, *John Hawkesworth: Eighteenth Century Man of Letters* (Madison: Wisconsin University Press, 1983), 161—a sympathetic study.

21. William H. Pearson. "Hawkesworth's Alterations," *Journal of Pacific History* 7 (1972): 45–72, 64 (quotation).

22. Beaglehole, *Journals of Captain Cook* 1:ccli.

23. Pearson, "Hawkesworth's *Voyages,*" 253.

24. Ibid., 242–244; Bernard Smith, *European Vision and the South Pacific, 1768–1850* (2d ed., Sydney: Harper and Row, [1985], 38–42).

25. Beaglehole, *Journals of Captain Cook* 2:cxliii.

26. Ibid. 2:xlvi, cliii.

27. M. A. Milet-Mureau, *A Voyage round the World . . . by J. F. G. de la Pérouse,* J. Johnson, ed. (London, 1798), 1:323; J. Dunmore and M. de Brossard, *Le Voyage de Lapérouse, 1785–1788* (Paris: Imprimerie Nationale, 1985), 2:57.

28. See D. E. Allen, "The Lost Limb: Geology and Natural History," in L. J. Jordanova and R. S. Porter, eds., *Images of the Earth,* British Society for the History of Science, Monograph 1 (Chalfont St. Giles, England, 1979).

29. F. Péron and L. C. D. de Freycinet, *Voyage de découvertes aux terres Australes* (Paris, 1807), vol. 1.

30. M. E. Hoare, *The Tactless Philosopher* (Melbourne: Hawthorn Press, 1976).

31. Smith, *European Vision,* 55.

32. H. Carrington, ed., *The Discovery of Tahiti* (Robertson's journal), Hakluyt Society, 2d Ser., 97 (London, 1948), 144–158; Rodríguez's most lively jour-

nal takes up most of volume 3 of B. G. Corney, ed., *The Quest and Occupation of Tahiti by Emissaries of Spain during the years 1772–1776,* Hakluyt Society, 2d Ser., 32, 36, 43 (London, 1913, 1914, 1919).

33. J. R. Forster, *Observations made during a Voyage round the World* (London, 1778), 397; G. Forster, *A Voyage round the World* (London, 1777), 2:230.

34. M. E. Hoare, ed., *The Resolution Journals of Johann Reinhold Forster, 1772–1775,* Hakluyt Society, 2d Ser., 152–155 (London, 1982), 4:661; G. Forster, *Voyage* 2:434–438; Beaglehole, *Journals of Captain Cook* 2:550–552, 554, 549; J. R. Forster, *Observations,* 69–102.

35. J. R. Forster, *Observations,* 149–151, my italics.

36. R. Hartshorne, *The Nature of Geography* (Lancaster, Pa.: Association of American Geographers, 1949), 42.

37. G. Forster, *Voyage* 1:165–166, 253–254.

38. Alexander von Humboldt, *Cosmos: A Sketch of a Physical Description of the Universe,* English translation by E. C. Otté (London, 1864), 2:371–372, 436–437, where Forster is bracketed with Darwin; cf. W. T. Stearn, "The Botanical Results of Captain Cook's Three Voyages," *Pacific Studies* 1 (1978): 147–162, esp. 156.

39. I owe this point to my colleague Mrs. Honore Forster.

40. Amasa Delano, *Narrative of Voyages and Travels* (Boston, 1817; Upper Saddle River, N.J., 1970).

2

Science for Political Purposes: European Explorations of the Pacific Ocean, 1764–1806

ALAN FROST

*I*T is now a commonplace that the period 1764–1806 constitutes a second great age of European exploration. The explorers of that era—Byron, Wallis and Carteret, Bougainville, Cook, Surville, La Pérouse, Phillip, Malaspina, Vancouver, d'Entrecasteaux, Baudin, and Flinders—vastly extended European knowledge of the world's oceans and islands, of the coastlines of the continents shaping the Pacific Ocean, and of the peoples inhabiting them. These expeditions form one of the bases of our present science. For the most part well-equipped for scientific investigation, they gave rise to immense natural history and ethnographic collections, which scientists at home then examined, classified, and used in the development of the modern disciplines.

The historiography of these voyages is now immense.[1] In their attention to the great scientific achievements, however, historians have often overlooked the extent to which these expeditions also had distinct political purposes that gave a global dimension to the European nations' continental and imperial rivalry. Each commander sailed with the intention of obtaining detailed information about the resources and defenses of rivals' existing empires, of acquiring knowledge of unknown coasts and harbors, and of obtaining possession of new territories promising strategic or commercial advantage. The rivalry expressed by the competing scientific expeditions was intense; and there are some good grounds for finding their underlying political impulse more important than the scientific one.

The origins of this rivalry lie in the development of the modern European states and in their overseas expansion during the Renaissance; but we may conveniently take George Anson's famous circumnavigation of 1740–1744 as a starting point. Anson sailed with the immediate purposes of raiding the Spanish settlements on the western coasts of America and capturing the annual treasure galleon; but in the longer term, he sought to encourage rebellion in the Spanish dominions, which might lead to the British gaining access to rich new markets. When he returned, he did so not only with treasure, but also with well-developed ideas of how best to promote the "important purposes of navigation, commerce, and national interest."[2]

Anson's scheme involved establishing a way station to the Pacific where ships could refresh and refit, and he saw the Falkland Islands as being well-situated for this purpose. In 1749, at his urging, the British Admiralty set about equipping two ships to sail to these islands and then to proceed into the Pacific, but the Lords Commissioners put off this scheme "for discovery of New Countries & Islands in the American Seas" in the face of Spanish resentment. A dozen years later the British revived it in another guise when they sent an expedition to capture Manila from the Spanish as a first step to opening trade with the Pacific region at large. While the expedition succeeded, the government at home failed to gain the hoped-for advantage because news of the result did not reach Europe in time to influence the peace settlement.[3]

The British Admiralty then reverted to Anson's scheme. Pretending they were intended for the East Indies, the Lords Commissioners fitted out two ships for a lengthy voyage. They told the commander, Captain John Byron, that his immediate task was to survey the Falkland Islands and locate a suitable site for a base; afterwards he was to examine the coast of New Albion for Juan de Fuca's Strait and to return via the strait if found.[4]

That the accomplishment of these specific purposes was a prelude to the more general and grander one of acquiring empire in the southern hemisphere the Lords Commissioners showed when they began their secret instructions with the rubric developed by predecessors over the previous two hundred years:

> Whereas nothing can redound more to the honor of this Nation as a Maritime Power, to the dignity of the Crown of Great Britain, and

to the advancement of the Trade and Navigation thereof, than to make Discoveries of Countries hitherto unknown, and to attain a perfect Knowledge of the distant Parts of the British Empire, which though formerly discovered by His Majesty's Subjects have been as yet but imperfectly explored. . . .[5]

Byron sailed in June 1764. After searching unsuccessfully in the South Atlantic for Pepys's Island (thought to be an outlier of the southern continent), he surveyed the Falklands and decided that Port Egmont on the western island was suitable for a base. Byron relayed this information via a storeship, and the British sent a small party to settle it. Byron proceeded through the Straits of Magellan into the Pacific. Once there, however, he made no attempt to look for the Straits of Anian. His idea was instead "to make a NW Course til we get the true Trade wind, and then to shape a Course to the W^{t·}ward in hopes of falling in with Solomons Islands if there are such, or else to make some new Discovery."[6] This route would have been along the coast of Terra Australis as depicted by Ortelius, the Mercators, and their successors, but Byron found neither the southern continent nor the Islands of Solomon. Taking his course at 23 °S, he crossed too far north to run among the great atoll clusters of the central Pacific. He reached the Ladrones at the end of July 1765 and then proceeded home by way of Batavia.

Unknown to the British, the French, who also considered the Falklands the "key" to the Pacific, had anticipated them, for Louis de Bougainville had placed a colony on East Falkland early in 1764.[7] On learning of these settlements, the Spanish protested to both Britain and France that the islands belonged to them. The issue was not simply about possession of these small specks bounded by a bleak ocean. Spain claimed the exclusive right both to hold South America apart from Brazil and to navigate the southern Atlantic Ocean and the entire Pacific. The claim was based on the "Law of the Americas," the Papal Bulls of 1493 and the Spanish and Portuguese practice based upon them; and on the guarantee to respect the status quo in Spanish America given by the other European nations in the Treaty of Utrecht in 1713. Accordingly, the Spanish envoy told the British that their penetration of the Southern oceans gave his nation "occasion to . . . Suspect a War."[8]

The British considered Spain's claim that its American possessions "included the A[merican] and S[outh] Seas" preposterous and said that they would not shrink from war if Spain "insisted on reviving such a vague & strange pretension, long since wore out, as the exclusive right of [navigation in] those Seas."[9] But Britain was nonetheless worried that Spain might be able to enforce the claim and therefore hastened to take advantage of the new settlement on the Falklands to discover Terra Australis about which Europeans had for so long held such rich expectations. In June and July 1766 the Admiralty fitted out the *Dolphin* and the *Tamar* for another voyage of exploration and gave the command to Captain Samuel Wallis. The Lords Commissioners told Wallis to begin looking for the southern continent, which they supposed to lie between "Cape Horn and New Zealand" directly west of the Straits of Magellan. If following its coast took him a good distance northwards, he was to return via the East Indies. Otherwise, he should return by way of Cape Horn and the Falklands. He was to cultivate friendships with any peoples not previously visited by Europeans whom he should discover, and, with their permission, "take Possession of convenient Situations in the Country." If uninhabited, he was to take possession of it "for His Majesty, by setting up proper Marks and Inscriptions as first Discoverers and Possessors." If, "contrary to Expectation," he did not find the continent, he should proceed across the Pacific to China or the East Indies, seeking out islands on the way.[10]

In a later note, the First Lord of the Admiralty sketched the context of the voyage:

After the Return of Commadore Biron from the Expedition . . . and his discovery of Falklands Islands, together with other Islands in his Track thro yᵉ Pacifick Ocean; Upon Representation . . . to the King, that the Knowledge of the Ports in Falklands Islands, & of the Streights of Magellan would greatly facilitate farther discoveries in yᵉ Pacifick Ocean, South of the Line, if pursued, before a War with France or Spain, or the Jealousy of those two Powers should oblige Great Britain to part with yᵉ Possession of Falklands Islands, or otherwise Interrupt yᵉ attempts of Great Britain in that Part of yᵉ World, His Majesty was graciously pleased to Authorize this second Expedition to be undertaken, in hopes of finding a Continent of Great Extent never yet Explored or seen between the Streights of Magellan and New Zeeland.[11]

To assist in these tasks, the Admiralty recruited a Mr. Harrison, the purser of a sixty-gun ship, who, having "a very Mathematical Turn," was sent to calculate longitude according to Maskelyne's method.[12]

Wallis sailed through the Tuamotus to Tahiti, which he claimed for the King. Near this island, he and his men thought that they saw the coastline of the mysterious southern continent, "but afterwards thought [it] most prudent . . . not to take Notice that they had Ever seen it at all."[13] They discovered other islands as they continued across the Pacific; and on their return in May 1768, Wallis gave all Harrison's observations, "together with Plans, Views & Charts of the whole Voyage" to the Admiralty, reporting secretly on the discovery of Terra Australis and on the many islands offering safe anchorage and refreshment—which were, in Wallis's words, "a Happiness to be greatly esteemed for the Benefit of future Adventures, & may be the Means of making them usefull Settlements hereafter."[14]

Wallis's expedition marked the beginning of the scientific exploration of the Pacific. Even as he sailed, another navigator, Bougainville, began his circumnavigation in November 1766. Its immediate occasion was formally to hand over the East Falkland settlement to Spain, whose claim France had conceded, but its larger purpose was to lay a basis for imperial expansion in the Pacific such as envisaged by Charles de Brosses.[15] The ships' complement included the naturalist Philibert Commerson and the astronomer Pierre Véron (also there to solve the problem of determining longitude at sea). Bougainville too came through the Tuamotu archipelago to Tahiti, then west through the Samoan islands and the New Hebrides (Vanuatu) to the coral fringe of Australia, before turning north for the East Indies. The scientific importance of the voyage proved to be less than expected, for Bougainville's published charts lacked details, and Commerson died at Mauritius before he was able to write up his notes and organize his collections. Nonetheless, in the location and charting of the western Pacific islands, there were distinct results; and Bougainville also brought back up-to-date information concerning navigation to and the state of such European outposts as the river Plate settlements, Rio de Janeiro, and Batavia.[16]

Immediately, French adventurers sought to build on the results of these voyages. At the Cape of Good Hope, some of Wallis's men had been "so enthusiastic" about their discovery of Tahiti that they were "unable to stop themselves from gossiping," from which came a garbled story of a very rich island settled by Jews. Considering the adventure worth attempting and that its success "could become too important for our nation for me not to be in honour bound to sacrifice everything to make it succeed," Jean-Baptiste Chevalier sent Jean de Surville "to take possession of this island."[17] Then in 1770 Marion du Fresne began planning his voyage, making the return of the Tahitian Bougainville had brought to France the occasion of discovering Terra Australis and providing a basis for an imperial resurgence in the East.[18]

Nor were the British behindhand. In 1768 Captain James Cook began the first of his three voyages. This was intended as an explicitly scientific voyage. Cook himself was skilled in survey and astronomical observation, and the *Endeavour* carried besides the astronomer Charles Green and Joseph Banks's party, which included the naturalists Daniel Solander and Herman Spöring, and the draughtsmen Sydney Parkinson and Alexander Buchan.[19] An English correspondent told Linnaeus that "no people ever went to sea better fitted out for the purpose of Natural History, nor more elegantly"; and, as is well-known, the scientific results were stunning, the explorers returning in 1770 with a large number of specimens from South America, the Pacific Islands, New Zealand, and Australia, many of which were entirely new to science. Linnaeus was moved to speak of a "matchless and truly astonishing collection, such as has never been seen before, nor may ever be seen again."[20]

The voyage of the *Endeavour* was a great feat of science. Nonetheless, while its scientific purposes provided its occasion, they do not represent its most important impulse. Of profounder import was that purpose which the Lords Commissioners of the Admiralty conveyed to Cook in their secret instructions:

> Whereas the making Discoverys of Countries hitherto unknown, and the attaining a Knowledge of distant Parts which though formerly discover'd have yet been but imperfectly explored, will redound greatly to the Honour of this nation as a Maritime Power, as well as to the Dignity of the Crown of Great Britain, and may tend greatly to the advancement of the Trade and Navigation thereof; and Whereas there is reason to imagine that a Continent or

Land of great extent, may be found to the Southward of the Tract lately made by Captn Wallis in His Majesty's Ship the Dolphin . . . or of the Tract of any former Navigators in Pursuits of the like kind; You are therefore in Pursuance of His Majesty's Pleasure hereby requir'd and directed to put to Sea with the Bark you Command so soon as the Observation of the Transit of the Planet Venus shall be finished and observe the following Instructions. [21]

Cook was further instructed to:

- carefully observe the location of the coast of any land discovered and chart it accurately;
- carefully observe the "Nature of the Soil, and the Products thereof";
- observe "the Genuis, Temper, Disposition and Number of the Natives," and cultivate friendships with them;
- with the consent of the inhabitants take possession of "Convenient Situations in the Country in the Name of the King of Great Britain; or, if you find the Country uninhabited take Possession for His Majesty by setting up Proper Marks and Inscriptions, as first discoverers and possessors";
- accurately observe "the Situation of such Islands as you may discover in the Course of your Voyage that have not hitherto been discover'd by any Europeans, and take possession for His Majesty and make Surveys and Draughts of such of them as may appear to be of Consequence, without Suffering yourself however to be thereby diverted from the Object which you are always to have in View, the Discovery of the Southern Continent so often Mentioned." [22]

Careful commander that he was, Cook followed these injunctions diligently. He rather disingenuously professed himself surprised at the viceroy of Brazil's wariness; but while the Marquis of Lavradio was wrong to suspect a smuggling venture, he was not wrong to consider that the expedition comprehended more than its announced scientific purpose. Its fundamental purpose was— no more and no less, as the above quotations indicate—to ensure that the British reached Terra Australis before their European rivals, and, by this discovery or by others, to give themselves the means to a rich Pacific trade. As they proceeded, Cook and his companions charted islands, coastlines, and harbors; they noted local resources; and they established preliminary rights of possession. And although they effectively abolished the southern continent so beloved of theoretical geographers, they established Tahiti as a focus for future voyaging in the Pacific. They decided that, if the colonization of New Zealand should become an object, then either the river Thames estuary or the Bay of Islands would be suitable locations, both of which offered "the advantage of a good harbour and by means of the former an easy communication would be had and settlements might be extended into the inland parts of the Country."[23] And they claimed all of eastern Australia (New South Wales) for the British Crown, also with the idea that parts of it might be suitable for settlement.

Cook returned to England with a precise scheme for finally settling the question of Terra Australis and for making further discoveries:

> the most feasable Method of making further discoveries in the South Sea is to enter it by the way of New Zeland, first touching and refreshing at the Cape of Good Hope, from thence proceed to the Southward of New Holland for Queen Charlottes Sound where again refresh Wood and Water, takeing care to be ready to leave that place by the latter end of September or beginning of October at farthest, when you would have the whole summer before you and after geting through the Straight might, with the prevailing Westerly winds, run to the Eastward in as high a Latitude as you please and, if you met with no lands, would have time enough to get round Cape Horne before the summer was too far spent, but if after meeting with no Continent & you had other Objects in View, than haul to the northward and after visiting some of the Islands already discover'd, after which proceed with the trade wind back to the Westward in search of those before Mintioned thus the discoveries in the South Sea would be compleat.[24]

This was the scheme which Cook pursued with such relentless vigor on his great second voyage, in two ships carrying, again, astronomers and naturalists. The collections from this voyage were as extensive as those from the first, with the addition of Johann Reinhold Forster's pioneering attempt toward a world climatology. Yet political considerations loomed as large as scientific ones, with the explorers charting, drawing, observing, and hypothesizing as assiduously as before. Like Cook and Banks before him, J. R. Forster thought that a settlement might profitably be made in the North Island of New Zealand, partly to take advantage of its naval materials; and the subsequent discovery of New Caledonia and Norfolk Island, with their stands of striking trees, added to the sense of the Pacific's potential as a convenient source of naval materials and offered further incentive for colonization.[25]

On his third voyage, Cook turned his attention to the northern Pacific, seeking (among other things) the entrance of a northwest passage above 65°N. As before, his exploring and charting were impressive, and the collecting of his scientifically minded colleagues extensive. However, his scientific complement was much slighter than on his previous voyages. This might be a sign of the lessening importance of the scientific motive, and an increase of that of the political and commercial ones. In any case, he and his companions observed with a political eye, finding that the Hawaiian Islands might admirably play the role that Tahiti had in the southern Pacific; and gathering information about the Russian settlements in northern Asia.[26]

The American War of Independence, which in 1778 became in effect a global conflict, put a temporary halt to further European exploration and to any expansion based upon it. But no sooner was the war concluded (1783) than the maritime nations turned again to scientific expeditions designed to promote their abiding quest for trade, empire, and strategic advantage. During the first half of 1785 the French mounted La Pérouse's voyage. The most lavishly equipped French scientific expedition to this time, it carried a retinue of scientists, who received fulsome instructions concerning matters of interest in the fields of geography, geometry, astronomy, mechanics, physics, chemistry, anatomy, zoology, mineralogy, botany, medicine, and ethnology.[27]

Though secret instructions of the sort issued to Cook are lacking, the French—both those who sent the expedition and those who went on it—well knew that it might also have important political and commercial consequences. Indeed, the earliest schemes stress these above likely scientific ones.[28] In his public instructions La Pérouse was told to observe and report on the forces in and trade of the colonies he visited, on the commercial potential of the products of the lands in and about the Pacific, and on the purpose of any settlement the British may have formed in the southern half of the Pacific. The navigator and his companions followed these instructions assiduously, recording strategic details of the settlements at Teneriffe, Trinidada, Santa Catarina, Conception, Monterey, Manila, and Formosa. And when he learned in Kamchatka of the British settlement of Botany Bay in New South Wales, he sailed there to investigate it.[29]

As La Pérouse was preparing to leave France, the British heard a rumor that he was taking along sixty convicts to found a ship-building colony in New Zealand. The idea certainly was believable. Cook's voyages had shown the potential; and such a move would have significantly affected the balance of power in the East, where the European nations often had difficulty refitting their ships. The forestalling of the move was a powerful motive in the British decision to colonize Botany Bay.[30] As Evan Nepean, under secretary at the Home Office and the official most concerned with colonization, said on one occasion, the venture would be "a means of preventing the emigration of Our European Neighbours to that Quarter, which might be attended with infinite prejudice to the [East India] Company's Affairs." And, apart from "the removal of a dreadful Banditti" from Britain, the principal advantages to be expected were supplies of masts "which the Fleet employed occasionally in the East Indies frequently stand[s] in need of," and the cultivation of the New Zealand flax plant for cordage and canvas. Accordingly, Captain Arthur Phillip, the founding governor, was instructed to "send a small Establishment [to Norfolk Island] to secure [it] to Us, and prevent its being occupied by the Subjects of any other European Power."[31]

Earl Howe, the First Lord of the Admiralty, described the Botany Bay venture as a "Voyage of discovery & Settlement";[32] and while it was not fundamentally scientific in orientation, a scientific component was originally planned for it, which rather foundered when the botanist Francis Masson, then collecting at the Cape of Good Hope, decided that he did not wish to go to New South Wales. Nonetheless, there were men in the First Fleet who knew enough of botany and zoology to know what would interest the learned in Europe, and they sent back specimens in large numbers, together with ethnographic details. It was as a consequence of this data, added to that earlier obtained by Banks and Solander, that scientists in England began to understand how much Australia was scientifically a "new world." As Linnean Society founder J. E. Smith remarked in 1793:

When a botanist first enters on the investigation of so remote a country as New Holland, he finds himself as it were in a new world. He can scarcely meet with any fixed points from whence to draw his analogies; and even those that appear most promising, are frequently in danger of misleading, instead of informing him. The whole tribes of plants, which at first sight seem familiar to his acquaintance, as occupying links in Nature's chain . . . prove, on a nearer examination, total strangers, with other configurations, other economy, and other qualities; not only the species themselves are new, but most of the genera, and even natural orders.[33]

In the manner by now well-established, this scientific activity went hand in hand with political and strategic ones. By their settlement of New South Wales, the British gained an advantage in the Pacific not only over the French, but also over the Spanish. In 1788, one Spanish commentator observed: "The endeavours of [the] energetic [Cook], his perseverance and labours, besides enriching the sciences of geography and Hydrography by new discoveries, have placed his Nation in a position to compensate itself for the loss of North America by the acquisition of a country almost as vast, and with possibilities for becoming one of the most flourishing and advantageous on account of its position." After describing how a settlement in New Holland offered advantages in navigation to China and created a threat to Spanish trade in the Pacific, he continued: "These possessions will have a Navy of their own, obtaining from the southern region everything necessary to create it, and when they have it ready formed they will be able to invade our neighbouring possessions with expeditions less costly & surer than from the ports of England, & it will not be difficult to foretell even now, which will be their first conquests."[34]

Nor was this an uninformed or idiosyncratic speculation, as the British choice of Arthur Phillip as founding governor of the colony shows. One of Phillip's qualifications was that he was a "discreet" officer who had previously collected information concerning South American coastlines and the Spanish settlements about the river Plate, and spied in France. On his way to New South Wales, he gathered more information about the forces at Montevideo and Buenos Aires;[35] and once there, he saw the settlement as capable of being a way station to the west coasts of America. So, too, did his counterparts in the Spanish dominions. In December 1788, one viceroy of Mexico reported that "the Russian projects and those which the English may make from Botany Bay . . . already menace us"; and in 1790, when the Nootka Sound crisis had made that menace actual, another wrote: "[There are] not enough forces in our South Sea and the Department of San Blas to counteract those which the English have at their Botany Bay, and I think therefore we should withdraw those we have in the pretended establishment at Nootka so that, instead of exposing them to be readily made prisoner, they can fall back to redouble the defences of our older and established possessions."[36]

The Nootka Sound crisis wove these various threads tightly together. By the late 1780s, British traders had begun to frequent the southern Atlantic and the Pacific in search of the whales and seals whose numbers Cook had so tellingly described. The presence of British whalers off the South American coasts and British fur traders at Nootka Sound mightily disturbed the Spanish, who continued to believe that they had an exclusive right to the trade and navigation of these areas, and who therefore protested to Britain. The Spanish did more than protest, though. In 1788 the Spanish court accepted Alejandro Malaspina's proposal for a voyage of scientific discovery to outshine Cook's. It was hoped that this would bring "new discoveries, careful cartographic surveys, important geodesic experiments in gravity and magnetism, botanical collections, and descriptions of each region's geography, mineral resources, commercial possibilities, political status, native peoples, and customs." But behind these scientific purposes lurked the usual political ones, for planners were aware of how much the voyage might do "to explore, examine, and knit together Madrid's far-flung empire, report on problems and possible reforms, and counter the efforts of rivals to obtain colonial possessions at Spain's expense."[37]

Inevitably, the northwest coast of America was on Malaspina's agenda, but as his grand expedition was being mounted, the viceroy at Mexico City sent a small expedition to Nootka Sound to assert Spain's priority there and to expel the interlopers. Commodore Martinez's seizure of the British traders' ships and his detention of their crews led to a diplomatic crisis. The Pitt Administration's first response, in February and March 1790, was to propose an expedition to "lay the foundation of an establishment for the assistance of His Majesty's subjects in the prosecution of the Fur trade from the North West Coast of America," which should sail via New South Wales so as to take on convict artificers.[38] In April the British put off this expedition in favor of forcing the Spanish to retract their claims. With the issue settled in Europe, the British returned to the idea of an expedition, which then sailed under George Vancouver's command.

Vancouver's voyage, like the others, is famous for its contribution to geographical and oceanic knowledge, but it carried only one person who can be considered a scientist, and its political significance can scarcely be exaggerated. Indeed, the idea of the voyage had emerged from the dispute over the right to navigate in, trade with, and possess territory in and about the Pacific. The British developed the idea conscious of the need to counteract the likely political and commercial effects of Malaspina's voyage; and a central purpose of the proposed scientific activity was to be the securing of all of what is now western Canada for Britain:

> [It being his Majesty's intention] that an Establishment should be formed at one of those ports or places, [of which His Subjects have been dispossessed] or in such other situation as shall appear to be more advantageous with a view to the opening a Commercial intercourse with the Natives, as also for establishing a line of communication across the Continent of America, and thereby to prevent any future intrusion, by securing to this Country the possession of those parts which lye at the back of Canada and Hudson's Bay, as well as the Navigation by such Lakes as are already known or may hereafter be discovered. [39]

Among the consequences of Vancouver's voyage were that the Spanish effectively relinquished their centuries-old claim to enjoying the Pacific as their "lake," and Britain forestalled an American territorial claim to what is now British Columbia.

But if Britain settled its imperial rivalry in the Pacific with Spain by the Nootka Sound crisis and Vancouver's voyage, that with France continued unabated. In 1791 the French National Assembly authorized d'Entrecasteaux's expedition. The immediate occasion was the need, if possible, to succor the missing La Pérouse expedition. Like its predecessors, this was an explicitly scientific voyage. Again, however, it had important political consequences, for d'Entrecasteaux charted the southwestern corner of Australia and the southeastern corner of Tasmania, enabling France to claim an interest in the continent Britain was settling, even if war and the fact that British authorities retained the records of the voyage delayed any realization of this interest for some years.[40]

Napoléon took the matter up even before the Peace of Amiens (1802) when he mounted Nicolas Baudin's expedition. Like that of La Pérouse, this was intended as an exemplar of modern science. It sailed with a specialist complement; and it returned with very extensive collections:

> Apart from a multitude of cases of minerals, dried plants, shells, fishes, reptiles, and zoophytes preserved in alcohol, of quadrupeds and birds stuffed or dissected, we still had seventy great cases full of plants in their natural state, comprising nearly two hundred different species of useful plants, approximately six hundred types of seeds contained in several thousand small bags, and finally, about a hundred living animals, rare or absolutely new.[41]

And Antoine Laurent de Jussieu, professor of botany at the Muséum d'Histoire Naturelle, considered this the greatest collection to be brought from different lands to France.[42] Nonetheless, the voyage was also intended to achieve a distinct political purpose —the reconnaissance of the western coasts of New Holland. This would allow the entire coastline of "this great south land" to be known and therefore provide for a French presence, for though it was "situated not far from the countries of *Asia* where, for three centuries, Europeans have been forming settlements, [it] seemed until recently to [have been] condemned to a sort of oblivion."[43] Baudin and his officers reflected this purpose in naming the area of which Adelaide is now the center "Terre Napoléon" and in their loose talk at Sydney of intentions to form one or more settlements in the Bass Strait region.

Alarmed by these rumors, Governor Philip Gidley King immediately dispatched an officer to ask an explanation of the French, whom he found at King Island in Bass Strait. There, the much inferior British party insisted on hoisting the Union Jack above the French camp. While Baudin accepted this charade in a good-natured way, he pointed out that Tasman was the discoverer of Van Diemen's Land, and that the British party had found him only several days after the French had "left in prominent parts of the island . . . proofs of the period at which we visited it." (With studied generosity he also announced that he would nonetheless name the island after the governor.) King sent another party to form a settlement at Storm Bay, near D'Entrecasteaux Channel (Hobart); and, simultaneously, the equally anxious home government sent a much larger expedition to settle Port Phillip (Melbourne), so as to forestall the French and ensure control of Bass Strait.[44]

The British made another countermove at this time, too. In keeping with his generosity of outlook and his sense that science overrode nationalism, Sir Joseph Banks had assisted Baudin's expedition. However, with the French threat apparent, he also contributed massively to that which the British mounted in opposition, commanded by Matthew Flinders. During his three-and-a-half-year survey of the Australian coastline, Flinders and his party of natural historians, draughtsmen, and mineralogists made extensive and important collections. Robert Brown's, for example, numbered thirty-four hundred items, of which approximately two thousand were new. The political results of the voyage were equally important, for it established Britain's interest in the whole continent, an interest that would be substantiated twenty years later by additional settlements (Melville Island, King George's Sound, Swan River) after the French again made their presence felt by such striking scientific voyages as those of Louis de Freycinet and Jules Dumont d'Urville.

That his voyage should so much have helped to establish Britain's control of the real southern continent, and that his narrative of his arduous work should have given this continent its modern name, could have been of little comfort to Matthew Flinders, who —legend has it—died with the first copy of his *Voyage* in his hand.[45] The privations of the years at sea joined to the anxieties of the confinement at Mauritius had exhausted him. There, he was no ordinary prisoner of war. As a principal in imperial rivalries he was a state prisoner whom the governor could not exchange without explicit approval from France. This approval was years in coming, for while Banks organized his scientific acquaintances in France to intercede on his protégé's behalf, political considerations proved stronger. In Flinders's sad fate we see reflected the fundamental reality of the great age of scientific exploration as a whole —that imperial interests ultimately had precedence over scientific ones.

Notes

1. The relevant scholarship makes for a very long list. Particularly noteworthy are J. C. Beaglehole's editions of Cook's and Banks's journals (cited below); Bernard Smith, *European Vision and the South Pacific, 1768–1850,* 2d ed. (Sydney: Harper and Row, [1985]); Bernard Smith and Rudiger Joppien, *The Descriptive Cataloque of the Art and the Charts and Views of Captain James Cook's Voyages of Discovery to the South Pacific,* 2 vols. (Melbourne: Oxford University Press, 1985). See also the various essays in *Captain Cook: Navigator & Scientist,* ed. G. M. Badger (Canberra: Australian National University Press, 1970); *Employ'd as a Discoverer,* ed. J. V. S. Megaw (Sydney: A. H. and A. W. Reed, 1971); *Captain James Cook and His Times,* ed. Robin Fisher and Hugh Johnson (Vancouver: Douglas and McIntyre, 1979); *Captain Cook and the South Pacific* (Canberra: Australian National University Press, 1979); and *Sydney Parkinson,* ed. D. J. Carr (Canberra: Australian National University Press in association with the British Museum [Natural History], 1983). Other works include John Dunmore, *French Explorers in the Pacific,* 2 vols. (1965; Oxford: Oxford University Press, 1969); John Dunmore and M. R. de Brossard, *Le Voyage de Lapérouse,* 2 vols. (Paris: Imprimerie Nationale, 1985); M. Dolores Higueras Rodriguez, *Catalogo Critico de los Documentos de la Expedicion Malaspina (1789–1794) del Museo Naval* (Madrid: Museo Naval, 1985); *La Expedicion Malaspina 1789–1794* ([Madrid]: Ministerio de Cultura, 1984); David Mackay, *In the Wake of Cook: Exploration, Science & Empire, 1780–1801* (Wellington: Victoria University Press, 1985); J. E. Martin-Allanic, *Bougainville,* 2 vols. (Paris: Presses Universitaires de France, 1964); Étienne Taillemite, ed., *Bougainville et ses companions autour de monde, 1766–1769,* 2 vols. (Paris: Imprimerie Nationale, 1977).

2. See Glyndwr Williams, ed., *A Voyage round the World* (London: Oxford University Press, 1974), 9, for quotation; *Documents Relating to Anson's Voyage round the World, 1740–1744* (London: Navy Records Society, 1967).

3. Synopsis of Admiralty Correspondence, and Lenox to Shelburne, 17 September 1766, Shelburne Papers, vol. 75: 321–325, 331–332, William L. Clements Library, Ann Arbor, Michigan; and N. P. Cushner, ed., *Documents Relating to the Fall of Manila* (London: The Royal Historical Society, 1971).

4. Lords Commissioners of the Admiralty, Secret Instructions to Byron, 17 June 1764, in *Byron's Journal of His Circumnavigation, 1764–1766,* ed. R. E. Gallagher (Cambridge: At the University Press for the Hakluyt Society, 1964), 3–8.

5. Ibid., 3. These instructions were modeled on earlier ones to Sir John Narborough (1669).

6. Ibid., 89.

7. For an account of the settlements, see Julius Goebel, *The Struggle for the Falkland Islands* (1927; New Haven: Yale University Press, 1982), 221–270.

8. "Notes on a Conversation with Prince Masserano," 26 September 1766, Shelburne Papers, vol. 166, item 7.

9. Ibid.

10. Helen Wallis, ed., *Carteret's Voyage round the World,* 2 vols. (Cambridge: At the University Press for the Hakluyt Society, 1965). Includes the Lords Commissioners' Secret Instructions to Wallis, 16 August 1766, vol. 2:302–306.

11. Egmont, Notes on the Voyage, undated but probably June–December 1768, in ibid., 2:311–312.

12. Wallis to Egmont, 19 May 1768, Shelburne Papers, vol. 75:435–445.

13. Egmont, Notes on the Voyage, 2:312 (quotation); George Robertson, *The Discovery of Tahiti,* ed. Hugh Carrington (London: The Hakluyt Society, 1948), 189, 233.

14. Wallis to Egmont, 19 May 1768, Shelburne Papers, vol. 75:435–445.

15. Charles de Brosses, *Histoire des navigations aux terres Australes* (1756; Amsterdam: N. Israel, 1967), 1:1–81.

16. Louis de Bougainville, *A Voyage round the World,* trans. J. R. Forster (1772; Amsterdam: N. Israel, 1967).

17. Quoted in John Dunmore, ed., "Introduction," in *The Expedition of the 'St Jean-Baptiste' to the Pacific, 1769–1770* (London: The Hakluyt Society, 1981), 21–23.

18. See John Dunmore, *French Explorers in the Pacific* (Oxford: Clarendon Press, 1965–1969), 1:166–168.

19. See J. C. Beaglehole, ed., *The Journals of Captain James Cook,* vol. 1: *The Voyage of the 'Endeavour,' 1768–1771* (1955; Cambridge: Cambridge University Press for the Hakluyt Society, 1968).

20. Quoted in J. C. Beaglehole, ed., "Introduction," to *The 'Endeavour' Journal of Joseph Banks,* 2d ed. (Sydney: Public Library of New South Wales in association with Angus and Robertson, 1963), 1:30, 70.

21. Beaglehole, *Journals of Captain Cook* 1:cclxxxii.

22. Ibid., cclxxxii–cclxxxiii.

23. Ibid., 278.

24. Ibid., 479.

25. Michael Hoare, ed., *The "Resolution" Journal of Johann Reinhold Forster, 1772–1775* (London: The Hakluyt Society, 1982), 3:429; J. C. Beaglehole, ed., *The Journals of Captain James Cook,* vol. 2: *The Voyage of the "Resolution" and "Adventure"* (1961; Cambridge: Cambridge University Press for the Hakluyt Society, 1969), 527–561, 565–568, 868–869.

26. J. C. Beaglehole, ed., *The Journals of Captain James Cook,* vol. 3: *The Voyage of the "Resolution" and "Discovery,"* 2 vols. (Cambridge: Cambridge University Press for the Hakluyt Society, 1967).

27. See L. A. Milet-Mureau, ed., *A Voyage round the World* (London: G. G. and J. Robinson, 1799), 1:1–255.

28. See Catherine Gaziello, *L'Expédition de Lapérouse, 1785–1788* (Paris: C. T. H. S., 1984), 52–54. I am grateful to Madame Carpine-Lancre for referring me to this work.

29. La Pérouse, "Subjects Relating to Politics and Commerce," in Milet-Mureau, *A Voyage round the World* 1:24–32; Monneron, "Observations on different places," in ibid., 2:391–404; La Pérouse, "Account of Manila and Formosa," in ibid., 2:405–411; La Pérouse to Fleurieu, 28 September 1787 and 7 February 1788, in ibid., 2:499–500, 501–508.

30. See Alan Frost, *Convicts and Empire: A Naval Question, 1776–1811* (Melbourne: Oxford University Press, 1980).

31. [Nepean/Sydney] to Chairmen of the East India Company, 15 September 1786, India Office Records, E/1/79:187; Nepean to Sackville Hamilton, 24 October 1786 (draft), Public Record Office, HO 100/18:369–372; George III, Instructions to Phillip, 25 April 1787, PRO, CO 202/5:35.

32. Howe to Blankett, 19 August 1786 (draft), National Maritime Museum, HOW 3.

33. Quoted in Smith, *European Vision,* 5.

34. Francisco Munoz y San Clemente, "Discurso politico sobre los establici-mientos Ingleses de la Nueva-Holanda" [20 September 1788], English version in the British Library, Add. MS. 19264.

35. See Frost, *Convicts and Empire,* 133; and Phillip to Nepean, 2 September 1787, *Historical Records of New South Wales* (Sydney: Government Printer, 1892–1901), 1:ii, 114.

36. Quoted in Robert King, "The Territorial Boundaries of New South Wales in 1788," *The Great Circle* 3 (1981): 74, and in Warren L. Cook, *Flood Tide of Empire: Spain and the Pacific Northwest, 1543–1819* (New Haven: Yale University Press, 1973), 300–301.

37. Cook, *Flood Tide,* 118; see also chapter 5 for a detailed account of events at Nootka Sound.

38. See Frost, *Convicts and Empire,* 154–157.

39. [Nepean] to Lords Commissioners of the Admiralty, December 1790 (draft), PRO, HO 28/7:392–399.

40. See Dunmore, *French Explorers* 1:283–341, and Hélène Richard, "L'Ex-pédition de d'Entrecasteaux (1791–1794) et les origines de l'implantation anglaise en Tasmanie," *Revue française d'histoire d'outre-mer* 69 (1982): 289–306.

41. Péron, quoted in Dunmore, *French Explorers* 2:37–38.

42. Jussieu is quoted in Christine Cornell, *Questions Relating to Nicolas Baudin's Australian Expedition, 1800–1804* (Adelaide: Libraries Board of South Australia, 1965), 83.

43. Christine Cornell, trans. and ed., *The Journal of Post Captain Nicolas Baudin* (Adelaide: Libraries Board of South Australia, 1974), 1.

44. Baudin to King, [23 December 1802], *Historical Records of New South Wales* 4:1008–1010; Frost, *Convicts and Empire,* 166–167.

45. Matthew Flinders, *A Voyage to Terra Australis,* 2 vols. (1814; Adelaide: Libraries Board of South Australia, 1966).

3

Pierre-Adolphe Lesson, Surgeon-Naturalist: A Misfit in a Successful System

ISABEL OLLIVIER

FRANCE'S growing awareness of the Pacific in the last quarter of the eighteenth century prompted a succession of voyages to the region. As the blank spaces on the map were rapidly eliminated, largely as a result of the voyages of James Cook, the French concentrated increasingly on detailed scientific studies of reduced areas. By 1830 their scientific missions had become very precise and worked efficiently toward clearly defined goals.[1]

From about 1770, major French voyages had generally included at least one naturalist. By the end of the eighteenth century, the number of civilian scientists embarked on naval expeditions was often considerable. Armed with instructions from the Académie des sciences, these men carried out the work of compiling and preserving the natural history collections often destined for the Cabinet du Roi, later to become the Muséum National d'Histoire Naturelle.

Initially, the naturalist-voyagers were civilians and professional naturalists. But, unaccustomed to naval discipline and the privations and dangers of long sea voyages, they frequently proved a source of tension on board. The voyage of the *Géographe* and the *Naturaliste,* under the command of capitaine de vaisseau Nicolas-Thomas Baudin (1800–1804), was the last to suffer the inconveniences of this uneasy partnership. Of the twenty-three scholars embarked, many of whom died or left the expedition, the anthropologist François Péron was to attract the most attention.[2] The voyage became notorious for difficulties between civilian and

45

naval camps, focused largely on the stormy relationship between Baudin (himself an amateur botanist) and Péron. But Péron had been assisted in his work by the two surgeons François Lharidon and Jérôme Bellefin, and their contribution did not pass unnoticed. Inspecteur-général Pierre-François Keraudren of the Service de Santé, Navy Medical Corps, who had drawn up a part of Péron's instructions, was quick to see the advantages of encouraging the *conseils de santé,* or medical boards, in the ports to direct young surgeons in training toward the study of natural history.[3]

In the decades that followed, the double preoccupation of naval medical officers became widespread. A constant supply of natural history specimens found its way back to the Ecoles de médecine navale, the medical school in Brest benefiting more than the others because of the high number of ships outfitted in the port of Brest. Keraudren and the *Annales Maritimes et Coloniales* encouraged this effort, drawing up instructions and publishing lists of donations and of gaps still to be filled on a regional basis. In 1818, at the navy's request, the Muséum Royal d'Histoire Naturelle put out a booklet of detailed practical instructions on the compilation and preservation of natural history collections, aimed specifically at voyagers and colonial staff.[4]

It is against this background of modest and diligent activity that we must consider the more prestigious work of the surgeon-naturalists assigned to the great scientific expeditions around the world. On the instigation of Louis de Freycinet, and with the enthusiastic support of Keraudren, the navy decided in 1816 to replace civilian naturalists with naval personnel. The surgeons Jean-René Quoy and Paul Gaimard and the pharmacist Charles Gaudichaud-Beaupré were invited to further their instruction in natural history in Paris with teachers at the Collège de France and the Sorbonne (notably Jean-Baptiste Lamarck and Georges Cuvier). Thus, when they embarked on the *Uranie* under the command of capitaine de vaisseau Louis de Freycinet in 1817, they were equipped with scientific instructions drawn up by the Académie des sciences and newly coached in the practical and theoretical details of their task.

In the Pacific, Freycinet's voyage on the *Uranie* was followed in quick succession by two others: the *Coquille* under the command of lieutenant de vaisseau Louis-Isidore Duperrey (1822–1825); then the same ship, renamed the *Astrolabe,* under her former second officer, Jules Dumont d'Urville, now capitaine de frégate (1826–1829).

The naturalists on these voyages were chosen from among the officers of the Service de Santé. In his study of the Service de Santé from 1814 to 1835, Jacques Léonard notes that of thirty-five hundred students instructed by the Ecoles de médecine navale in that generation, twenty-three hundred later served in the navy; nearly five hundred obtained a doctorate in medicine; a few dozen won renown for their merit and a handful of scholars crowned the academic pyramid. The naturalists on the *Uranie,* the *Coquille,* and the *Astrolabe* were all to be found near the top of the pyramid, an elite whose careers were already promising at the time they were assigned their task.[5]

The most outstanding figure was undoubtedly Jean-René Quoy (1790–1869). Trained at the Ecole de médecine navale at Rochefort and a keen botanist, he had already enriched his school's natural history collections from a voyage to Bourbon (Réunion Island) in 1814–1815. He was twenty-six when he volunteered for service on the *Uranie,* and his work won him the praise of the Académie des sciences (report read by Arago on 23 April 1821). He wrote the zoological part of the official account of the voyage and, along with Paul Gaimard, was invited to join Dumont d'Urville's expedition on the *Astrolabe* in 1827. He became professor of anatomy of Rochefort, rose to the rank of premier médecin en chef in 1835, and held the post of inspecteur-général from 1848 to 1858. As a corresponding member of the Académie des sciences and of the Académie de médecine, he was clearly one of the handful at the summit of the pyramid.[6]

The pharmacist Charles Gaudichaud-Beaupré (1789–1854) would become no less distinguished. Another dedicated botanist, who had collected specimens in such illustrious company as Laurent de Jussieu, Achille Richard, and Dumont d'Urville,[7] he published the botanical part of the official account of the voyage of the *Uranie.* He became pharmacien en chef and member of the Institut de France and also sailed on the *Bonite* (1836–1837) as botanist under the command of M. Vaillant.

The *Coquille* too had her share of famous men, notably the pharmacist and botanist René-Primevère Lesson. He had already proven his worth as a botanist and zoologist in Rochefort and, in collaboration with Dumont d'Urville, he put together a collection of insects and a herbarium of three thousand species during the voyage of the *Coquille*. The Académie des sciences devoted no fewer than two sessions to his achievements (18 and 22 August 1825) and honored him with the position of corresponding member.

From a naval point of view the new system was a convincing success. Difficulties due to the autonomy of civilian naturalists were eliminated and the naval naturalists carried out their task with laudable disinterest. Several were launched on brilliant careers as a result of the renown the voyage brought them and the exceptional opportunities it offered to develop and display their talents.

The savants of the Académie des sciences were more reticent at the outset, but the quality of the results of the *Uranie* expedition won their grudging praise. Speaking of Quoy and Gaimard in his report to the académie on 23 April 1821, François Arago pointed out that: "The zeal of these two voyagers deserves even more praise in that, not being naturalists by profession, they were able to bring to the task only a general training, covering the different aspects of zoology."[8]

While the scientific establishment cooperated with the navy in drawing up instructions for the naturalists and in assessing the scientific results of the voyages, it also played a watchdog role and provided professional backing where competence or time was lacking. Parts of the official publications following the voyages were taken in hand by civilian naturalists (Bory de Saint Vincent worked on the botanical part of the voyage of the *Coquille,* for example, and Achille Richard on that of the *Astrolabe*). Reports read to the Académie des sciences contained passages underlining the limitations of the role they expected their naval colleagues to fulfill. A distinction between naval and "true" naturalists continued to be made and praise was tinged with condescension. The zoologist Georges Cuvier, reporting to the académie in 1825 that the officers of the *Coquille* had carried out their task as required, said:

> like true naturalists, [they] collected everything, right down to the smallest species, including some they may have suspected to be common, even on our shores: they did not follow the example of so many voyagers, who, in their pretention to make a selection and to

bring back only what strikes them as remarkable, neglect precisely what would have been interesting. We repeat, because voyagers cannot be told too often: the most learned naturalist, faced with an isolated species, is incapable of saying whether it is new or not: it is only when he has before him the series of related species that he can be sure of its characteristics. Thus it is a great error, while on a voyage, to do anything but collect the raw material for study, either by preparing specimens or by drawing what cannot be preserved, or, finally, by writing down the ephemeral details that the specimen does not retain. It is likewise a mistake to waste time with descriptions or in the search for nomenclature, work which will always have to be started afresh once back in the laboratory.[9]

Old wounds were slow to heal and as late as 1825, in a report to the Académie des sciences on the publication of the zoological results of the *Uranie,* the zoologist Etienne-Geoffroy Saint Hilaire again invoked the bitterness of the professional naturalists at their exclusion. He emphasized that France had previously been exemplary in the place she had granted natural history on her great voyages, and that he considered the decision to rely wholly on naval naturalists tantamount to sending no naturalists at all. The distinction between "true" and "false" naturalists could not have been more clearly drawn: "I admit that too much emphasis was perhaps placed on philosophical research; but to go to the other extreme, to announce that there would be no one to represent natural history on board the corvettes the *Uranie* and the *Physicienne* and that science would have to be satisfied with charity from the hand of sailors—that, I may be so bold as to say, was not good enough either."[10] Quoy, Gaimard, and Gaudichaud were outstanding individuals and Geoffroy Saint Hilaire was not niggardly in their praise, but he saw the hand of Providence in their appointment and his deep mistrust of the system itself remained unaffected by that stroke of luck. We shall see that his fears were not wholly unfounded and that the new system did indeed contain flaws, masked though they were by the brilliance of individual performances.

The navy made an effort to mollify the naturalists and to ensure that the success of its missions was not compromised by their exclusion. At the time of the outfitting of the *Astrolabe,* the Comte de Chabrol, ministre et secrétaire d'état de la marine et colonies, instructed Dumont d'Urville:

You are to assemble and send to me on your return to Toulon, the
journals, charts, plans and other documents constituting the fruit of
the voyage. The same goes for natural history collections of all
kinds. No items are to be removed from the mass of the products of
the expedition and it is my express request that you give me an
account of the contribution made by each of your colleagues to the
work to be done in common. On earlier voyages, officers, masters
and even sailors, purchased and kept for themselves natural history
specimens, which have been neither described nor published, as
they were not included in the collections destined for the Cabinet du
Roi. In the interests of science and for the renown that ought to
accrue to the *Astrolabe*, it is desirable that the same thing should
not happen on this new voyage. [11]

It should be noted that the naturalists on the *Uranie* at least
were above suspicion in this respect, Quoy and Gaimard having
handed over to the museum specimens purchased out of their own
pockets. [12]

The use of naval surgeons as naturalists was thus a practice that
developed in the early nineteenth century with conspicuous success. Candidates for the posts were invariably of above average
talent, and the opportunity such voyages offered them in furthering their academic careers was frequently taken up.

The case of Pierre Adolphe Lesson, botanist on the *Astrolabe*,
presents a curious contrast to this tableau. His background, training, and early voyages seemed to have prepared him for a brilliant
career as a naturalist in emulation of Gaudichaud, Quoy, or his
elder brother, René-Primevère Lesson. Nonetheless, he remained
relatively obscure. His journal reveals a misfit in a system that
worked well for others and brings us insight into the difficulties
encountered by surgeon-naturalists in the execution of their dual
role.

The Career of Pierre-Adolphe Lesson

The illustrious career of René-Primevère Lesson has so overshadowed the more modest achievements of his younger brother that
Pierre-Adolphe is rather cruelly remembered by history as "brother of the above." [13] Born to René-Clément Lesson and Marie-Eus-
telle Nicolas in 1794 and 1805 respectively, the Lesson brothers

belonged to a modest family from Rochefort, in Charente-Inféri-
eure on the French Atlantic coast. Their father's administrative
position in the navy, where he was *commis de la marine,* a naval
clerk, helped orient them toward a naval career. Preference given
to sons of naval personnel facilitated their admission to the prestigious Ecole de médecine navale de Rochefort, France's first naval
medical school, set up in 1696.

René-Primevère showed early promise as a botanist and was
rapidly oriented toward pharmaceutical studies. From 1816 to
1821 he was in charge of the school's botanical garden, established in 1722, and soon won acclaim both as a botanist and as a
zoologist. After sailing in the Pacific as a naturalist on the *Coquille*
(1822–1825), he became professor of botany at his old school in
Rochefort in 1829. A prolific writer, he published forty-four
works and numerous papers and left his name to thirty-four animals, twenty-four plants, and two botanical genres.

He was clearly a formidable role model for his brother, who
was anxious to win his approval. Eleven years his junior, Adolphe
was known as Lesson jeune, or Lesson the Younger, to avoid con-
fusion. He was admitted to the Rochefort medical school in 1821,
but became a surgeon, not a pharmacist. Botany was Rochefort's
specialty. From 1817, the conseil de santé organized natural history rambles every Sunday from 15 April to 15 September, led by a
first class medical officer, which all pupils and officers of the second and third classes were required to take part in.[14] All students
therefore received elementary instruction in botany as part of their
general studies before later specializing in medicine, surgery, or
pharmacy, a direct result of Keraudren's policy.

Adolphe was a student during his brother's voyage on the
Coquille, and was away on a voyage to Newfoundland in 1825
when the *Coquille* returned. Renamed the *Astrolabe,* and now
under the command of Dumont d'Urville, the corvette was to set
off again almost immediately on another voyage to the Pacific. On
his return from Newfoundland, Adolphe Lesson found himself
posted as second surgeon and botanist on the *Astrolabe,* due to
leave Toulon early in 1826, a prospect he greeted with enthusiasm.

At this point the careers of the two brothers diverge. René-Primevère devoted himself increasingly to his work as a naturalist
and the enormous academic labor that implied. Adolphe continued his career as a surgeon, embarked frequently on long sea voy-

ages, some of them under wartime conditions, and rose up through the ranks to become *second chirurgien en chef,* second chief surgeon, in the Society Islands in 1846. He accumulated nearly twelve years' service at sea and was decorated chevalier de la Légion d'honneur in 1831. Plagued by ill health, a direct result of his voyaging, he took an early but honorable retirement in 1854.

Both brothers remained faithful to Rochefort. Between voyages Adolphe was almost invariably posted to the Hôpital Maritime de Rochefort, and on the rare occasion of his being stationed at Brest, his brother, then premier pharmacien en chef at Rochefort, pleaded family reasons and used his influence to have him transferred to Rochefort. They both died there, in the same house, the elder in 1849 and the younger in 1888, in the street that now bears their name. As a final gesture, Adolphe Lesson left their combined libraries to the Bibliothèque Municipale de Rochefort, the local public library where his manuscripts can still be consulted.

Leaving Toulon on 25 April 1826, the *Astrolabe* sailed via the Cape route to Australia, across to New Zealand, where she passed through Cook Strait and followed the east coast of the North Island, before sailing on to Tonga, the Fijis, New Caledonia, the Louisiade archipelago, New Guinea, and the Carolines, and then returning to France via Mauritius. The voyage lasted three years and ended on 25 March 1829. For Lesson it was a first glimpse of the Pacific, a world that was to become a lifelong passion and the subject of much of his writing. For the surgeon and botanist, this voyage furnished the data for a doctoral thesis in medicine and for the publication of an essay on New Zealand flora.[15] But Lesson's interests ranged well beyond his official tasks on the *Astrolabe,* and later experiences of the Pacific were to reinforce these early leanings, to draw him away from the study of botany to that of the inhabitants of the Pacific.

An examination of his service record and the list of his publications shows an active surgical career, with frequent embarkments leaving little opportunity for the editing of his manuscripts. Apart from the botanical section of the *Astrolabe,* and *Voyage aux îles de Mangareva (Océanie),* published and annotated by his brother (Rochefort, Mercier et Devais, 1846), almost all his published work appeared more than twenty years after his retirement. A spate of short articles in the *Revue d'anthropologie* 1876–1877 was followed by a further series in the *Bulletin de la Société de géographie de Rochefort* between 1883 and 1885.[16] In 1883–1884 appeared his major work, *Les Polynésiens, leur origine, leurs migrations, leur langage* (Paris, Ernest Leroux), edited from his manuscripts by his friend and fellow member of the Société d'anthropologie, Ludovic Martinet. Controversial at the time, this work has been largely neglected because his theory of a wave of migrations beginning in New Zealand and spreading up through the Pacific toward the islands of Malaysia won little support.

Many of the manuscripts he accumulated remain unpublished, and the relative poverty and obscurity of his publications contrast curiously with his prolific note-taking. He was an exuberant critic of everyone about him: his journal on the *Astrolabe* included a wealth of detail about the banal aspects of the voyage along with descriptions of all that was exotic or new. In fact, he kept no fewer than six journals on the *Astrolabe*—medical, surgical, botanical, historical, nautical, and miscellaneous notes[17]—seeking, as he wrote to his brother, to compensate by the quantity of his works their lack of real value and to make sure no one could accuse him of laziness.[18] Whatever his faults, Adolphe Lesson was far from lazy. The specialized scientific journals range from detailed case notes to collections of excerpts drawn from a variety of printed sources, some of which Lesson translated from the English.

His historical journal, which contains a general record of the voyage, runs to over two thousand manuscript pages. It is this journal I have chosen to deal with here because it shows the young surgeon-naturalist in action and brings out the difficulties he encountered in learning his role. I have focused particularly on the New Zealand section for more detailed study because it represents Lesson's first contact with the Pacific and the real beginning of the voyage: "We all felt that the voyage was, so to speak, about to begin, because we were going to visit peoples and places that were new or little known. Everything there was going to be matter for observation."[19]

The form of organization Lesson chose for his historical journal was simple and cyclic, with clear divisions between time spent at sea and periods at anchor. A section of general remarks as each country was left behind broke the journey into its separate stages, a pattern that was not unusual in travelers' journals of the period. Entries were strictly chronological, and Lesson's movements and those of other officers were subject to fairly precise timing. The general historical sections, while obviously falling outside the time context of the voyage itself, were not atemporal and aimed to summarize the state of existing knowledge about each country visited.

Lesson manipulated the genre of the traveler's tale with ease. Without being exhaustive, he gave sufficient meteorological and nautical details to set the scene for dramatic accounts of storms and near shipwreck. He accumulated topographical descriptions and place names regularly enough to situate the ship in a general way, without allowing an exact tracing of her course, and he noted sightings of birds and fish. Into this framework he set his encounters with the local people, incidents on board ship, his adventures in port, and his botanical excursions like so many tableaux, picking up the rhythm of the voyage again to mark the end of each episode. Rapid, entertaining, it could be fiction. It is intriguing therefore to try to assess the historical value of such a document and to follow one surgeon-naturalist through the tribulations hidden by the much-acclaimed success of the new system.

The difficulties experienced by Lesson can be divided into three categories: those affecting all naval surgeons at the time; practical difficulties faced by all naturalists on itinerant expeditions; and tensions arising from the attempt to fulfill a double and often conflicting role.

Just twenty at the outset of the voyage, Lesson was keen to perform his task. His conscientiousness can be seen in the care with which he copied his instructions (drawn up by René Desfontaines and M. Mérat)[20] into the front of his journal. In Toulon awaiting the completion of the final preparations, he made a few botanical excursions in the hills surrounding the town in the company of Dumont d'Urville. The latter, an experienced botanist, could have proved an ideal companion for the novice he had chosen for that post on the *Astrolabe*. But it was not to be so. Tensions developed between the two men that were given full rein in Lesson's journal, culminating in a cruel thumbnail sketch calling into doubt his superior's competence as an officer and a sailor.

For his part, Dumont d'Urville, bitter at the official indifference that greeted his return, contented himself with a dry remark in the published account of the voyage. In his view, Lesson, worthy as he might be, certainly did not figure among the people who had

rendered the most important services to the mission. He emphasized that Lesson's promotion from third to second class surgeon,
granted in the course of the voyage, had not been at his instigation.[21] In fact, this promotion, the only one granted to an officer
of the *Astrolabe,* had been requested by Quoy, who, already by
the end of the New Zealand visit, was delighted with the number
of specimens Lesson had collected and the special care he took of
them. Keraudren, taking notice of Quoy's recommendation,
granted the promotion in July 1827.[22]

That a certain friction should develop between men obliged to
live at close quarters for several years is only to be expected, but
this clash of temperaments exacerbated one of the sore points for
the Service de Santé de la Marine under the Restoration—the inferior status of the naval surgeons in relation to both the naval hierarchy and to their colleagues in the army. It would be 1835 before
the "skills" of the naval surgeons would win sufficient recognition
to class them with the combattants rather than the administration.
Long and bitter battles over inferior status, a humiliating dependence on the naval officers, an over-flamboyant uniform, insuffi-
cient numbers, and low wages were being fought at the time Lesson was in training and on the *Astrolabe.*[23]

Seemingly trivial matters betray Lesson's awareness that the
surgeons were not accorded the status they considered their due.
He was vexed to find himself classed with the *aspirants,* the mid-
shipmen, who in terms of training and service were indeed his infe-
riors. When the medals to commemorate the expedition were distributed among the officers, Lesson and the aspirants received the
bronze, their superiors the silver.[24] In Port Jackson (Sydney) society invitations excluded him along with the aspirants, and only
other naval ships accorded him what he considered appropriate
courtesy.[25]

However, these were minor irritations beside the dependence of
the surgeons on the whims of the naval officers. Surgeons with
only a medical function to fulfill had complained of petty humilia-
tions and obstruction in the execution of their duty. With a dual
task to carry out, how much more vulnerable were the surgeon-
naturalists? Lesson goes so far as to ascribe most of his difficulties
to a willful attempt on the part of the captain to hamper his work
as a botanist. But it is clear from the detail of his complaints that
the conditions under which he was obliged to work were those of

any naturalist on board an expedition of this sort. It is interesting to note in passing that he saw in his difficulties with the captain a reflection of the troubled Baudin-Péron duo:

> I was delighted with the load of plants I had gathered, but if I was happy in that respect, I could not help feeling that it cost me a bit much, in fact, to climb hills, go through thickets and cover whole valleys with an enormous box on my back, a spade in my hand, a big cutlass at my waist and sometimes a packet of plants in my handkerchief. It was, as one will understand, as arduous as could be, and I needed no less than my zeal to help me bear the fatigue resulting from an excursion conducted in that way. And even then, our excursion today took place within a limited circumference and lasted no longer than five or six hours. What will it be like when I go on a day-long excursion? Never mind, unless I fall ill, I feel my zeal will not fail me; but it is nonetheless true, that if a certain person was as interested in botany as he says, he would know how to make my excursions less exhausting, which would enable me at the same time to double my collections. Since masters are employed as hunters, and sailors act as companions or carry out other tasks, it seems to me that for my long excursions I could be assigned some willing fellow, such as several who have already offered me their services. I ought to have all the more right to someone, in that I am not collecting plants for myself and that it is part of my duty to do so, since I have been embarked as botanist, just as much as being a naval observer is part of the naval officer's duty, or being a zoologist is other people's duty. Admittedly, the latter are scarcely better treated than I am in this respect. As we know only too well, the naval officer, in general and the one on board, is infatuated with the pre-eminence of his own specialty: go and ask Péron, Labillardière and others. But what inevitably comes of this unfair treatment? If the person who receives no help is not completely put off, he at least misses the opportunity and possibility of making an abundant collection, or of going any distance from the shore, and he is frequently reduced to going back on board exhausted and consequently less capable of starting again next day. He is certainly less to blame than his superiors, who refuse him the only means he might have of doing better.[26]

Lesson's fears concerning an all-day excursion were to prove unfounded, at least in New Zealand. Only half of his trips ashore lasted six hours or so, the others being short rambles of two or three hours. According to his own testimony, we can estimate the total time spent ashore in New Zealand as only about sixty hours over a period of two months, including the time spent between ship and shore—the equivalent of an hour a day. Even taking into account the time required for the preparation of specimens and accompanying notes, this left a considerable amount of time available for other activities.

Relatively few of the five hundred pages written in or about New Zealand are devoted to botany. The strictly scientific material was recorded in a separate botanical journal, and Lesson used his historical journal to note details of the conditions under which he worked, incidents that occurred during his rambles, and botanical information gleaned from written or oral sources—Maori names for plants, or generalizations about the flora contributed by the English missionaries or by earlier naturalists such as Joseph Banks and J. R. Forster.

Exasperating as they may have been to Lesson, his difficulties were common to other surgeons and to other naturalists. More pertinent are the problems arising from the conflict between the two roles. Lesson's case reveals two flaws in the system: inadequate training, which was not necessarily compensated for by personal aptitude; and the need to have a surgeon on duty at all times, meaning that the time theoretically available for collecting was curtailed.

Arago's remarks about the general nature of the training received by Quoy and Gaimard, justified as they may have been when the *Uranie* sailed, were no longer true ten years later. Quoy was professor of anatomy at the time of the voyage of the *Astrolabe* and the worth of both men had already been well demonstrated. This was not the case with their young colleague, however, and it would appear that Adolphe Lesson's knowledge and experience in botany were not yet very wide. This was shown in Quoy's remarks to René-Primevère Lesson shortly before the beginning of the voyage: "It gives me real pleasure to initiate your brother into comparative anatomy and natural history. He has just what is required to make good progress in those sciences."[27] Quoy did not appear unduly alarmed by this lack of experience, but Lesson himself was more ill at ease. He confessed his ignorance in a letter to his brother from Sydney nearly a year later. Listing among his pursuits during the long days and nights at sea the study of medicine, surgery, botany, and a little drawing and philosophy, he justified the small proportion of time he devoted to botany by a lack of relevant books. He then declared that the little he had read was neither interesting nor agreeable, a distaste he hoped would not be permanent: "Admittedly that is always the case when one is restricted, as I am, to looking at plants solely in view of their forms and structure—but I hope that generalizations and comparisons will appeal to me more once I get back to France."[28]

The guiding hand of the scientific establishment is clearly apparent in the truncated role assigned to Lesson. His initial enthusiasm for his task had already been sapped, and even his vague hope that the subsequent laboratory work would be more stimulating was to be disappointed. His contribution to botany would not go far beyond his fieldwork. Reporting to the Académie des sciences on 30 November 1829 about the botanical achievements of the expedition, René Desfontaines counted some fifteen hundred to sixteen hundred botanical species, quite a number of which were new. The New Zealand and Tasmanian specimens were worthy of particular note and Lesson also received his due: "We cannot praise too highly the zeal and knowledge demonstrated by M. Lesson, *jeune,* in collecting and preparing these plants and in writing the notes to accompany them."[29]

His work as a field-worker had thus been satisfactory. But the Muséum d'Histoire Naturelle had no intention of leaving the important theoretical follow-up solely in the hands of so inexperienced a naturalist. At Dumont d'Urville's request, Lesson was seconded to work on the official account of the voyage, but the preparation of the formal botanical section, including the *Flore de la Nouvelle-Zélande,* was carried out jointly by Lesson and the professional botanist Achille Richard. Indeed, the manuscript of Lesson's botanical journal found its way into Richard's personal library.

Quoy and Gaimard completed the zoological account of the voyage with its accompanying atlases themselves, thereby greatly enhancing their reputation as zoologists. Lesson made his useful but obscure contribution as a field-worker and, returning to the Hôpital Maritime at Rochefort in 1831, faded out of botanical history. Indeed, even as a naval surgeon he is barely remembered: specialized works dealing with surgeon-naturalists neglect to include him, or at best give him a cursory mention.[30]

Yet a conduct report written by M. de Cambray, captain of the *Hussard,* on which Lesson served for three years (1834–1837) indicated that he continued to devote his spare time to botany and conchology. If he had any academic pretensions in those fields, they did not bear fruit. Lesson's contribution to botany is a fine example of the efficiency of the cooperation between the navy and the scientific establishment. Ensuring that fieldwork carried out by naval personnel was guided along standard lines, this cooperative arrangement effectively avoided any lowering of standards in the results of the mission as a whole.

But Lesson illustrated another weakness in the system that was not so easy to resolve: the conflict of interests between the two aspects of the surgeon-naturalist's role. Fears expressed by professional naturalists on this account were summed up by Geoffroy Saint Hilaire: "When the corvettes departed, we were afraid that the ships' doctors would not be able, as was nonetheless proclaimed, to take care of both the crew and of natural history in such a way as to fulfill the two kinds of occupations equally well. Hence the dismay experienced by the naturalists at that time."[31] The scope and quality of the results of the expeditions tended to mask the importance of this objection. It is certain that, although the botanical results of the voyage of the *Astrolabe* were judged satisfactory, they would have been a great deal better had the botanist not chanced to be the junior surgeon and therefore frequently on duty in the infirmary while his superiors were off on scientific excursions. On 6 December 1826 at Port Jackson, Lesson wrote: "Mr. Gaimard, who had not appeared on board since the first days here, relying on me as usual to take care of the infirmary, came to see us for a moment and set off again to spend several days at Parramatta."[32]

While on duty, Lesson was restricted to brief excursions near the ship, although lack of available transport sometimes prevented even that. The problem was aggravated by the fact that the two senior naturalists were both zoologists and worked as a team, an imbalance for which the presence of Dumont d'Urville, whose experience in botany was uncontested, made some compensation. Lesson was not to draw much profit from his knowledge, however, as he learned as early as June 1826, only a few months into the voyage. Left in charge of the infirmary while both zoologists accompanied the captain on an excursion to Teyde Peak in

Tenerife, he was embittered to find that botanical specimens given to Dumont d'Urville by M. Berthelot, head of the local botanical gardens, were destined for the captain's private collection. Disheartened, he felt his appointment as botanist to be hollow and worthless.

It is clear, however, that this journal was also a safety valve for strong emotions inadmissible in a confined space. Lesson's timetable for the two months spent on the coast of New Zealand shows a surprisingly different picture. Out of nineteen possible excursions, Lesson made thirteen. Of the six occasions when he stayed on board, only twice did he feel cheated of his due, and on one occasion only was there any evidence that Dumont d'Urville may have deliberately excluded him. Such a proportion can hardly be considered victimization, although it is true that most of the New Zealand excursions were brief and within a short distance of the ship. Inevitable tensions on board heightened Lesson's criticism of his captain and for personal reasons his resentment due to his exclusion was focused more often on Dumont d'Urville than on Quoy or Gaimard.

The problem was not one of personalities but of the incompatibility of the tasks assigned to Lesson. The proportion of time Lesson spent in sole charge of the infirmary may seem inordinately high, but Gaimard was considered a superior naturalist whose services were more valuable to the mission in that capacity than Lesson's. To his credit, he frequently brought back from his excursions a few botanical specimens for the young colleague he had left behind.

But botany was not in fact Lesson's main preoccupation, and he was far from being impassioned for this branch of natural history. He had confessed in a letter to his brother that "whatever does not touch the soul has, indeed, always seemed to me insipid."[33] In New Zealand, his historical journal recorded the beginning of a drift away from botany toward ethnology. Off Tolaga Bay he wrote: "Since M. Gaimard had gone ashore, I had no choice but to stay on board, considering the distance, and to regret not being able to take part in that scientific ramble; but I was luckily to be amply compensated for staying on board out of duty in witnessing a spectacle which is certainly but rarely to be seen in a lifetime."[34]

He threw himself enthusiastically into meticulously recording the confrontation he witnessed between groups of Maoris on board. The interest he took in this "spectacle" was maintained throughout his journal and was to extend beyond the voyage of the *Astrolabe*. He later used these early observations to construct a theory about the origin of the Polynesians. Discussions with other officers on board, especially Dumont d'Urville, along with his reading of texts written by earlier explorers, stimulated his interest on this subject while the ship was still off the coast of the first Polynesian country he had encountered. Finding his pretensions as a botanist checked as much by his subordinate situation as his lack of adequate training and real taste for the subject, Lesson was not long in finding a field that better suited his temperament and his position.

Conclusion

Adolphe Lesson's journal throws light on several aspects of the condition of surgeon-naturalists, whose presence on scientific missions set up by the French navy became the norm after 1817. The part assigned to Lesson, as a young and inexperienced botanist, was deliberately limited to that of a field-worker, although his older and more experienced colleagues had a much more extensive role to play. He was thus a living example of the cooperation between the navy and the scientific establishment, which ensured that the success of the missions was not compromised by the exclusive use of naval surgeons and amateur naturalists among the officers to fulfill the scientific part of the expeditions.

A man of modest talents, catapulted into a demanding situation through the accidents of family background and early training, he was unable or unwilling to take up the challenge facing him. Turning away from a potential career as a botanist, he chose to remain active in naval medicine, taking up a colonial posting in the Pacific, where he channeled his academic interests into the study of the Polynesians. His historical journal on the *Astrolabe* records the beginning of this drift. Taken in conjunction with his medical and botanical journals, it gives us the measure of the man, such as he was in 1827 and such as he would become in later years.

The document he has left us is a small but telling measure of the methods of observation employed by an educated if unexceptional European confronted with different tribal groups in the Pacific. It reveals the limitations imposed upon him by the practical difficulties of his situation as surgeon-naturalist and consequently the precarious nature of the communication on which his observations of the people were based. Ingenuous, malicious, and eminently readable, it is a useful contribution to our knowledge of this period of early cultural contact in New Zealand and in the Pacific as a whole.

Notes

All translations of Pierre-Adolphe Lesson's texts used in this article are by Isabel Ollivier.

1. John Dunmore, *French Explorers in the Pacific* (Oxford: Oxford University Press, 1969).

2. François Péron (1775–1810) studied for three years at the Ecole de médecine de Paris and trained as a naturalist under Cuvier. He was recruited for the Baudin expedition after his memoir on anthropology was presented to the members of the institute. See G. Hervé, "Les Premiers Armes de François Péron," *Revue anthropologique* 23 (1913): 1–16.

3. Pierre-François Keraudren (1769–1845) held the post of inspecteur-général from 1813 to 1845. His role in transforming the Service de Santé was capital. Dating from the Revolution, the conseils de santé were intermediary bodies between the inspecteur-général and the officiers de santé. They directed the studies of trainee surgeons in the hospitals, designated those who were to embark on each voyage, and supervised the professional and private life of medical personnel in the ports. See Amédée Lefèvre, *Histoire du service de santé et de la Marine militaire* (Paris: J. B. Baillière et fils, 1867), 361.

4. L'Administration du Muséum Royal d'Histoire Naturelle, *Instructions pour les voyageurs et pour les employés dans les colonies, sur la manière de recueillir, de conserver et d'envoyer les objets d'histoire naturelle* (Paris, A. Belin, 1818).

5. Jacques Léonard, *Les Officiers de santé de la Marine française de 1814 à 1835* (Paris: C. Klincksieck, 1967), 290.

6. For biographical details of the surgeon-naturalists, see J. P. Noel, "Quoy, médecin naturaliste navigateur (sa vie, son milieu, son oeuvre)," doctoral thesis, University of Bordeaux, 1960); Pierre Huard and Ming Wong, "Biobibliographie de quelques médecins naturalistes voyageurs de la marine au début du XIXe siècle," in *Vie et milieu,* supplement no. 19 (1965): 163–217; Maurice Zobel, "Les Naturalistes voyageurs français et les grands voyages maritimes du XVIIIe et XIXe siècle" (doctoral thesis, University of Paris, 1967); Patrick Haddou, "Notices biographiques de chirurgiens navigans rochefortais XVIIIe–XIXe siècles" (doctoral thesis, University of Nantes, 1983).

7. Laurent de Jussieu (1748–1836), botanist, was the organizer of the Muséum National d'Histoire Naturelle and a member of the Académie des sciences. Achille Richard (1794–1859), doctor and botanist, was a professor at the

Ecole de médecine de Paris and a member of the Académie des sciences. Jules-Sébastien-César Dumont d'Urville (1790–1842) had established a solid reputation as an amateur botanist.

8. *Rapport lu à l'Académie des sciences le 23 avril 1821,* by Jacques Arago, comptes-rendus de l'Académie des sciences, 1821.

9. *Rapport fait à l'Académie des sciences le 22 août 1825 sur la voyage autour de monde de la corvette de S. M. la Coquille commandée par M. L-I Duperrey,* by M. M. Humboldt, Cuvier, Desfontaines, Cordier, Latreille, de Rossel, Arago. Published in L. I. Duperrey, [*Voyage autour de monde. Partie historique*] [Paris: Arthus Bertrand, 1831]. Georges Cuvier (1769–1832), zoologist, was director of the Muséum d'Histoire Naturelle, 1822–1823 and 1826–1827.

10. Report to Académie published in *Annales des sciences naturelles* 5 (1825): 341. Etienne Geoffroy Saint Hilaire (1772–1844) was a member of the Académie des sciences and professor of zoology at the Faculté des sciences de Paris and at the muséum.

11. In J. S. C. Dumont d'Urville, *Voyage de la corvette L'Astrolabe* (Paris: J. Tastu, 1830), 1:lv.

12. Report to Académie, 351.

13. *Nouvelle biographie générale* (Paris, 1859). The biographical details that follow can be found in Personal file: P. A. Lesson, Marine CC⁷1565, Service Historique de la Marine, Château de Vincennes; Gustave Regelsperger, "Explorateurs océaniens: les deux frères Lesson," *L'Océanie française* (1922): 13–17; "Notices et mentions nécrologiques," *Bulletin de la Société de géographie de Rochefort* 9 (1888): 128.

14. Décision du 11 juin 1817, Bibliothèque de l'Hôpital Maritime de Rochefort 61F, 10873(1); Léonard, *Officiers de santé,* 76.

15. "Quelques mots sur la dysenterie aiguë en général, et particulièrement sur celle qui a été observée à bord de l'Astrolabe pendant son voyage de découvertes" (doctoral thesis, Faculté de Montpellier, 1834). Lesson himself suffered from dysentery and kept detailed case notes on the progress of his own illness.

Achille Richard and Adolphe Lesson, "Essai d'une flore de la Nouvelle Zélande," in *Voyage de la corvette l'Astrolabe . . . Botanique* (Paris: J. Tastu, 1832), part 1 [1]–376. Part 2, *Sertum Astrolabianum* (Paris: J. Tastu, 1834), was edited by Achille Richard from Adolphe Lesson's notes.

16. Some articles that appeared in *Revue d'anthropologie* were republished separately: *Vanikoro et ses habitants* (Paris: E. Leroux, 1876); *Traditions des îles Samoa* (Paris: E. Leroux, 1876); "Les races noires de Timor," *Revue d'anthropologie* (1877). Those published in *Bulletin de la Société de géographie de Rochefort* were: "Notice biographique sur Quiros" 5 (1883–1884): 3–5; "Légende géographique des îles Marquises" 5 (1883–1884): 286–289; "Migrations des Polynésiens" 6 (1884–1885): 74–79; "Iles Marquises: Lettre sur les migrations de leurs habitants" 6 (1884–1885): 77–79; "Tukopia" 7 (1885–1886): 54–58.

17. On Lesson's medical writings, see Anne Bataille, "Le Journal médical de A-P Lesson, chirurgien de Dumont d'Urville sur l'Astrolabe" (doctoral thesis, University of Nantes, 1978), which includes a transcript of Lesson's medical journal. The original is held by the Bibliothèque Municipale de Rochefort (hereafter BMR). For Lesson's medical report, see "Rapports de fin de campagne,

1800–1904," vol. 1: années 1800–1833, no. 20, *Astrolabe,* 25 May 1829, Bibliothèque de l'Hôpital Maritime de Toulon.

For Lesson's botanical and historical journals, see "Voyage de l'Astrolabe: Botanique," Ms. 62, Muséum National d'Histoire Naturelle, Paris, and "Voyage de découvertes de l'Astrolabe," BMR, Ms. 8122, Res. 1-B.

18. P. A. Lesson to R. P. Lesson, Sydney, 17 December 1826, Lettres familières, no. 4, BMR, Ms. 8160.

19. BMR, Ms. 8122, Res. 1-B, 391.

20. René-Louiche Desfontaines (1750–1833), member of the Académie des sciences, botanist, professor at the muséum and later administrator; M. Mérat, botanist at Rochefort.

21. Dumont d'Urville, *Voyage,* 5:588.

22. M. Keraudren, Memorandum to Rochefort Medical Board, 22 June 1827, Personal file: P. A. Lesson.

23. Léonard, *Officiers de santé,* 150–165.

24. BMR, Ms. 8122, Res. 1-B, 316, 339.

25. Ibid., 397.

26. Ibid., 430–432.

27. Quoy to R. P. Lesson, Rochefort, 15 January 1826, Lettres familières, 243.

28. P. A. Lesson to R. P. Lesson, Sydney, 17 December 1826, Lettres familières, no. 4, 15.

29. Dumont d'Urville, *Voyage,* cxvi.

30. See the works listed in note 6 above. Beside his illustrious colleagues, Lesson is a minor figure. Amédée Lefèvre (1798–1869), directeur du Service de Santé from 1854, speaks well of him (Lefèvre, *Histoire,* 366), but the series of essays under the direction of Pierre Pluchon, *Histoire des médecins et pharmaciens de marine et des colonies* (Toulouse: Ed. Privat, 1985), ignores him completely.

31. Report to Académie, 343.

32. BMR, Ms. 8122, Res. 1-B, 329.

33. P. A. Lesson to R. P. Lesson, Sydney, 17 Dec. 1826, Lettres familières, no. 4.

34. BMR, Ms. 8122, Res. 1-B, 509.

4

Tall Tales or True Stories?
Baudin, Péron, and the
Tasmanians, 1802

MIRANDA HUGHES

IN the history of Pacific exploration, the French voyages of Bougainville, La Pérouse, Freycinet, and Dumont d'Urville are well known. A lesser-known voyage, but one equally impressive in its scientific results, was that by Captain Nicolas Baudin to Australia between 1800 and 1804. The naturalist François Péron's *Voyage des découvertes aux terres australes* was the only first-hand account available for over one hundred and fifty years.[1] The *Voyage,* as well as exaggerating the author's own achievements in all aspects of the expedition, presents a biased narrative against Baudin, for whom Péron had much personal animosity. As a result, historians have used this voyage to exemplify the consequences of a tyrant captain who ignored the health of his men and the advice of his peers. An examination of Baudin's *Journal*[2] and other documents from the voyage shows that this reputation is unwarranted, and that the difficulties were due to a combination of inopportune factors. Despite problems, more specimens and descriptions of new specimens were discovered or recorded on this voyage than in all the previous voyages combined (including those of Cook),[3] indicating its importance in the history of science.

The most novel and significant aspect of this voyage was the inclusion of anthropology among its scientific objectives. Savants, artists, and officers alike were aware of the importance of studying "natural man" in his "natural habitat" in a systematic, scientific way. The observations were guided by anthropological instructions specifically written for the expedition. However, as in all such endeavors, the actual execution of these programs was problematic given the intrinsic difficulties of moving from the armchair to the field. This does not, of course, deny the validity of either proposing approaches or of forming conclusions from fieldwork, but the difficulties that arose do illustrate some of the methodological problems of the field sciences generally.

Two principal sets of documents relating to the Tasmanians resulted from this voyage: one by the captain, Nicolas Baudin, the other by the chronicler, François Péron. As well, numerous illustrations, accounts, and reports by the ships' crews and savants survive.[4] The collection forms a valuable resource for the history of anthropology and especially for knowledge of the Tasmanian aborigines. Yet the accounts do not present unbiased observations of the Tasmanians, for the cultural baggage of the French colored their perceptions. The purpose of this chapter, however, is not to establish a checklist of known facts about the Tasmanians and criticize the French for their misconceptions, for such a simple, clear list cannot be obtained: all "facts" contain theory at some level. A more interesting task is to examine how the implicit biases and assumptions of European philosophy and "science of Man" transform a complex society of human beings into a group of savages who are barely surviving.[5] The voyage's anthropological investigations of the Tasmanians—the Diemenese, as the Europeans called them—enable us to examine the manner in which the prejudices and opinions of a particular society come to be reinforced and reified.[6] In any period, the form that knowledge takes to justify a particular opinion is the one that is seen at the time to be the most indisputable. During the Renaissance, arguments concerning man's place in the universe appealed to theologians. At the end of the eighteenth century, the "scientization" of knowledge resulted in the creation of anthropology, physiognomy, and scientific instruments to augment and validate the conclusions and beliefs of observers of man.

The first section of this chapter considers the Société des Observateurs de l'Homme, the anthropological instructions it prepared, and the organization and execution of the voyage. The second section relates the encounter between the French and the Tasmanians, with emphasis on the not insignificant contrasts in the accounts of Baudin and Péron concerning the inherent nature of the Diemenese. The third, concluding section analyzes the effect of the instructions on the observations, and whether the use of a science, with its implication of adherence to an objective truth, resulted in qualitatively better results.

Instructions of the Observateurs

The little-known Société des Observateurs de l'Homme existed for a mere five years in Paris at the beginning of the nineteenth century.[7] Both its emergence and its subsequent obscurity pose a puzzle to the historical sociology of science, for this birth of a social science was still-born. The content of the writings produced by the société justifies the term "social science," for in the papers presented to the meetings are perceptive analyses of the problems of anthropology: the application of a psychology to the individual and to society; and a conscious attempt to apply the methodologies of the established "hard" sciences to fields that had previously come within the domain of law or philosophy.[8]

The Société des Observateurs de l'Homme was established in December 1799 by its future secrétaire perpetuelle, Louis-François Jauffret, a former journalist who would become a teacher, an author of science books for children, and an organizer of nature walks. During this period, Jauffret aspired to a career as a savant but earned his income lecturing on his "Cours d'Anthropologie" and editing a dictionary of science. He had the friendship of many Parisian savants, obtaining for the société the membership of such illustrious figures as Lamarck, Cuvier, Hallé, Pinel, and Bougainville.[9] The Société des Observateurs de l'Homme attracted over eighty members whose self-appointed aim was to examine "man in all his different moral, physical and intellectual relations" through the use of anatomy, physiology, hygiene, history, language, voyages, and jurisprudence. Seven of the société's members would become "philosophical travelers" on Baudin's voyage. Over half its members were trained in medicine and science; many were idéologues and interested in the relationship of ideas and language, through which, it was believed, cultures developed.[10] Enlightenment theories concerning the nature of man underlay the beliefs of the observateurs, for the philosophes were their intellectual parents. However, no longer could "vain theories" or "rash speculation" (French: *hasardées*) suffice for reliable knowledge: the human sciences could only progress, as the physical sciences had done, by "the gathering of many facts and observations."[11]

The impetus for the studies on anthropology was precisely the proposed voyage of Baudin to the southern hemisphere. The African explorer François Levaillant asked that the société issue "particular instructions on the research to be done in relation to man in the diverse countries which will be visited by Captain Baudin." Baudin also requested anthropological instructions. The Institut de France organized the issuance of scientific instructions for naval hygiene, the collection of plants and animals, geographical and astronomical observations, and reissuance of instructions given to La Pérouse. As with all the scientific instructions for the voyage, the task of compiling the anthropological ones was assigned to the most appropriate group: in this instance, the Société des Observateurs de l'Homme. From the société, the Institut de France selected Cuvier, Hallé, Sicard, and Degérando, but unfortunately the instructions of Hallé and Sicard are lost.[12]

The instructions of Cuvier and Degérando focus primarily on physical anthropology and cultural ethnology respectively, although for the observateurs the classification of man and the study of "savage" tribes used both approaches simultaneously. The differences between races, families, and individuals—defined as physical anthropology or physiognomy—were based on such physical features as build, cranial and skeletal structure, hair type, and muscular strength. Comparative anthropology (or what we would label "ethnology") was defined as "the moral and cultural differences between the races" and was considered inseparable from the study of physical anthropology, for the dominant medical theory of hygiene postulated an intrinsic, continual interaction of the mind and body.[13]

Georges Cuvier's guidelines for studying the anatomical differences between the races essentially constitute a work of physical anthropology, of craniometry. He appealed to the need to adopt a systematic, scientific approach to gathering details about races rather than using the vague and inaccurate information typically provided by travelers and sailors. Ideally, the voyagers would collect living human beings, but, failing these, Cuvier advised the gathering of skulls and skeletons, for which he gave methods of preservation, and the making of exact drawings. Paintings of savages and their life-styles were important, and for Cuvier, painter-travelers must forget the precepts of art school, whose rules resulted in such distortions as negroes being painted as "whites smeared with soot." Instead, he requested artists to portray the character of diverse races by applying principles of craniometry and anatomy. Facial portraits must be painted from a specific angle and "delicate observations" must be made to reveal "the true character of the physiognomy." The hair was to be drawn in such a manner as to least hide the forehead and to least alter the shape of the head, and all extraneous ornaments, rings, pendants, and tattoos were to be omitted.[14]

Cuvier, following a tradition begun by Linnaeus, listed the external (such as cranial) characteristics that enable ready demarcation between the races. Cuvier's recommendation for the removal of all decoration shows the trend toward a purely biological approach as opposed to one incorporating cultural features such as ornamentation, an important means by which groups can be distinguished. By attempting to establish a correlation between structures of skulls and skeletons and levels of intelligence and culture, these trends clearly display the Eurocentricity and implicit biases of craniology. The skull of an unknown but non-Caucasian person was already assumed to have belonged to a race that possessed less intelligence and morality. Cuvier's notes belong to the nineteenth-century biological tradition with its differentiation between a concept of race with unalterable characteristics, and an environmentalism allowing the possibility of change, especially for the beneficial improvement of savage society in this philanthropic period. For Cuvier, skeletal differences between races were not contingent on the environment, but were due to hereditary factors. Cuvier cites the example of the "pointedness" of some African heads. The shape of a race's head was not achieved by "squashing" the baby's skull at birth, as had long been suggested; rather, it was an inherited characteristic that was independent of human intervention.[15]

For the voyage of Baudin, Joseph-Marie Degérando produced an essay of some seventy pages on the observation of savage races.[16] This treatise must qualify as the first scientific work of anthropology, for it contains many features essential to scientific research in that discipline. It includes a detailed analysis of the problems associated with examining tribes of an unknown language and culture; it proposes the features of alien cultures that must be observed; and it gives a "scientific" method for learning their languages. Following the system of ideology,[17] which Degérando had helped develop, the philosophical traveler would achieve linguistic fluency by generating the systematic grammar that arises with the "natural" acquisition of language. According to the system, would-be linguists first begin to understand the gestures and signs of the natives, then proceed to concrete objects and their nouns and adjectives, and finally to a comprehension of the more complex and abstract ideas. Knowledge of the language of a tribe is deemed necessary to achieve proper understanding of the range and extent of the savages' ideas.[18]

According to Degérando, the development of ideas is similar to the acquisition of language; indeed, the two are inextricably entwined within the framework of the idéologues upon which Degérando's work is based. Both ideas and language depend on the natives' capacity to experience sensation, for "our ideas are nothing more than elaborated sensations," and language is dependent on this. As with language, ideas are to be examined in the order in which they are generated. Degérando does not expect many higher-order ideas, perhaps not because of an incapacity on the natives' part, but due to a lack of complex stimuli in their environment. It is important to study the visual means of communication—the emblems, the allegories, and the signs—to see how they function as symbols within the culture. In rituals such as dances, which are "sometimes so mysterious for a stranger," the functions are not just to be described: "[the explorer] will try as far as possible to reach an understanding of the sense attached to them, the effects they produce and the origin from which they spring."[19]

The last third of Degérando's treatise is concerned with the disparities between savage and European thought and society. It utilizes an environmentalist approach to investigate how the form of ideas and society is influenced by such factors as climate, food, physical needs, and the flora and fauna of the region: they reflect on the underlying philosophical doctrine, and the developmental stage of the relevent scientific theory.[20]

Finally, the explorer should examine the individual in his physiological sense, including physical strength, actions, and needs; the number of hours and regularity of sleep; clothing; and the illnesses to which the savages are prone. Degérando distinguishes between the functional sense of clothes and sleep and the ritualistic or symbolic aspects of such actions.[21]

Degérando continues with a detailed discussion of the aspects of society with which the philosophical traveler needs to acquaint himself, reflecting political and social preoccupations as well as cultural biases. His suggestions form the basis of a comprehensive ethnology that is qualitatively richer than previous travelers' tales (armchair or otherwise), and a precursor of modern research on primitive tribes. "Aggregates of families" form "society at large" and an understanding of these will follow from an examination of the savages' ideas of the basic unit, the family, and their attitude to love, marriage, divorce, education, fathers, and women. He argues that "all these observations can be grouped in two main categories: the state of the individual, and that of the society." Degérando suggests a comprehensive list of features of political, civil, religious, and economic life about which information can be gathered. These include: hierarchy of power and whether it is elected or hereditary; how and why wars arise; military art; crime; industries; commerce; and religious ceremonies, buildings, traditions, and priests.[22]

These instructions, prepared for Baudin's voyage, were issued in an attempt to raise the quality of the savants' and the officers' reports on the native inhabitants encountered, although it is not known if they were widely read. Moreover, familiarity with the anthropological issues raised by Degérando and Cuvier could not obviate the influence of a personality fundamentally at odds with a perspective of "scientific" neutrality. It appears that the different characters and backgrounds of Péron and Baudin influenced their perceptions. Their anthropological reports were not the product of mere observation alone.

The first protagonist, twenty-five-year-old François Péron, had fought, been imprisoned, and lost an eye during the French Revolution. In June 1797 he arrived in Paris to study at the Ecole de Médecine, but it appears his interests lay more in natural history for he frequently attended the lectures of Cuvier, Lamarck, and Geoffroy Saint-Hilaire at the Muséum d'Histoire Naturelle. But both poverty and a refusal in marriage fueled his desire to join the voyage of Baudin to the southern hemisphere. Discovering that all the savants' positions had been filled, Péron presented a paper to the Institut de France arguing that "anthropology, or the natural history of man," was crucial to the success of the voyage. He noted that although plants and animals were to be examined in detail, no special "anthropologiste" had been commissioned to study the habitats and morals of the diverse peoples the expedition would encounter. As a result, not only would Europeans remain ignorant of their life-styles; they would also be deprived of the opportunity to utilize the remedies that "instinct and experience have made known to these savage men." Péron cited quinine and sassafras as examples. Moreover, study of native societies could provide useful data for the doctrines of hygiene, which postulated that the constitution of a society was contingent on the environment in which it was situated. On the strength of this paper he was admitted to the voyage, but in the class of zoologist rather than anthropologist. Hints of a "zealous" and "impetuous" nature emerge from this brief portrait.[23]

Forty-five-year-old Nicolas Baudin, a much more cautious person, had captained three earlier scientific voyages (including one for the Austrian emperor, Joseph II). These he had executed with success, and exotic specimens from one voyage had featured in the victory parade for Napoléon after Marengo.[24] In 1798 Baudin proposed a grand enterprise for the "glory of France" in which a flotilla of ships would engage in world exploration to the Americas as well as the southern hemisphere. The expenses of a country at war did not allow such a grandiose scheme, but with Napoléon's aid, a modified version was accepted in 1799.[25]

Baudin was versed in natural science and was respected by many officers of the Muséum d'Histoire Naturelle. Lamarck described him as "a most enlightened man," while the professor of natural history Jussieu told Napoléon's Directory that "of all the voyagers, he is the one whose achievements in the sphere of natural history are the most meritorious." Baudin was an active member of the Société des Observateurs de l'Homme and undoubtedly would have been familiar with the anthropological instructions they prepared.[26] Observations and reports of a similar reliable standard could be expected from Baudin's work on this new expedition.

Sailing to the Extremities of the Globe

Equipped with these instructions, the *Géographe* and the *Naturaliste* sailed from Le Havre in March 1800. It was a slow, wearying passage to Timor, with adverse winds, slow-drawing sails, and (owing to political factors) no access to supplies at the Canary

Islands and Île de France (Mauritius).[27] The original plan of circumnavigating Australia and exploring the coastline of both the mainland and Van Diemen's Land was altered because of the onset of winter. Instead, months were spent in carefully exploring the western coast of Australia, and the expedition returned to Timor before sailing south again.[28]

Finally, Van Diemen's Land was reached, and on 24 nivoîse, an X (14 January 1802), two French longboats landed on the beach of D'Entrecasteaux Channel in the south-east corner of Tasmania. Baudin and Péron were among those who went ashore and were greeted by small groups of Diemenese. Baudin, providing descriptive rather than interpretative details, observed that the natives approached "without the slightest distrust," with "no harmful design," "behaving in a very friendly way toward us," establishing "mutual trust."[29] In contrast, Péron speculates on the intention and personality of the Diemenese. The two men and two women, he writes, showed "the most extraordinary gestures of surprise and admiration." The first male's features "were not the least austere or fierce. His eyes were bright and spiritual, and his countenence expressed at the same time benevolence and surprise." The second, a man in his fifties, also had features that "were open and frank [and] in spite of some unmistakable signs of uneasiness and fright, we could readily perceive his artlessness and good nature." The younger man examined the longboat, giving Péron "the most striking example we ever had of attention and reason among savage people." To the two young women, Péron attributes kindness and benevolence, and to the younger one, "an expressiveness and something spiritual about her eyes which surprised us and which since then we have not encountered in any other woman of this nation."[30]

Thus, initially, the Tasmanians made a favorable and friendly impression on the French. But, had the observateurs influenced the observations? Had the philosophical travelers proceeded according to Degérando's treatise and produced a veritable anthropology? The answer, in both cases, is no. The noble savage fell from a state of grace into one of near beastiality within a few weeks as impressions changed from preconceptions based on a Rousseauesque philosophy to misconceptions apparently derived from experiences, but actually only based on a different set of beliefs.

The French explored D'Entrecasteaux Channel for five weeks,

Figure 1. "Terre de Diémen," showing native habitations, from L. Freycinet, Atlas deuxième (2d ed., 1824) of *Voyage de découvertes aux terres australes.* (Courtesy of Baillieu Library, University of Melbourne)

and then Maria Island, two days sailing further north, for eight days, before heading to Kangaroo Island off the coast of South Australia.[31] In his report to the ministre de la marine, Baudin concludes that: "whilst not being entirely devoid of humanity, the Diemenese are at the least degree of civilization imaginable."[32] Péron characterizes them as

> having no true chiefs, without laws, without any form of regular government, without arts of any sort, without any idea of agriculture or the use of metals or animal husbandry, without clothing, or fixed habitations, without any other retreat than a miserable windbreak of bark to shield them from the cold winds of the south, lacking any weapons except the waddy and the spear, always wandering through the forests or along the seashore, the inhabitants of these regions doubtless combine all the characteristics of non-social man. He is in truth the very *child of nature.*[33]

The explanation of this transition does not lie in a simple realization of the true nature of the Tasmanians. Rather, it requires a closer examination of the dynamics of the encounter, the personalities of the French protagonists, and the manner in which interpretations were affected by actual confrontation with these "savage children of nature."

There was a total of thirteen meetings with the Tasmanians varying both in duration and in number of natives present. In general, the encounters were amicable, with enthusiasm for anthropology shown by both parties. At one level these encounters parody the archetypal field anthropology, for the Tasmanians were not as passive as "the studied tribe" ought to be; instead, they were enthusiastic about the whole enterprise. While the French, with an eye on their instructions, busily carried out their measurements, made their sketches, built their vocabulary, and pursued their investigation of aboriginal cultural life, the Tasmanians carried out investigations of their own.

Aborigines believed that ancestors reappear with white skins, and they may have considered Caucasians to be ghosts of their ancestors. The Tasmanians were stunned by the removal of gloves, which appeared to be a removal of skin. Péron comments: "The natives wanted to examine the calves of our legs and our chests, and so far as these were concerned we allowed them to do everything they wished, oft repeated cries expressing the surprise which the whiteness of our skin seemed to arouse in them."[34]

This preoccupation of the Tasmanians is not surprising, for the French, having no women and children among them, presented a far more unnatural group of people than the Diemenese. The blacks were puzzled by the whites' refusal of offers of sexual intercourse with the women, and their keenness to engage merely in arm-wrestling and other physical games with the men. Péron discusses at length why the acts of kissing and caressing appear to be unknown to the savages and suggests that they are the result of civilization.[35] Yet, Péron appears to have hugged only the *males* of the group, or, at the least, sees nothing inappropriate in writing: "However, I do not positively assert as a fact, what may only be a conjecture; but I can assert that I never saw, either on Diemen's Land or New Holland, any savage embrace another of his own sex, or *even* of a different sex" (my emphasis).[36]

Péron spends a quarter of this report discussing kissing, caressing, and male potency. When an examined sailor "suddenly exhibited striking proof of his virility," Péron surmises that the Tasmanians "had the air of applauding the condition as if they were men in whom it was not very common." He continues: "Several of them showed with a sort of scorn their soft and flaccid organs and shook them briskly with an expression of regret and desire which seemed to indicate that they did not experience it as often as we did."[37] The anthropological treatise reverts back to such topics a few pages later where Péron spells out the "cause of the feeling of pleasure that most people experience from a kiss": "The kiss on the mouth is much more tender and much more delicate; and that which a happy lover savours rapturously on the palpitating bosom of his mistress is undeniably one of the most profound sensations and the most voluptuous which one can experience."[38] Given the space devoted to the description of genitalia and interpretations of the "savage" sexuality, it is difficult to say whether we see the preoccupation of the Diemenese, or the obsession of European men after two years at sea.[39]

Clearly, the assumptions of European philosophy about the nature of savages structured communication and trade with the Tasmanians. The instructions "of the Conduct to be observed towards the Natives" issued to La Pérouse, and reissued to Baudin, discussed the need to establish a good rate for traded articles: "[The traveler] will regulate the value of the articles of exchange, and he will never allow the price fixed to be exceeded, lest, if he should grant in the beginning too high a price for the commodities he wishes to procure, the natives might take advantage of it not to part with them afterwards for less." The commander "will forbid them, under pain of severest punishment, ever to employ force to procure from the inhabitants what they may refuse to part with voluntarily." Moreover, the voyagers were to encourage and demonstrate the usefulness of cultivation and animal husbandry to civilize the savages.[40] Degérando suggested Baudin discover the fate of animals previous explorers had left behind and introduce natives to the ship's livestock. The first few encounters between islanders and sheep involved, however, the Diemenese trying to talk to the animals and wondering why there was no response. In the native belief system and experience, all creatures were either human-like or like Australian fauna. No sheep were in the Dreamtime—the legendary period of aboriginal origins—thus the sheep were as likely to be human as the whites.[41]

Implicit in the types of gifts offered to the Tasmanians is the then common comparison between natives and children and, furthermore, the Europeans' lack of understanding of the natives' needs and interests. The voyagers offered them the usual trinkets of buttons, glass beads, bottles, handkerchiefs, and looking glasses. But "everything that we offered them was received with an indifference that surprised us, and which we had often occasion to observe amongst individuals of the same country."[42] The French were made aware that little value was placed on the trinkets, which could have told them that the Tasmanians were mentally more advanced than children. There are many references to the enthusiasm that the natives had for gleaming, glinting metals. Yet only Leschenault, the draftsman, reported the reason why the natives were persistently attracted to the bottles. It was not from a simple fascination for the glass, as implied by the other reports, but rather that "they considered bottles to be of particular value, not to use as containers, but to break them up so as to use the fragments to scrape and point their spears, which as a rule they do with pieces of granite."[43]

The Tasmanians tired of the tokens they received, and by the end of each encounter the French found that most of the trinkets had been abandoned. Péron comments: "we were convinced that after satisfying a puerile curiosity, these uninformed men threw away what no longer pleased or amused them."[44] This statement conveys the implicit assumptions of the childish intelligence of savages: it ignores the indifference to possessions that is characteristic of nomadic hunter gatherers and distorts the act of rejecting something of no use into an immature response of lack of amusement. The trinkets were of a type given to satisfy an impetuous, angry child or to amuse a bored child. The gifts were also given with the aim of gaining unconditional trust and friendship. More importantly, the trade transactions were uneven in terms of the power symbols they expressed. What the French gave was not only worthless, but also, for the most part, harmless. Although they did give knives and axes, which were no more lethal than the native weapons, they did not offer guns, the potential of which the Tasmanians were well aware. Yet the French expected native assagais and spears in exchange and thought it unreasonable when the Tasmanians refused.[45]

In general, the interactions between the French and the Tasmanians were amicable, and the native hosts were as helpful and excited as their guests. Yet some farewells were marred by the Tasmanians throwing spears at the backs of the retreating whites. The most striking instance of this occurred when a sailor, Maurouard, won an arm-wrestling contest against a Tasmanian. The rest of the meeting had apparently passed amicably, but when the French were boarding the longboats, a Tasmanian threw a spear and wounded Maurouard in the neck. Neither Baudin nor Péron were present, but both record the incident.[46] Baudin describes the event and attempts to rationalize the attack. First he suggests that "it can be attributed to some treachery and their slight fear of those who were still ashore." But then he offers an alternative: "Nevertheless, it seems likely to me that the natives, upon seeing their comrades defeated by strength, sought to make it known that they were not the weaker in skill and cunning. This is perhaps what brought about the throwing of the spear, for there was just the one."[47] Contrast this with Péron's account, where after the contest the Diemenese was "compelled to acknowledge his inferiority" and for which during the rest of the afternoon "it was impossible to have the smallest suspicion of any change in the sentiments." (Péron here is applying the science of physiognomy to a field situation.) After the midshipman was hit, Péron reports that "the boat's crew, provoked at the perfidious and cowardly brutality would have pursued the savages and punished them as they deserve."[48]

There is a qualitative difference in these two accounts of the same event. Baudin blames neither side. He attempts to explain the Tasmanians' inconsistent behavior within the framework of their essential good-nature: that the same individuals could reappear the next day "without the slightest sign of distrust . . . alone proved to me that either they are not naturally wicked or they consider us incapable of doing them harm."[49] Péron, self-proclaimed anthropologist, mentions only their "perfidious and cowardly brutality." Without including any possibility of native resentment, he suggests that the savagery of the Tasmanians *alone* suffices as an explanation, agreeing with the crew's desire to punish the entire group of savages rather than the single native.[50] This is a response perhaps expected of a sailor, but surely inexcusable for an "observer of man."

The attacks by the Tasmanians on the French exemplify the problem of interpreting the actions of foreigners, a perennial problem for any traveler. Degérando warned that "careful precautions must be taken before making a judgement. Fear and ferocity can equally put arms in the hands of people visited: good nature, trust, timidity or perfidy can equally lead him to accord strangers a favourable welcome."[51] Despite this advice, the French hastily arrived at conclusions that failed to reflect adequately their role in the encounters. For the most part, the reports emphasize the apparent injustice of giving "gifts" and yet not getting "civilized" treatment in return rather than the need to explain such inconsistencies. There are some attempts at explanation—Baudin suggests fear—but generally these are secondary to the sense of injustice.[52]

For the historian, the number of expeditions that had visited the area in the intervening period provides a feasible explanation of the different welcomes given to La Billardière in 1792 and Baudin ten years later. Sealers and explorers had made indiscriminate use of firearms, both in hunting and in maintaining control over the Tasmanians. All the Tasmanians whom Baudin met were aware of the potential of firearms: the French had only to raise the weapon in threat to get them to "behave."[53] Thus, the occasional unfavorable interpretation of the Frenchmen's motives on the part of the Diemenese in the early stages of encounter seems a reasonable response. Once trust was established, no further attacks were perpetrated.

Conclusion

The voyage of Baudin to Australia is representative of European exploration of the Pacific region. Although the general scientific and navigational instructions issued for the expedition utilized previously gained experience, they reflect more on the expected outcome of the voyage. This is especially true of the anthropological instructions issued by the Société des Observateurs de l'Homme. As well as containing sound advice for a methodical approach to anthropology, the instructions include many assumptions concerning the expected nature of the inhabitants of countries to be visited.

The two main assumptions underlying this theoretical discourse are the identification of so-called primitive tribes with early humans and the notion of primitives as children. Parallels are drawn between the imagined first stages of civilization and newly discovered hunter gatherer tribes, where "primitive" connotes both simplicity and immaturity. The fallacy, however, is twofold: first, that a discovered tribe was of recent origins; and, second, that a society at the first stage of development is also mentally at a childish level.

These ideas appear in the writings of the Société des Observateurs de l'Homme. Degérando states: "The philosophical traveller, sailing to the ends of the earth is, in fact, travelling through time: he is exploring the past; every step that he takes is the passage of an age. Those unknown islands that he reaches are for him the cradle of human society." Jauffret, in *Introduction aux mémoires,* argues that the work of the explorers will aid the "science of Antiquities," for the "observations of navigators on the actual habitats of diverse regions ought to furnish precise light on the first epochs of the human species [French: *genre*]."[54] Here, the comparison is clear and follows the tradition that traversed the globe with the explorers. From the Americas through the Pacific to Australia, the original race of humankind was thought to have been discovered.

The interactions between the French and the Tasmanians also illustrate two major problems of anthropology: namely, the problem of applying written instructions, and the influence of observer bias. Both Péron and Baudin made assumptions and errors that could have been avoided had they followed assiduously the advice of the Société des Observateurs de l'Homme, but this was an un-achievable, perhaps impossible task. Eurocentricity pervades the observations made about the Tasmanians, with the standards of beauty, morality, and intelligence set by Caucasians. Although many features of the Tasmanian physique are noted—such as skull shape; the woolly hair (French: *laineaux*); the color of the skin, which varies from copper to dark brown; the proportion of the limbs; and the gleaming white teeth—the tone of the commentary is generally derogatory.

The attitude toward female beauty provides a characteristic example. Perhaps Péron sums up his own opinion of Tasmanian beauty best in this sentence: "In a word, all the particulars of their natural constitution were in the highest degree disgusting." To Péron, the West Australian women differ little from the Tasmanians. They are "horribly ugly and disgusting, and enough to disgust the most depraved amongst our sailors." Péron is perceptive enough to realize that the Tasmanians likewise regarded the white-skinned foreigners as ugly (partly because the natives attempted to cover his face with charcoal or ochre), but this does not lead him to modify his position on the supremacy of white beauty.[55]

Despite the observer bias inevitably permeating the reports, it is still valid to criticize their relative quality. Péron's writings appear much more effusive and extravagant than those of Baudin—which is not to argue that Baudin is "right" about his observations, only that his descriptions are more informative than Péron's. Moreover, comparison with other writings from the voyage show that Péron's accounts, despite a superior literary style, stand less well as anthropological treatises. Indeed, they are little improvement on the work of an amateur traveler. Baudin, however, has presented a more thorough account of the Tasmanians, which displays an awareness of how the French presence will alter native behavior. He is worthy of Degérando's title, "Philosophical Traveler."

Notes

Rod Home, Homer LeGrand, and especially the editors of this volume, Roy MacLeod and Fritz Rehbock, made helpful comments on an earlier draft of this chapter. I would also like to thank the archivists at the Académie des sciences, the Archives Nationales, the Muséum d'Histoire Naturelle in Paris, and the Muséum d'Histoire Naturelle at Le Havre, for their help and permission to use material.

1. François Auguste Péron, *A Voyage of Discovery to the Southern Hemisphere, performed by order of the Emperor Napoléon, during the years 1801, 1802, 1803, and 1804* (1809; Melbourne: Marsh Walsh Publishing, 1975). Originally published as the first volume of François Auguste Péron and Louis Claude Desaulses de Freycinet, *Voyage de découvertes aux terres australes, executé par ordre de Sa Majesté l'Empereur et Roi, sur les corvettes le Géographe, le Naturaliste, et la göelette le Casuarina, pendant les années 1800, 1801, 1802 et 1804; (Historique)* (Paris: Imprimerie impériale, 1807–1816). Two volumes of text and atlas in two parts.

2. Nicolas Baudin, *Journal of Baudin, 1800–1803,* trans. Christine Cornell (Adelaide: Library Board of South Australia, 1974). This work has yet to be published in France. Other primary sources are Archives Nationales AJ[15] 565–576 and Marine BB[4] 995–997, Paris.

3. Jussieu reported to the Institut de France that over eighteen thousand individual specimens were gathered, which resulted in the discovery of 2,542 new species. Archives Nationales AJ[15] 569.

4. The illustrations and paintings are at Le Havre, as are some of Péron's manuscripts. The most accessible collection of reports and observations is to be found in N. J. B. Plomley, *The Baudin Expedition and the Tasmanian Aborigines, 1802* (Hobart, Tasmania: Blubberhead Press, 1983). No published French collection exists.

5. This problem of observer bias has become a common theme in recent works of anthropology. The debate concerning Margaret Mead and her version of Samoa centers on this. Greg Dening's *Islands and Beaches: Discourse on a Silent Land, Marquesas 1774–1880* (Hawaii: University of Hawaii Press, 1980) provides an excellent analysis of the interplay of the social theory of the observer and the social structure of the islanders.

6. Society itself is not, of course, a monolithic edifice. Here reference is to the educated parts of French and especially Parisian society.

7. The symbolism of creating a new science in the last few weeks of the eighteenth century was hidden, for the adoption of the Republican calendar meant that the société merely appeared in "frimaire, an VIII." Its last meeting was in 1805. The société was rediscovered at the turn of this century by the anthropologists E. T. Hamy and G. Hevre of the Musée de l'Homme. In 1978 it was again found, and a collection of papers appeared, with an introduction by Jean Copans and Jean Jamin, as *Aux origines de l'anthropologie française: Les Mémoires de la Société des Observateurs de l'Homme en l'an VIII* (Paris: Le Sycamore, 1978). In French there is also M. Bouteiller, "La Société des Observateurs de l'Homme, ancêtre de la Société d'anthropologie de Paris," *Bulletin et mémoires de la Société anthropologique de Paris,* 10th ser., 7 (1956): 448–465. The best English-language paper on this topic is George Stocking, "French Anthropology in 1800," *Isis* 55 (1964): 134–150.

8. The aims and aspirations of the société are discussed in Louis-François Jauffret, "Introduction aux mémoires de la Société des Observateurs de l'Homme," in Copans and Jamin, eds., *Aux origines,* 73–85.

9. R. M. Reboul, *Louis-François Jauffret, sa vie et ses oeuvres* (Paris: Six, 1869), 24–36. The "Cours d'Anthropologie" was never published. Jauffret lec-

tured on this theme in the Louvre in winter and during promenades around Versailles during the summer months. Jean-Baptiste de Lamarck postulated a system of inheritance of acquired characteristics, while Georges Cuvier is best remembered for his extensive and detailed classificatory systems for the animal and vegetable worlds. Jean-Noël Hallé and Philippe Pinel pursued medicine, the latter being famous for removing the chains from the insane at the Salpêtrière Asylum. Bougainville explored the Americas and the South Pacific.

10. No membership list of the société seems to have survived. It appears that Reboul had a list of the names of members from which all other lists are derived. Membership did not have to imply active participation in the société. On the aims of the société, see Jauffret, "Introduction."

The "philosophical travelers" were Nicolas Baudin, commander; Pierre-François Bernier and Frédéric Bissy, astronomers; René Maugé and Anselme Rièdle, botanists; Emmanuel Hamelin, second-in-command; Andre Michaud, botanist (who left the voyage at Île de France). Péron had some contact with the société but was not himself a formal member. Idéology was defined as the science of the generation of ideas. Following methodological notions of simplicity and observation, it was assumed that deaf-mutes, wild children, and savage tribes would acquire language similarly, and that their languages would be primitive, natural, and simple versions of sophisticated civilized ones. Members who were idéologues included Antoine-Louis-Claude Destutt de Tracy, Pierre-Jean-Georges Cabanis, Constantin-François Boisgiray de Chassebeuf de Volney, Dominique-Joseph Garat, Abbé Roche-Ambroise Cucurron Sicard, Jean Itard, Philippe Pinel, Pierre Sue, Jean-Noël Hallé, and Joseph-Marie Degérando. On the relationship of ideas and language, see, for example, Harlan Lane, *The Wild Boy of Aveyron* (Cambridge, Mass.: Harvard University Press, 1976). For idéology, see François Picavet, *Les Idéologues* (Paris: Alcan, 1891), and Georges Gusdorf, *La Conscience revolutionnaire: Les Idéologues* (Paris: Payot, 1978).

11. The late eighteenth century saw a narrowing of the generalities of Enlightenment thought, and treatises became more formalized by the application of a scientific method. This is apparent in the physical sciences, in the development of chemistry following the revolution in its nomenclature, and with the development of the biological sciences. Jauffret, "Introduction," 73.

12. Reboul, *Louis-François Jauffret,* 127 (quotation). Reboul comments: "The intrepid Baudin had asked Jauffret for instructions, especially to make on anthropology" (ibid., 38). The instructions to La Pérouse are printed at the beginning of J. F. G. de la Pérouse, *A Voyage around the World performed in the years 1785–1788 by the Boussole and Astrolabe* (Amsterdam: N. Israel Press, Bibliotheca Australiana #27 [facsimile: 1799], 1968).

The société itself had proposed the four selected as *commissaires.* See Reboul, *Louis-François Jauffret,* 127. The Abbé Sicard was director of the Parisian institution for deaf-mutes, whilst Degérando, who was primarily an administrator and politician, achieved academic fame with his publications on the relationship between language and thought.

13. Jauffret, "Introduction," passim; Georges Cuvier, "Note instructive sur les recherches à faire aux différences anatomiques des diverses races de l'homme," in Copans and Jamin, eds., *Aux origines,* 173 (definition). Of the observateurs,

Cabanis, Hallé, Sue, and Pinel were medical men who utilized the theory of hygiene. See Gusdorf, *La Conscience révolutionnaire,* Picavet, *Les Idéologues,* and Martin Staum, *Cabanis: Enlightenment and Medical Philosophy in the French Revolution* (Princeton, N.J.: Princeton University Press, 1980).

    14. Cuvier, "Note instructive," 174, 175.

    15. Stocking, "French Anthropology," discusses the nineteenth-century features of Cuvier's work. Although dealing with a different period from this paper, Stephen Jay Gould's *The Mismeasure of Man* (London: Penguin, 1984) also discusses this issue.

    16. Degérando, *The Observation of Savage Peoples,* trans. F. T. C. Moore (Berkeley and Los Angeles: University of California Press, 1969). The original French version ("Considérations sur les diverses méthodes à suivre dans l'observation des peuples sauvages") can be found in Copans and Jamin, *Aux origines,* 127–169.

    17. See note 10.

    18. Degérando, *Observation of Savage Peoples,* 73–76.

    19. Ibid., 83, 77.

    20. Ibid., 78. For example, although food is important, the water must also be "carefully analysed," which reflects the preoccupation of the French with the consititution of mineral waters and their benefits to health.

    21. Ibid., 78–79.

    22. Ibid., 78, 88–91. For Degérando's list, see pp. 91–101. Constraints on the length and direction of this chapter restrict further discussion of this issue.

    23. See Colin Wallace, *The Lost Australia of François Péron* (London: Nottingham Court Press, 1984), for a basically accurate, but rather simplistic account of the life of Péron. Péron's paper, *Observations sur l'anthropologie, ou l'histoire naturelle de l'homme, la nécessité de s'occuper de l'avancement de cette science, et l'importance de l'admission sur la flotte du Captain Baudin d'un ou plusieurs naturalistes, spécialement chargés des recherches à faire sur ce sujet* (originally published in "an VIII"), has been reprinted in Copans and Jamin, *Aux origines,* 177–185 (see p. 180 for quotations, my translations). The procès-verbaux of the Institut de France of I thermidor, an VIII, state: "L'Ecole de Médecine, ayant étendu dans sa dernière séance des *Observations sur l'anthropologie* . . . , communique à l'Institut ses idées à cet égard et lui recommende le C. Péron de l'Allier, auteur des observations citées."

Hygiene was an elaborated version of the Enlightenment doctrine of environmentalism. Many of its proponents were also *idéologues.* Cf. Piçavet, *Les Idéologues;* Gusdorf, *La Conscience revolutionnaire;* and Staum, *Cabanis.* Archives Nationales, Marine BB[4] 995, AJ[15] 569 feuille 367, lists Péron under the zoologists as "élève, chargé spécialement de l'anatomie comparée." On Péron's nature see the letter from the Ecole de Médecine to the Institut de France recommending Péron, signed by Hallé, Lassus, and Thouret (director), in Dossier, Lassus, Académie des sciences, Archives. See also Baudin, *Journal.*

    24. Archives Nationales, Marine BB[4] 995, Arthur W. Jose, "Nicholas Baudin," *Royal Australian Historical Society, Journals and Proceedings* 20 (1934): 337–396.

    25. Archives Nationales, Marine BB[4] 995.

26. Degérando, *Observation of Savage Peoples*, 9 (quotation from Moore's introduction); Reboul, *Louis-François Jauffret*.

27. "Sailing to the extremities of the globe" is Degérando's phrase from *Observation of Savage Peoples*, 101. Political strife in the Canary Islands and a minor mutiny by the French governors at Mauritius, which threatened to abolish slavery, prevented Baudin from obtaining good quality supplies at either port. When his carte blanche was not honored by his countrymen, Baudin was forced to buy supplies from traders.

28. Péron, *Voyage;* Baudin, *Journal.* For secondary accounts see Ernest Scott, *Terre Napoléon* (London: Meuthen, 1910); John Dunmore, *French Explorers in the Pacific* (Oxford: Oxford University Press, 1969).

29. Baudin, *Journal*, 304–306.

30. Péron, *Voyage*, 174.

31. Baudin, *Journal*, 304–350.

32. Baudin, "Des naturels que nous trouvions et de leur conduite envers nous," report to the ministre de la Marine and to the Muséum d'Histoire Naturelle, Archives Nationales, Marine BB[4] 995:5, and Muséum d'Histoire Naturelle, 2082, respectively. Translation from Plomley, *The Baudin Expedition*, 107.

33. Péron, "Experiments on the physical strength of the savage people of Van Diemen's Land and New Holland, and of the inhabitants of Timor," in Plomley, *The Baudin Expedition*, 147.

34. Péron, "Maria Island: Anthropological Observations," in Plomley, *The Baudin Expedition*, 84. Péron prepared this report of his fieldwork for Baudin soon after leaving Tasmania. The theme of whites as ghosts occurs throughout the initial contact period. A most readable account is Henry Reynolds, *The Other Side of the Frontier* (Brisbane: Queensland University Press, 1981). In this voyage, there are numerous references to the Aborigines' reaction to clothes. For example, Péron and Freycinet, *Voyage*, 175–176.

35. Péron, "Maria Island." The Tasmanians were curious to see whether the white males were identical in anatomy to themselves. They were keen to examine the young beardless sailors, aged about fifteen, presumably because they were the ones among the whites most likely to be female. Once or twice, a sailor was dragged into the bushes where "scrupulous inspections of the entire body" were made during which the Tasmanians would "utter great bursts of laughter" (ibid., 91), and then allow the youths to return unharmed. Baudin comments that it would be interesting for the science of man to know what thoughts passed through the minds of these young sailors (Baudin, "Des naturels," 109).

36. Péron, *Voyage*, 219.

37. Péron, "Maria Island," 84.

38. Ibid., 87.

39. Jean Jamin, "Faibles sauvages . . . corps indigènes corps indigent le désenchantement de F. Péron," in Hainard and Koehr, eds., *Le Corps en Jeu* (Neuchâtel: Musée d'ethnographie, 1983), 45–76; Jean Jamin, "De la génération perdue: L'Indigent, l'indigène et les Idéologues," *Anthropologie et sociétés* 3, no. 2 (1979): 55–78.

40. La Pérouse, *Voyage around the World*, 39–42.

41. Degérando, *Observation of Savage Peoples*, 95–97; Baudin, "Des natu-

rels." Translation from Plomley, *The Baudin Expedition,* 108. For the belief system of the Aborigines, see Reynolds, *Other Side.*

42. Péron, *Voyage,* 175.

43. Leschenault, "Journal," in Plomley, *The Baudin Expedition,* 136.

44. Péron, *Voyage,* 200.

45. This is a common complaint throughout the journals. See, e.g., Baudin, *Journal,* 104.

46. Péron, *Voyage,* 184–186; Plomley, *The Baudin Expedition,* 25; Péron, "Experiments on physical strength," 148; Baudin, *Journal,* 305.

47. Baudin, *Journal,* 305.

48. Péron, *Voyage,* 184–185.

49. Baudin, *Journal,* 305.

50. Péron, *Voyage,* 185.

51. Degérando, *Observation of Savage Peoples,* 94.

52. Péron writes: "In a word, we have done everything to deserve their goodwill and to maintain their confidence. By such means it seems to me that we deserve it wholly, and I perceived with regret that, along with the expressions of their joy and the evidence of their friendship, there was I know not what depth of ingratitude, of suspicion and of wickedness which they sought vainly to conceal from us" (Péron, "Maria Island," 88).

53. Baudin, for example, comments: ". . . for they are extremely frightened by a gun, even if one just touches it" (Baudin, *Journal,* 305). Leschenault notes, "They seem to be familiar with the power of firearms. . . . As they did not appear to be at all frightened, I took aim at the bird, whereupon they all ran away, very much terrified" (Leschenault, "Journal," 131).

54. Degérando, *Observation of Savage Peoples,* 63; Jauffret, "Introduction," 77.

55. Péron, *Voyage,* 197. Péron continues: "From this general picture, however, we must always except two or three young girls of fifteen or sixteen years of age, in whom we could perceive an agreeable form, and pleasant features, with a round well formed bosom, though the nipples were rather too large and long. These young girls had also something ingenuous in the expression of the countenance, something soft and tender in their manners, as if the most amiable qualities of the mind were always, even among the most savage hordes of the human species, the more particular appendages of youth and beauty."

PART II
METROPOLITAN PERSPECTIVES
AND COLONIAL SCIENCE

5

The Natural World of New Guinea: Hopes, Realities, and Legacies

DAVID G. FRODIN

New Guinea was the golden dream of all naturalists and
few had the fortune to land there.
—Giacomo Doria, 1870

Why, then, would anyone visit Papua New Guinea? For
its spectacularly plumed birds of paradise, butterflies and
orchids. To snorkel or to dive, or to explore the rugged
terrain. . . . Or just to see the land of headhunters and
cannibals, of anthropologists like Margaret Mead.
—Heidi P. Sanchez, *Philadelphia Inquirer*,
18 January 1987

The Setting

*I*N the 1870s the idea of New Guinea as a new and exotic place
came into fashion in the Western world. The timing was perhaps
appropriate: it was the period of the Gilded Age in the United
States and Europe and the high point of the Victorian world's taste
for the exotic and outlandish. A strong popular interest in natural
history, as well as in geography and exploration, still prevailed,
although for the former in some respects the peak may have
passed.[1]

Hitherto the great dark island, second only to Greenland in size
and so named because of its seeming resemblance to western equatorial Africa, had remained largely a mystery. Trade and commerce had impinged on it but little. Seaborne explorers and scientists had touched at merely a few points. Writers as late as 1875
were able freely to indulge in all manner of fabulous tales. Even
those "productions" most associated in men's minds with New
Guinea, the birds of paradise and bower birds, remained known
largely from legless skins.[2]

Four developments finally brought New Guinea into sharper
focus: the increasing economic development of Australasia and the

Pacific Islands, an emerging awareness of the potential importance of the Pacific Ocean as a basin rather than a barrier, the coming into fashion of plumed ladies' hats, and, simply, a realization that it was "the last unknown."[3] It is with the third and fourth of these developments that the progress of knowledge in natural history, the main object of this chapter, is most closely linked. The exotic plumes most in demand for the new millinery were those of New Guinea's best-known birds; and, as the journalist and author Anthony Trollope was to write to the Liverpool *Mercury* in 1875, "I doubt whether they [the readers] will not find that they know less about New Guinea or Papua than any other inhabited portion of the earth's surface. Its size and position in seas that are now open to commerce have made [serious investigation] so much a necessity."[4]

Despite New Guinea's acknowledged attractions, hopes for the natural sciences early gave way to realities. The difficulties that penetration and control of the largest tropical island in the world would entail at relatively so late a date were such that acquisition of an "adequate" knowledge of the biota would largely depend on other than purely scientific considerations, and that development of any pertinent institutional system, including museums and herbaria, would be slow and imperfect. But in the context of the Pacific basin, New Guinea, and indeed all Papuasia,[5] can provide a tabula rasa wherein the approaches of differing metropolitan governments and concerned scientists in an imperial age can be compared. Here, too, the progress of the natural sciences in themselves can be observed in an atmosphere relatively free from the kinds of sociopolitical factors that Lewis Pyenson has suggested might complicate their development in economically more favorable environments.[6]

By the 1870s the New Guinea region was not unknown scientifically. Several oceanic exploring expeditions and coastal survey voyages and a number of government officials and missionaries had called at various parts of the island and its near neighbors. Many narrative accounts and scientific reports had been published. These, however, at best gave only a sketchy idea of the total biota, for fieldwork had been of necessity confined largely to coastal areas.

Some visits were indeed brief: the *Endeavour* on 3–4 September 1770 spent a mere day on the southwestern coast. Others, such as

Simon Provost in 1769, Pierre Sonnerat in 1772, and Thomas Forrest in 1774–1775 had fairly specific instructions: obtain spice plants. The early nineteenth-century voyages, particularly those of the French, were scientifically the most productive. On one of these voyages, that of Louis Duperrey in the *Coquille*, René P. Lesson, at Waigeo Island in 1823 and Dorei Bay on the northwestern mainland in 1824, became the first naturalist to observe birds of paradise in the wild—three hundred years after they had first become known in Europe following Magellan's voyage.[7]

In a world where in the absence of large mammals birds have played a preeminent role, it is only to be expected that knowledge of them would develop rapidly. Ornithology has always attracted great popular interest, and among the fields of natural history in the broad sense it can be regarded as a bellwether.[8] At the figurative (and in some respects the evolutionary) apex of the avifauna of New Guinea stand the fabulous birds of paradise and bower birds, comprising the avian families Paradiseidae and Ptilonorhynchidae. The number of full species now recognized from New Guinea stands at fifty; a further seven full species are endemic to Australia and two more to the northern Moluccas. The interest in these birds, commercially and scientifically as well as aesthetically, has been so great that the progress of their discovery alone could serve as a kind of backbone for any treatment, including that essayed here, of the golden age of Papuasian natural history exploration. Indeed it can fairly be said that the search for these birds and their natural haunts has in one form or another influenced progress in every other domain of natural history, at least up to 1942—a trend matched in few, if any, areas of comparable geographical magnitude.[9]

In 1870 the study of birds of paradise and bower birds had met a watershed. In the preceding year, Alfred Russel Wallace's epochal book *The Malay Archipelago* had appeared with the first extended descriptions of birds of paradise and their behavior in the wild. Hitherto a number of what ornithologists then considered species had been discovered in New Guinea, but most were only poorly known. Wallace's discoveries and observations greatly enhanced interest in New Guinea among scientists, and his book accomplished the same at a more popular level.[10]

As an impetus for further, more intensive exploration and study of the natural world of New Guinea, *The Malay Archipelago* was

Figure 2. Forest scene in Borneo illustrating some characteristic mammals, from A. R. Wallace, *The Geographical Distribution of Animals* (London, 1876), vol. 1, plate 8.

Figure 3. Forest scene in New Guinea illustrating some characteristic birds (especially birds of paradise) and mammals, from A. R. Wallace, *The Geographical Distribution of Animals* (London, 1876), vol. 1, plate 10.

timely; it raised hopes of new discoveries in an island still unknown beyond the coast. These hopes coincided with others: for new sources of gold, additional supplies of labor, new mountains and rivers, and potential places for white settlement. The prevailing temper of the time is well depicted in the early part of *New Guinea: The Last Unknown* and, with a narrower focus, in *Rape of the Fly.*[11] It is from this period that the golden age of New Guinea natural history exploration begins, an age that was to last until 1942.

This chapter will focus on the progress of this golden age, although some attention will be paid to more recent progress and current developments in the postimperial era. I shall also look briefly at ways in which these discoveries have contributed to the development of the present body of knowledge and concepts in biogeography and in systematic and evolutionary biology.

Before the Rush: Exploration to 1870

Among islands in the Pacific, New Guinea, along with the Solomon Islands and the New Hebrides (Vanuatu), were among the last in which large-scale natural history exploration commenced. Yet New Guinea is home to creatures with a special cachet, the birds of paradise and bower birds, known in Europe since 1522. Why, then, was the total, or nearly total, range of their forms not revealed until the eve of the twentieth century?

The pursuit of natural history cannot be divorced from human affairs in general, even though for many scientists their chosen studies form their mental universe. From the earliest days of European exploration in the area, New Guinea (and Melanesia) acquired a sinister reputation: the easy successes of the conquistadores in the Americas were not to be repeated. To the earliest voyagers, Jorge de Meneses, Alvaro de Saavedra, Alvaro Mendaña, and others,[12] the dark, densely forested masses of mainland New Guinea (in the sixteenth to eighteenth centuries seen largely from the north) and the Solomon Islands seemed forbidding. The people appeared savage and primitive to the Europeans, and any settlements soon succumbed to disease.[13] The Portuguese in the Moluccas, as well as their Dutch successors, confined themselves to indirect trade through such centers as Dobo in the Aru Islands;

Spanish energies meanwhile focused on the Marianas and the Philippines. Direct contact was considered too hazardous, not least because formal administration was largely wanting in western New Guinea, and the United East India Company's relations with the Sultanate of Tidore, the nominal overlord, although effective from as early as 1654, were purely feudal. As a result, the basic geography of New Guinea, with its neighboring islands and their relationship to "New Holland," was not worked out until the latter part of the eighteenth century. Indeed, knowledge of the East Indies as a whole was to lag seriously as Company attitudes toward exploration became increasingly negative.[14]

A systematic approach to the study of natural history in Melanesia would, as elsewhere, only effectively manifest itself during the age of Linnaeus. William Dampier in the *Roebuck* (1699–1701), in Papuasia as in Australia the first explorer on record to have collected any biota, concerned himself with careful and dispassionate observation, but to him specimens were largely curiosa. All that is known, for example, of his plant collections from New Guinea are floating seaweeds.[15]

Maluku (the Moluccas) was thus very fortunate indeed in the latter half of the seventeenth century to have been the home of perhaps the greatest pioneer of serious tropical natural history study, George Eberhard Rumpf, resident in Ambon (Amboina) for forty-nine years beginning in 1653. Although much has been written about him, he remains insufficiently appreciated in many anglophone circles; even his scientific work has in the past been dismissed as of little modern value. His major works, including *D'Amboinsche Rariteitskamer* (1705) and *Herbarium Amboinense/Het Amboinsch Kruidboek* (1741–1755), are filled with careful factual observations and include some Papuan fauna and flora.[16] However, despite his remarks to the contrary, myths such as the one that birds of paradise had no legs would persist until the late 1700s.[17]

Only in the period from 1760 into the 1840s did outside knowledge of Papuasia improve. Even then direct contact by the exploring voyages was limited largely to certain safe havens such as Port Praslin, a sheltered system of bays in southwestern New Ireland, and Rawak, a small island off northern Waigeo. In later years Dorei Bay (and its offshore islet of Mansinam) on the eastern shore of Jazirah Doberai (the Vogelkop peninsula) gained favor and it was here that René Lesson in 1824 made part of his field observations of birds of paradise.[18] Lesson's work, however, formed but part of the overall French contribution to natural history in Papuasia, then the largest of any nation but one for which a retrospective evaluation has yet to be made.[19]

The Pacific voyages had general aims.[20] They represented primarily expressions of interest from nations new to the field, eager to break (as it happened, successfully) the Dutch spice monopoly as well as Spanish hegemony in the Pacific and elsewhere, and to extend their own mercantilist and colonial spheres. Reconnaissance of New Guinea was but a small part of their activities. The inclusion of scientists, and at a later date scientifically qualified naval personnel, represented a significant step for the progress of natural history. Nonetheless, the ultimate concern was with the progress of (European) human affairs in the economic and social terms of the day, and in this respect New Guinea seemed unattractive: it was isolated from the major trade routes and whaling grounds, represented a limited market, had few premium commodities, and was inhabited by people considered unpredictable and savage. Moreover, further attempts at settlement had failed.

The growing British presence in New Zealand, Australia, and the southwestern Pacific, not to mention Britain's establishment in 1819 of Singapore, appears finally to have prompted direct Dutch interest in western New Guinea.[21] The former Dutch East Indian possessions had been restored by Great Britain in 1814 in return for Dutch renunciation of interests in South Asia, Sri Lanka (Ceylon), and the Cape Colony in southern Africa. Following a mutual guarantee of rights with Britain in 1824, which among other provisions admitted Dutch claims to northwestern New Guinea, the Dutch embarked on a long-term policy of bringing all of what would become Indonesia under centralized rule. This led to a new phase of exploration of the New Guinea coastline, along with additional territorial claims, and cleared the way for a pioneer Dutch settlement. In 1828 the government ships *Triton* and *Iris* were dispatched, and Merkusoord, with its defense post Fort du Bus, was established in Triton Bay east of the present village of Kaimana.

In the colonization party were three scientists, Heinrich Christian Macklot, G. van Raalten, and Alexander Zipelius, and their assistants Pieter van Oort and Salomon Müller. All were members of the Natuurkundige Commissie (Dutch Natural Sciences Commission for the Indies), one of the creations of King Willem I as part of his efforts to revive the sciences in the Netherlands.[22] Inspired by the earlier work of the Batavian Society of Arts and Sciences (founded in 1778), Thomas Horsfield (from Bethlehem, Pennsylvania—the first United States–born scientist active in the archipelago), and Stamford Raffles, the commission from 1819 to 1850 carried out extensive investigations of the still poorly-known East Indian territories, including the largely neglected interiors of the large islands.[23]

Much has been written about Merkusoord, the first white settlement in New Guinea, and its ultimate failure after seven years of hardship.[24] The scientists, however, had the unprecedented opportunity of working from a nominally permanent base on the New Guinea mainland. Unfortunately, Zipelius died in Timor at the close of the year and the results of his work only slowly and incompletely came into circulation. Müller, however, went on to propose the first serious scheme of zoogeographic regions in the archipelago, inclusive of the biogeographic "line" that Wallace would later make famous.[25] In the 1850s, Zipelius's results, as far as they had been published, were utilized by Miquel for his *Flora Indiae batavae* and in turn by the Swiss botanist Heinrich Zollinger in developing his unifying *Idee* of a single flora Malesiana ranging over the whole of the archipelago and beyond.[26]

The Dutch withdrawal from Merkusoord, confirmed by Jules Dumont d'Urville on a visit to Triton Bay with his *Astrolabe* and *Zelée* expedition in April 1839, began a period of some thirty years during which scientific contacts with New Guinea were much reduced. Until the 1870s no European settlements existed save for the short-lived Marist mission at Woodlark Island (1847–1852) and the dogged Dutch Protestant mission at Dorei Bay (established in 1855). It was among the Marists that Père Xavier Montrouzier, later to settle in New Caledonia, began his career as a naturalist. However, improved means of communication within the Netherlands East Indies began to enable privately sponsored naturalists to make visits, notably to western New Guinea and the neighboring islands of Japen, Biak, Waigeo, Salawati, Batanta, and Misoöl. This was far less possible in the east, but it was during the 1840s that the Torres Strait and much of the southeastern coast were carefully surveyed by British naval vessels, first the *Fly* and *Bramble* (the former giving its name to the great river), and then the *Rattlesnake,* whose captain Owen Stanley is commemorated in the long mountain range that dominates the southeastern peninsula.[27] Hitherto the Coral Sea and Torres Strait coasts of New Guinea and the Gulf of Papua had been only poorly known.

For posterity, the outstanding visit of this period was made by one of the first independent naturalists, Alfred Russel Wallace, who spent a month at Dorei Bay in 1857. He and his assistant Charles Allen between them also visited Waigeo, Misoöl, and the Aru Islands, as well as many parts of Maluku, much of the time sailing on native *proas* that were very much at the mercy of wind and weather. Wallace did not collect any new birds of paradise in New Guinea, but he made classic field observations on two known species: *Paradisaea apoda* in the Aru Islands and *P. rubra* in Waigeo.

A number of factors combined in the mid-nineteenth century to encourage both independently supported naturalists such as Wallace and, in time, government-sponsored expeditions. Among these were the Victorian popularity of natural history; an interest in things exotic, including tropical orchids and conservatory plants; and the search for additional sources of tropical resources. Patterns of world trade were also changing; with industrialization came a gradual shift from mercantilism to an economic system that required regular supplies of raw materials. The need for such commodities in bulk brought pressures for plantation expansion, the introduction of new crops and the improvement of existing ones, and the regularization of production and transport.[28]

These factors prompted naturalists, as well as officially sponsored voyages, to enter the archipelago from the German states and Austria-Hungary, lands hitherto undistinguished in seaborne trade. From mid-century the Hamburg firm of J. C. Godeffroy und Sohn became active in the Pacific, notably in Samoa, where it acquired a substantial interest in the growing copra trade. The firm was unusual in encouraging natural history, engaging collectors and even founding a private museum. From Samoa, German interests spread out over other parts of the Pacific, and it was only a matter of time before attention was directed toward New Guinea and its neighboring islands, especially following establishment of a trading center at Jaluit in the southern Marshall Islands.

Developments were also taking place to the south. Settlement and economic growth in Australia and a rising local interest in organized natural history gave a new dimension to New Guinea.[29] The Australian north became a kind of frontier. Much of it proved to be all but uninhabitable in a conventional sense, but the moist east coast proved suitable for sugarcane and cotton; in Queensland this developed rapidly from about 1860. An early emphasis on cotton during the American Civil War gave way afterwards entirely to sugar, and with this and the associated mining boom the establishment of such towns as Mackay, Bowen, Townsville, Cairns, and Cooktown rapidly followed. A sense of manifest destiny surfaced, and with it the idea that Australia had an "imperial mission" in the Pacific based on needs different from those of the United Kingdom.[30] Beyond Queensland, to the north, lay New Guinea—on the far side of the increasingly strategic Torres Strait, where at Cape York a government post, Somerset, was established in 1864. The sense of mission began to communicate itself to naturalists, but it was not until the 1870s that this urge was translated into action.

The world economy was thus moving in on New Guinea (and other parts of Melanesia not yet formally organized into states or territories) from three directions: west, south, and east. This "closing of the ring" can be shown to coincide approximately with the opening of the Suez Canal, which profoundly altered world trade routes. Regionally, trade was increasing between Australian and New Zealand ports and those of eastern Asia such as Hong Kong, Shanghai, and Tokyo. New Guinea was thus losing its former isolation and, as Imperial Russia, Germany, and the United States became more active in the Pacific, its strategic value was increasing. These developments raised hopes that more official attention might at last be given to the problems and challenges posed by what was still largely a black spot on the map. The perceived nature of New Guinean geography and peoples was such that for many naturalists no real exploration was deemed possible without some form of infrastructure, which only government could provide on any scale.

The 1870s: Golden Dreams

The seeming reluctance of governments to become seriously involved in New Guinea—the presence of the Dutch in the western half was still little more than nominal—did not, however, act as a deterrent to two intrepid young naturalists, the Italian Luigi M. d'Albertis and the Russian Nikolai N. de Miklouho-Maclay. In 1871–1872 they separately conducted the first serious extended scientific expeditions within New Guinea.[31] Both were from the relatively well-to-do middle classes in the rising nations of Europe; both had doubtless been inspired by the publication of Wallace's book; and both shared the research interests of leading scientists of the day. Indeed, the time may have been ripe for a serious opening to the sustained study of natural history in New Guinea; its scientific importance had been made more effectively known and the Victorian spirit of boundless optimism was approaching its height. Miklouho-Maclay had established links with the German academic community, and d'Albertis, who had served under Giuseppe Garibaldi, was a creature of the Italian Risorgimento. The prevailing spirit, aptly summarized by Giacomo Doria, leader of the Museo Civico di Storia Naturale in Genoa and one of d'Albertis's mentors, viewed New Guinea as a "golden dream" for naturalists.

Both Miklouho-Maclay and d'Albertis were privately sponsored, but received indirect government support in the form of naval passages and other favors in kind (d'Albertis would later get similar aid from the colonial government of New South Wales), as well as support from their national geographical societies. Neither of them represented the mainline powers who were, or would become, involved in New Guinea. Both were young and relatively inexperienced, and both were to a degree eccentric, d'Albertis perhaps the more so (his sponsors arranged for the very able and level-headed botanist and veteran Borneo explorer Odoardo Beccari to accompany him).[32]

Notable firsts were achieved by both parties. The Italians in the west penetrated into the Arfak Mountains, a journey never before attempted by Europeans, and among their many finds were some new species of birds of paradise and bower birds. The Russian and his party were the first to live peaceably among inhabitants of the eastern part of the great island and to make observations of them. Both d'Albertis and Miklouho-Maclay were to return for further extended visits; both made contacts with their counterparts in Australia. Beccari also returned to New Guinea in 1875 but remained entirely in Dutch lands; d'Albertis shifted his focus to the southern and southeastern parts with which he remains most closely associated.

The work of these naturalists did much to increase interest in New Guinea. The elderly botanist Johannes Teijsmann, first appointed to the Bogor Botanical Garden in 1830, in connection with other scientists resumed Dutch geographical and biological work in surveys lasting from 1871 to 1876 and from 1879 to 1882. In 1873 came the visit of the zoologist Albert B. Meyer from Dresden, also in western New Guinea. At the same time, mission societies, with the London Missionary Society in the lead, began serious moves aimed at opening New Guinea to Christian evangelism on a larger scale. This was a fortunate development for the natural sciences, as this Congregational group seems to have had among its membership many individuals, not only in New Guinea, who were, or could be, interested in various aspects of natural history.[33] The British navy completed its survey of the coasts of the southeastern peninsula in 1871–1874 during a series of cruises by the steam-sailship *Basilisk* commanded by John Moresby; although the cruises incorporated natural history work, the most important discovery was the protected harbor of Port Moresby, the best of its kind on the south coast. A head L.M.S. mission-station was shortly after established, and "Port Moresby" became a major jumping-off point for explorers and naturalists interested in the great Owen Stanley Range system. Captain (later Admiral) Moresby afterwards became a strong advocate of intensified exploration and settlement in New Guinea.

The New Guinea "fever" first climaxed in 1875, when hopes and dreams were at their highest.[34] A veritable flood of expeditions and individual naturalists appeared that year on the shores of New Guinea: Beccari was active in the west; Miklouho-Maclay returned to the northeast in the following year; the circumnavigating German *Gazelle* expedition, commanded by Georg Emil Gustav, Freiherr von Schleinitz, after a visit to McCluer Gulf arrived in northeastern New Britain;[35] the Methodist mission under George Brown began its work in the nearby Duke of York Islands; the great oceanographic *Challenger* expedition visited northwestern Manus in the Admiralty Islands; d'Albertis spent seven months at Yule Island northwest of Port Moresby; William John Macleay's *Chevert* expedition, the first to be sponsored from Australia, explored in the Torres Strait along the south coast adjacent to the strait and around Yule Island; and Samuel Macfarlane examined the lower Fly as well as the Kussa water system inland from the far south coast. While some cooperation has been recorded, a spirit of rivalry was more evident, as Goode has shown in his discussion of the relationship between Macfarlane, Macleay, and d'Albertis.[36] On top of all this, there also arrived the first dilettante-traveler, at least in eastern New Guinea: Octavius Stone, who spent some three months at Port Moresby. In the history of New Guinea, almost nothing like this kind of rush had happened before—or since—and it was not entirely coincidental.[37]

In 1876 and 1877 came the two long cruises up the Fly River by d'Albertis on the steam launch *Neva* (loaned by New South Wales) and the second stay by Miklouho-Maclay on the part of the north coast that came to be named after him. D'Albertis's trips became controversial, however, for the manner in which they were conducted, and his collecting has, on account of its scale, come to be viewed by some as plundering.[38] Geographically, his 1877 trip contributed nothing new; most notably, he did not take the opportunity to explore the Fly's most important tributary, now known as the Strickland River. More significantly, Miklouho-Maclay would conclude, as Macleay had done after his *Chevert* voyage, that the land was not fit for unrestricted white settlement and that the inhabitants were relatively more sophisticated than Australian aboriginals, a message very similar to that put out at Port Moresby by "Misi Lao," the Reverend William George Lawes, first of the English Protestant missionaries resident in eastern New Guinea.[39] These views would not only slow the entry of the outside world and sustained interior exploration, but in the longer term would strongly influence the future of what is now Papua New Guinea.

Scattered visits of naturalists and others continued, however, and a few Europeans settled into commerce at Port Moresby and in the Duke of York Islands. The number of missionaries increased, as did commercial stations associated with the growing local trade. Gold was discovered in 1877 near Port Moresby. The big rush of 1875 had given way, however, to a comparative quiescence as the realities of New Guinea became evident.

Among scientific results achieved during the 1870s were the discovery and description of more full species of birds of paradise and bower birds; the beginnings (after Montrouzier's pioneer work in Woodlark) of serious entomological collecting; the realization (with important future economic consequences) that the key timber-producing and botanically interesting "Philippine mahogany" family Dipterocarpaceae was, when compared with Borneo, poorly represented; and the first substantial zoological and botanical collections from southeastern New Guinea (from which Ferdinand von Mueller concluded that there existed a significant Australian element in the flora).[40] Although all this was but a beginning, the 1870s as a period will remain memorable for purely scientific exploration.[41]

Realities and Achievements, 1880–1885

As Lawes and Miklouho-Maclay had warned, the 1870s, while focusing a strong light on New Guinea, also brought a realization that its "civilization" would be a long, hard process. The geography proved to be some of the most awesome in the world, thus making basic exploration alone a slow, tedious, and expensive proposition. The task was effectively too great for any one outside power, and, with external involvement coming from three directions due to New Guinea's size and situation, it was perhaps inevitable that mainland New Guinea would eventually be further partitioned. Even then governments hesitated until rivalries, major commercial needs, and public opinion forced them into action. This fragmentation, the policies and activities of subsequent administrations, and differing perceptions of the sciences by the various metropolitan powers go far to explain the very chequered progress of natural history within Papuasia up to the mid-twentieth century.

Between the rush of the 1870s and 1884, government activity in Papuasia consisted largely of visits by naval vessels and assorted agents, and in Dutch lands this situation continued until the end of the century. Few opportunities for natural history work arose. Eventually, however, the need to protect commercial activities, most notably the infant coconut plantation industry in the Gazelle Peninsula, as well as an increasing desire that the native inhabitants be protected from what was considered excessive exploitation by Queensland, gave rise to the declaration of territorial rights by the United Kingdom and Germany in eastern New Guinea, the Bismarck Archipelago, and, later, the Solomons. "Imperial fever," expressed particularly as a belief that the region should be made secure for British and Australian interests, and a change of heart, if qualified and relatively short-lived, on the part of the German Chancellor Bismarck in 1884 favoring German overseas possessions, contributed also to the advent of formal government.[42]

Individuals who made visits during this period included F. H. Otto Finsch from Germany and Francis Henry Hill Guillemard and Henry Ogg Forbes from the United Kingdom. Finsch made extensive coastal explorations in 1880–1882, and his geographical and other information was later of material assistance to the German imperial government when determining the limits of their future protectorate; he returned in 1884–1885 as a participant in the annexation activities. Guillemard and Forbes were voyager-naturalists in the tradition of Wallace, in the northwest and southeast respectively. Forbes was the more active in inland work, and it was his failure to attain the principal goal of his New Guinea expedition, the highest peak of the Owen Stanley Range, that clarified the desirability of direct government participation in and control of geographical exploration where possible. Substantial collections did result, however, from his work as well as that of Guillemard and Finsch, both for research and for public display.[43]

The work of resident naturalists was also notable. The known diversity of birds of paradise and bower birds was greatly increased through the efforts of Andrew Goldie, Port Moresby's first storekeeper, and particularly his assistant Carl Hunstein, who penetrated far into the Owen Stanleys. By 1885 they were together responsible for the discovery of six full species as well as some seven others now considered to be geographical races. Hunstein moved north with the establishment of Deutsch-Neu-Guinea where as an employee of the Neu-Guinea-Kompagnie he traveled extensively, discovering one more species before his untimely death in New Britain in 1888. In the Gazelle Peninsula of New Britain, Richard Parkinson, a German national, from 1882 made extensive explorations, collections, and observations on the basis of which he and "Queen" Emma Forsayth established the first major commercial copra plantation in Papuasia. Continuing the example of the *Chevert* expedition of William Macleay, the collections of these residents, as well as missionaries such as W. George Lawes, James Chalmers, and George Brown, and others including Erik Edelfelt and William Armit, substantially enhanced natural history collections in Australia, including the herbarium of Ferdinand von Mueller in Melbourne. Many zoological results were published in the new *Proceedings of the Linnean Society of New South Wales* founded by Macleay.

The rise of imperial fever in the Australian colonies, aided by a booming economy, brought about a renewed interest there in organized New Guinea exploration, and from 1883 to 1890 a number of expeditions were mounted with varying degrees of success. In addition to geographical exploration, the expeditions undertook work in the natural sciences, and the sometimes considerable collections that resulted went to Australian museums and herbaria. The first two expeditions, both in 1883, were sponsored by rival Melbourne newspapers. The remainder, including that of Forbes in 1885, were sponsored wholly or partly by the various branches of the recently formed Geographical Society of Australasia, which received government subsidies to be used in aid of exploration.[44] These expeditions, and the work of the society, form part of the adolescence of organized science in Australia as distinct from the United Kingdom.

Commercial orchid collectors appeared in the 1880s. Information on their travels is scanty and specimen data meager, but the two most notable collectors, the Englishman David Burke and the German Wilhelm Micholitz, employed by two leading British horticultural houses, Veitch of Chelsea and Sander of St. Albans, visited many different parts of Papuasia and made many collections of living orchids and other plants for the trade.[45] Harvesting of the pearl-yielding trochus shell and the gelatin-producing sea cucumbers, starfish relatives known in the Pacific as bêche-de-mer or trepang, was also increasing, along with trade in village-prepared copra and other natural products.

It was, however, growth in the plume trade over the late nineteenth century that as far as natural history is concerned brought the most attention to New Guinea. The rise of this trade, as well as the flood of discoveries by field naturalists since 1871, revived scientific and popular interest in the birds of paradise and bower birds, and shipments of skins were regularly picked over by ornithologists for novelties.[46] A number of new forms were first made known to science in this fashion; many subsequently were collected in the field, but others remained enigmatic until 1928–1929 when an expedition was undertaken by Ernst Mayr to resolve their status.[47] Popular interest, including that of wealthy patrons, gave rise to a "Gould folio" especially dedicated to birds

of paradise and bower birds. Its author, the noted contemporary
ornithologist R. Bowdler Sharpe of the British Museum (Natural
History), was, however, intent on creating a serious scientific
work and in it lamented that the aim of the typical collector
seemed to be "not to furnish us with details of the nesting-habits of
the [birds], but to see how many of these beautiful creatures he can
procure for the decoration of the hats of the women of Europe and
America." Nevertheless, the quantities of bird skins procured in
field and market between 1871 and 1915 provided an indispens-
able foundation for future research.[48]

The five years to 1885 thus provide a contrast to the 1870s in
that the pursuit of natural history was now marked by an atmosphere of greater imperialism and territorial acquisition, with consequences for the independence of the sciences.[49] The limitations
on operations in Papuasia by more or less autonomous parties—
due to geography, climate, health problems, and human relations
—became evident. Indeed, the activities of naturalists as well as
traders in natural products and labor recruiters were among factors contributing to the advent of formal administration in all
areas by the turn of the century. At the same time, however, the
work of the naturalists had contributed significantly to government intelligence; it is probable, for instance, that the travels and
other activities of the strongly nationalistic Otto Finsch were, as
already noted, instrumental in determining the location and extent
of the German protectorate.

Comparative Progress in Natural History, 1885–1942

The imposition of external rule and formal administration in
Papuasia over the last fifteen years of the nineteenth century naturally brought about a closer relationship between the pursuit of
natural history and government and metropolitan interests. Exploration and fieldwork also became increasingly professional-
ized. To a historian, the real interest is in a comparative review of
the progress made, given a more or less common environment and
biota, in territories under different rule.

Control of the eastern part of New Guinea and the Bismarcks
had in 1884 come under different administrations, one German,
one British. German New Guinea was, with one interruption, the

responsibility of the Berlin banker Adolph von Hansemann's chartered Neu-Guinea-Kompagnie until 1899 when the charter was resumed by the Reich and the company reverted purely to commercial activities. In August 1914 control passed to Australia, first under military occupation and then, from 1921 to 1942, to a civilian administration under a Class C mandate from the League of Nations. British New Guinea began as a protectorate but in 1888 became a colony of the United Kingdom. In 1906 control passed to the new Australian Commonwealth government, and the name was changed to Papua. Western New Guinea remained under Dutch rule throughout this period, but its status within the Netherlands East Indies changed from time to time, and until 1902 it was without resident officials.

By 1885 the major features of the biota were known, although this meant mainly vertebrates, the more attractive insect groups, and ferns and flowering plants at low and moderate elevations. Little or no work had been done at higher altitudes; this remained a major objective until 1942 and beyond. Other than evidence that dipterocarps were few and Australian red cedar *(Toona surenii)* fairly plentiful, forest trees were scarcely known, and in the absence of any significant market or strong interest, information about them grew only slightly and spasmodically in the decades up to World War II.[50]

The growth of knowledge about Papuasia was influenced by certain factors common to other newly opened parts of the world. The flow of specimens from Papuasia in the late nineteenth and early twentieth centuries at times became so great that it could overwhelm the capabilities of the relatively few specialists. In some circumstances, resources were up to the task; in others, less spectacular finds were set aside, rarely or never to be fully documented unless by chance retrospective examination, often decades afterwards.[51] The development and activities of various applied sciences, more noticeable after 1885, also influenced the relative increase of knowledge among different biotic groups, as did changes in popular interests.

In the same period, professionalization of natural history, along with changes in institutional arrangements and the relationship between government and the sciences, was proceeding in metropolitan countries.[52] Nevertheless, significant work continued to be contributed by amateurs. Before 1942 the size of the local naturalists' community in a given territory in Papuasia was minute or nonexistent; scattered individuals largely worked independently.[53]

British New Guinea (Papua)

British New Guinea (later called Papua) was for nearly all of its existence relatively poor, and unlike the other territories never enjoyed much material support for scientific work from its successive metropolitan powers. What was accomplished depended very much on luck and a significant amount of private outside sponsorship of individuals and expeditions. British New Guinea was blessed with four able administrators, three of whom—General Peter Scratchley, George le Hunte, and especially William Mac-Gregor—were interested in the natural sciences and supported botanical, zoological, and geographical exploration. MacGregor, whose two terms lasted ten years, from 1888 to 1898, took a particular interest in the fostering of natural history, but Port Moresby was to him simply too underdeveloped for establishment of a local museum.[54] The task of exploration was made a government monopoly and officers were charged, among other duties, with making botanical and zoological collections. The MacGregor era was responsible for the first ascents of several mountains in the Owen Stanley Range (including, in 1889, the summit of Mount Victoria, which had eluded Forbes); significant collections of the highland and alpine flora (the latter revealed strong links with temperate Australia, New Zealand, and southern South America); and the discovery of three more full species of birds of paradise and bower birds, all described by Charles W. de Vis at the Queensland Museum. Certain individuals were also active: Henry Ogg Forbes was in the territory from 1885 to 1887 (for nine months, however, as a temporary district officer!), and from 1889 to 1896 Lamberto Loria and Amadeo Giulianetti (sponsored by Giacomo Doria at Genoa) collected extensively in the southeastern part, Giulianetti afterwards joining the government service. The government collections were sent out for study to the best men available, either in the United Kingdom or Australia, and summaries of their results (and sometimes original contributions) were published in the official *Annual Reports*. In botany the best meant von Mueller in Melbourne until his death late in 1896; then the Royal Botanic Gardens, Kew (where William Botting Hemsley reported on the plants collected during MacGregor's last mountain expeditions in 1896–1897); and then, even before assumption of authority by Le Hunte in 1899, Frederick Manson Bailey at the Queensland Herbarium. Most zoological and entomological material was deposited in the Queensland Museum, where it was studied by de Vis, Henry Tryon, and others.[55]

The scanty means available to the administration meant, however, that larger and more intensive field campaigns, necessary if good results in botany and entomology were to be obtained, were not possible. Expeditions from Australia ended after 1890, partly as a result of MacGregor's policies but also as a consequence of depressed economic conditions and changes in scientific fashion. After MacGregor's departure less emphasis was placed on natural science exploration, although Le Hunte continued MacGregor's practice of attaching natural history appendixes to the annual reports. With the de facto transfer of control to Australia, official interest rapidly declined, and it never revived. The widening gap between British and German New Guinea in terms of the degree of exploration, collection, and description of fauna and flora was already by 1906 the subject of unfavorable comment, but nothing was done.[56] It has been argued that this relative lack of direct official activity was due not only to limited means but also to long-standing personal rivalries.[57] The only botanical campaigns to be officially sponsored after 1906 were those of Cyril Tenison White in 1918 (by the Papuan administration) and the forester Charles Edward Lane-Poole in 1922–1923 (by the Australian Commonwealth government). Owing to the absence of any local depository, their collections were deposited in Australian, North American, and British herbaria.[58] A small entomological collection assembled in Port Moresby by agricultural personnel in the course of their duties was lost during World War II.

Thus from the end of the nineteenth century until 1942, virtually all progress in natural history was externally sponsored. Save for what duplicates have been returned since World War II, no collections came to Port Moresby although there is evidence that the question of local deposit was considered.[59] It is to the credit of the advocates and sponsors of the various campaigns, and to the expeditions and intrepid individuals who were prepared to spend many months in the field (as well as to the increasingly widespread and peaceful influence of the Papuan administration under Lieutenant

Governor Hubert Murray), that much was accomplished despite the low level of official activity. Otherwise, knowledge of the biota in this part of New Guinea would have lagged even more seriously behind German New Guinea. Indeed, it was this very disparity that evidently led the mammalogist and millionaire Richard Archbold to propose that the first of the American Museum of Natural History expeditions (which are unofficially but popularly named after him) be directed toward Papua. The choice appears also to have been influenced by Leonard J. Brass, a botanist who had collected in 1925–1926 on behalf of the Arnold Arboretum of Harvard University. Brass became the botanist on the first Archbold Expedition as well as on five of the subsequent Archbold Expeditions mounted in New Guinea, three of them in Papua. Each expedition concentrated on areas that biologically were scarcely known, although mostly previously explored and possessing a limited amount of nontraditional infrastructure. As a major sponsor, Archbold was the successor of Lord Rothschild, whose collectors, notably Albert S. Meek, had gathered birds and insects in the territory since the 1890s; from these many new species had been described, among them the largest butterfly in the world, *Ornithoptera alexandrae*.[60] Individuals who made significant collections included the entomologist Evelyn Cheesman and the botanist Cedric Errol Carr, both under external sponsorship, and the resident Anglican missionary-priest and amateur pteridologist Copland King.

The geographical pattern of collecting reflected the early objective of most explorers, adventurers, and administrators: to open up as much of the country as possible through rapid patrols and the establishment of a thin network of resident magistrates and village magistrates. MacGregor's policy of employing natural history agents meant that a certain amount of collecting was done in relatively remote areas. The lessening of official activity after 1898— including the thirty-four-year Murray regime during which not a single major mountain appears to have been biotically surveyed under government auspices—focused collecting areas more narrowly, though they were still widely dispersed. In a land where air transport was late in coming and economic activity limited, biotic exploration tended to become associated with points of settlement such as government stations, plantations, and missions, or such routes as the Fly River, the Kokoda Trail (a mail route first established in the 1900s between Port Moresby and Kokoda), and the Sacred Heart Mission's graded tracks from the coast into the present Goilala District. Vehicular roads were all but lacking and the availability of horses or other pack animals, themselves only introduced in the 1870s, was limited. Apart from coastal and river travel, this left as the sole alternative the traditional method of cartage, human porterage. Only in 1928 was this pattern broken through the use of aircraft by the sugarcane collecting expedition of Brandes, Jeswiet, and Pemberton, a development further pursued eight years later by the second of the Archbold Expeditions, responsible for the first truly effective campaigns in the upper Fly basin and in the extensive savannas south of the Fly River.[61]

By World War II, therefore, Papua had been extensively explored biotically but, with some localized exceptions, at a relatively superficial level. The considerable work accomplished under private sponsorship could not really make up for the virtual lack after 1900 of local government participation or, in turn, the absence of any interest on the part of the Australian Commonwealth—a reflection of the unfavorable atmosphere for biological survey that existed in Australia from Federation until well after 1945.[62] Thus, with limited exceptions such as geology and forest resources, basic knowledge of a territory already viewed as having limited resources and prospects lagged the more for want of a strong metropolitan commitment.

Dutch New Guinea

In the rest of New Guinea, the natural sciences were, in contrast, relatively generously supported by metropolitan governments and local authorities as well as by nonofficial bodies and institutions and private individuals. This was despite undeveloped or generally adverse local economies with uncertain prospects and, in Dutch lands, the late establishment of a resident official presence. For cultural and technical reasons, a stronger need was felt for a thorough knowledge of flora, fauna, and other natural features, which was deemed a job for professionals or semiprofessionals. There was also an associated belief that as far as possible research should be documented through scholarly publications.[63]

With the establishment of British and German New Guinea, followed by the British Solomon Islands, increasing pressure came upon the Dutch, both at home and in the Indies, to initiate some form of development in western New Guinea. Mere possession was in some quarters held to be no longer enough. An offer by interests in another country to buy the territory, the accession in 1898 of Queen Wilhelmina to the Dutch throne, and the concern of the successive Indies governors-general Willem Rooseboom (1899–1904) and especially Joannes B. van Heutsz (1904–1909) for an effective Dutch presence thr·)ughout the East Indies possessions finally brought about adoption of a higher profile and the initiation of a systematic program of exploration, control, and effective administration. Hitherto, little of the interior was known except in Jazirah Doberai (the Vogelkop) and Bomberai (the Onin Peninsula).

The Dutch effort, involving great expenditure but aided for the first twenty years after 1900 by conditions of relative prosperity in the Indies, was prosecuted on a large scale through both individual expeditions, and, from 1907 to 1915, a detailed survey by a military detachment. The Dutch maintained a relatively more liberal administrative policy toward the entry of expeditions than was the case in MacGregor's British New Guinea or in the lands under German rule. This, along with the contemporary view of the area as a "virgin field," resulted in British or German sponsorship of a considerable proportion of the exploration carried out before 1922. Individuals such as Lilian S. Gibbs, Thomas Barbour, and Max Moszkowski also contributed. A motivation for some expeditions was "the race to the snow," that is, the rivalry to first ascend one of the snow mountains, the only ones of their kind at lower latitudes between the Himalaya and the Andes.

The Dutch made relatively little effort, however, to extend effective administration except in areas where some form of social control was necessary or where economic, strategic, or other interests were concerned. This led in the mid-1930s to further criticism.[64] The Dutch practice resembled that prevailing in the German lands up to 1914, but stood in contrast to the British New Guinea tradition, wherein primary exploration, particularly after 1900, was organized with a view to extending administrative control as widely as possible, if only with a rudimentary presence. In Dutch as in German New Guinea, major expeditions were more purely geographical and scientific, combining metropolitan professional leadership and local logistical support; they were often lavishly funded and operated in advance of administrative penetration and control.

Notable achievements during the decades to 1922 included the first completed transect of the main body of the island; additional contributions to the knowledge of the alpine flora, building on the earlier work in British New Guinea; the discovery of "pygmy" peoples in the Sudirman (Nassau) Range; the first serious studies of vegetation;[65] great improvements in knowledge of bird and insect life (partly through the activities of Rothschild's collectors); and, finally, establishment at Leiden of the stately series *Nova Guinea,* whose first two volumes contain the invaluable chronological-topographical "Entdeckungsgeschichte von Neu-Guinea."[66] In marine biology, the *Siboga* expedition in 1899 visited various parts of the southwestern coast and some neighboring islands as part of a year-long cruise in the archipelago. A major, still-continuing series of publications, fundamental to marine research in the region, likewise arose from this undertaking.

Substantial improvements in institutional organization and resources also took place, notably at Buitenzorg (Bogor) near Batavia (Jakarta) where the visionary Melchior Treub, director from 1880 to 1909, and his immediate successors greatly expanded the facilities and scope of *s'Lands Plantentuin,* the Botanical Gardens, to include work in zoology, chemistry, agriculture, and marine biology and fisheries. Under their influence as well as that of Max Weber, the scientific leader of the *Siboga* expedition, and others in the Netherlands, some of the zoological results from the New Guinea expeditions were incorporated into a number of still-standard synthesis works treating the Indies as a whole. In botany, however, the overall contribution was somewhat less than for German New Guinea. There were relatively few Dutch taxonomic botanists, and fewer institutional resources than available in Berlin. Nonetheless, under the influence of August Pulle at Utrecht —himself a participant on one of the New Guinea expeditions—as well as Treub, more scientists entered the field and many useful contributions were made.[67]

In the early 1920s a serious economic slump developed in the Netherlands East Indies, forcing a curtailment of government activities.[68] Some recovery took place later in the decade, but this ultimately was negated by the Depression. The consequences have been well described from the point of view of an expedition partic-

ipant and subsequent lifelong advocate of New Guinea, Herman
Johannes Lam.[69] Between 1922 and 1935 there was only one
major government-supported geographical and scientific expedition, and that undertaken jointly with American personnel. For
more than a decade progress largely lay with individual explorers,
to some extent aided by greater extension of government control
and improved transportation. Notable visitors included Ernst
Mayr, Victor van Straelen (accompanying Crown Prince Leopold
of Belgium and Princess Astrid), Georg Stein, and Evelyn Cheesman. The relative lull in new collecting enabled metropolitan scientists to work up the results of the earlier expeditions in both
Dutch and German New Guinea; and in 1934, shortly after his
assumption of the directorship of the Rijksherbarium at Leiden,
Lam reviewed botanical progress for the whole island. Among his
conclusions was the suggestion that while there was a need for
continued fieldwork, it was as important to consolidate what had
already been done.[70]

German New Guinea (Mandated Territory of New Guinea)

In 1885 the part of New Guinea that had just become German territory—Kaiser-Wilhelmsland—was, of the three territories, biotically the least known. Collecting had largely been limited to the
vicinity of Blanche Bay on the Gazelle Peninsula. By 1914 German
New Guinea, although less extensively explored than British New
Guinea, had almost certainly been more *intensively* studied, collected, and mapped within its explored limits. The German predi-
lection for detail had manifested itself here as in so many other
areas of endeavor, aided by a belief that exploration and scientific
work was as much a cultural as well as practically useful activity.[71]

The history of biological and geographical exploration in German New Guinea, then, is one of well-supported expeditions and
individuals who were able to make large collections and obtain
extensive publication of their results. In thirty years the Germans
attained a preeminence that to this day remains unbeaten, with
parallels on the local economic and political scene. The destination of collections was, as in Dutch lands, less scattered than was
the case to the south. This was a result not only of policies
favoring centralization—Adolf Engler, director of the Berlin Botanical Garden and Museum from 1889 to 1921, was a strong

advocate of this—but also of the fact that by design or otherwise and in contrast to western New Guinea, non-German natural historians were few.[72] Moreover, at least some of the consequent museum and herbarium work was noticeably autarchic, which with the near-destruction of the Berlin Botanical Museum in 1943 would tragically impose a permanent handicap: descriptions lacking any authentic voucher plant specimens.

Exploration was not, however, a random process. Much of it appears ultimately to have been economically oriented—toward potential mineral and other natural resources, suitable plantation lands, or additional supplies of labor. Two expeditions, for instance, were organized with the primary aim of locating wild sources of gutta-percha and rubber and developing a system of "smallholder" collection of these resources for export. Development of the Bismarck Archipelago, which ultimately became a coconut economy, proved an easier proposition and thus more attractive to commercial interests. In the years before 1900 the chartered German Neu-Guinea-Kompagnie devoted more of its resources to the mainland, partly because of blind faith on the part of its director-in-chief, von Hansemann, that it could be another North Sumatra (where from about 1869 a large and very successful plantation economy had become established). With the permanent introduction in 1899 of imperial rule from Berlin, development became more methodical, but with a bias toward the Bismarcks.

Apart from a reconnaissance expedition in 1886–1887 and Carl Lauterbach's self-sponsored ascent of the Gogol River in 1890, the Kompagnie, early beset by mismanagement and financial woes, confined itself to the coast until 1896. Then economic and geographical interests led to the mounting of a series of expeditions on the Ramu River. In the subsequent era, local support for natural sciences was always favorable, notably under Governor Albert Hahl (1902–1914), but effective action depended very much on metropolitan support. Although this rose and fell by turns, it was quite substantial during 1907–1914, a time of general prosperity in Europe and North America. In those years four major campaigns and several lesser ones took place, resulting in a host of collections and other data that kept scientists occupied long after the loss of the territory to the Australians. Enough progress had been made by 1919, however, for the Berlin botanist and eventual successor of Adolf Engler as director of the Botanical Garden and Museum, Ludwig Diels, to produce a key summary paper on the biogeography of the montane vascular flora of New Guinea.[73] In it he argued that the flora of the rain-forest formations basically was part, but only part, of an "ancient" panaustral evergreen temperate or subtropical flora "complementary" to the panboreal, more or less deciduous, mesic temperate floras of Asia, Europe, and North America, and that the evergreen condition was related to high rainfall and nutrient-poor soils.

The progress of biological exploration under the Australian mandate in the northeastern quarter of the island, which with the Bismarck Archipelago and the northern Solomons became the Mandated Territory of New Guinea, was far less rapid. The economic traditions and practices of German New Guinea remained, but not the interest in the natural sciences. The kind of support the territory had enjoyed from Germany did not exist, or no longer existed, in Australia.[74] Certainly from the Commonwealth point of view such support would have involved a capital-expenditure commitment, which was alien to the still-prevailing official idea that a colony should pay its own way. Finance in the territory was very limited until the late 1920s, when gold royalties began to play an increasing role and more internal funds could be allocated for capital purposes. This was reflected in the establishment of modest local collections of insects and plants and, in Rabaul, the maintenance of an attractive botanical garden. The greatest share of the fieldwork and collecting of the interwar years was, however, undertaken by externally sponsored individuals—notably the indomitable Mary S. Clemens in Morobe Province; Fred Shaw Mayer in the Central Highlands, initially sponsored by Rothschild and the first significant collector in that newly opened area; and, in the northern Sepik region, Evelyn Cheesman. So far as is known, however, few of their collections remained in the territory, even duplicates. Long-resident collectors such as the Catholic missionary-priest Gerhard Peekel, author of one of the few regional floras (published only in 1985), also sent their collections away save what they may have kept for their own use.

As in other quarters of New Guinea, the 1930s were more productive for collections than the 1920s, particularly after the worst of the Depression. Botanical materials began again to flow to Berlin and elsewhere. Duplicates of specimens from Clemens and others were, however, more widely distributed, both for security and to garner more money. Thus, the materials utilized by Elmer D. Merrill and Lily Perry in their key series *Plantae papuanae archboldianae,* as well as other authors of the "Botanical Results of the Archbold Expeditions,"[75] are more widely available in institutions than many German, Dutch, or Australian/British specimens, fortunately so for post-1945 studies. The territorial Department of Agriculture even initiated a small herbarium, the only one definitely known to exist in the whole of Papuasia before 1944.[76]

The Framework Begins to Fill, 1942–1982

Our story cannot be complete without some reference to recent developments in the study of New Guinea natural history. More material was collected and results published between the close of World War II and the completion of the next great synthesis, *Biogeography and Ecology of New Guinea,* than in all the period from 1870 to 1942.[77]

A number of factors were responsible for this. Australia, the Netherlands, and the United Kingdom all sought after 1945 to increase capital expenditure, both in works and services, in their respective territories, and to initiate efforts in human development and social welfare. World War II had changed attitudes toward colonialism and had shown the world how little development had taken place in New Guinea. For native peoples, especially those in the theaters of war, there were new desires, of which the most striking manifestation was the upsurge in cargo cults. With the Indonesian declaration of independence in 1945, notice was served that, in New Guinea as elsewhere, the colonial order could not last.

For the natural sciences, this would mean a considerably higher level of participation by governments in biological exploration and research, of which, inevitably, much would be of an applied nature. New Guinea in this respect had hitherto been well behind its neighbors in the Malay Archipelago and Southeast Asia. With greater direct government involvement after 1945, a substantial body of locally based scientific units at last was developed.[78] The majority of these were in the Australian-controlled territories, from 1949 to 1971 known as the Territory of Papua and New

Guinea. During three decades a number of collections of biota came into being, mostly in units within the economic branches of government such as the Departments of Agriculture, Stock, and Fisheries (DASF), and Forests.[79] Some of these, such as the fish, pathological fungi, and insect collections of DASF and the plant collection of Forests, were substantial and became internationally recognized; the herbarium in Lae, for example, would in time accumulate upwards of 250,000 mounted plant specimens. No geological or paleontological collections were ever established, however, the local geological survey sending all material to Canberra.

Collections of other groups of biota, including land vertebrates, became the province of what is now the National Museum and Art Gallery of Papua New Guinea. This body was reestablished in 1954 from what had been a minute entity in Papua during the Murray administration. Natural history was a part of the museum's terms of reference, but few resources were available until the 1960s, and since then the field has played a relatively minor role in the museum's activities.[80] Additional contributions were made by the government's wildlife branch, which has continued its surveys up to the present time.

The development of these collections, a form of capital investment, was a belated acknowledgment by Australia of the changed circumstances. In the absence, however, of any firm *formal* policies in an administrative environment now more closely under metropolitan control, the establishment of these collections was for the most part ad hoc and their development largely isolated. Their growth, balance, and effectiveness depended very much on departmental means and policy and upon the relative resourcefulness of section heads, whose work at times became lost in public service empire-building and departmental rivalries. The establishment of the museum came too late and its effectiveness in the biological field was always too limited to counteract this situation. It was not until 1970 that the consequences of separate development began to be addressed, but the prospect of early independence for Papua and New Guinea forestalled any action.[81] Outside of Port Moresby and Lae, herbaria evolved in forestry centers at Bulolo in Papua New Guinea, Manokwari in Indonesian Irian Jaya, and Honiara in the Solomon Islands, while insect collections were developed in the Solomon Islands as well as at several entomological centers in Papua New Guinea. Collections were also established at the private Wau Ecology Institute, until 1971 known as the Bishop Museum Field Station.

Legislation first gazetted in Papua New Guinea in 1951, but since modified, now controls the export of plant and animal specimens. More recently, the country became a signatory to the Convention on International Trade in Endangered Species (CITES). Environmental legislation has been enacted, and a government Office (now Department) of Environment and Conservation, which now incorporates the Conservator of Fauna, has been established.

Besides the work of internal agencies, a great deal of collecting of all kinds of biota was carried out by expeditions and individuals from metropolitan countries (sometimes as joint undertakings involving an internal agency). The era of general-purpose expeditions was passing, however, and fieldwork became increasingly specialized; moreover, trips were usually of shorter duration than had been the case before World War II. With the advent of easier travel to, from, and within Papua and New Guinea and its neighbors, more individuals came for field studies in what were relatively liberal administrative climates. These good times, as evidenced by the level of fieldwork in progress and an explosion of publications, were certainly aided by favorable economic conditions and great interest in the sciences. However, the many scientific visitors, nearly all of them Europeans, were sometimes seen, especially from the 1960s, as exploiting the field for their own benefit. Their activities were "samting bilong witman"; and the relative lack of education among Papuans and outside preconceptions of native peoples in general left little place for them save as carriers, camp hands, or field assistants.[82] Some assistants, however, did become very skilled, in due time making collecting trips on their own, and they often developed a profound empirical knowledge of the biota.

Changes also occurred in the mix of metropolitan institutions and organizations concerned with New Guinea exploration in the postwar period. New Australian participants included the Commonwealth Scientific and Industrial Research Organization (CSIRO), whose land resource division was involved with basic surveys in Papua New Guinea for some twenty years, and students and staff from the new Australian National University, particularly its Research School of Pacific Studies. Elsewhere, the Dutch state herbarium (Rijksherbarium) in Leiden—under the initiative first of Lam (its director from 1933) and then, from 1962 to 1972, of Cornelis van Steenis—acted as a direct sponsor or part-sponsor of several botanical expeditions in both western and eastern New Guinea. Four more Archbold Expeditions, the last in 1964, as well as ornithological surveys by E. Thomas Gilliard, were mounted by the American Museum of Natural History in New York. In the remaining years of Dutch rule in western New Guinea, further large general expeditions were conducted, the last being the Star Mountains Expedition of 1959, which filled in "the last white spot on the map," as the expedition's leaders dubbed their field of operations.[83] Many other expeditions and investigators also visited all parts of Papuasia. Terrestrial biological stations were established, the first being the Bishop Museum Field Station in 1961 on the initiative of J. Linsley Gressitt, an active participant in entomological exploration from the mid-1950s until his death in 1982. Marine stations followed in the 1970s. The natural sciences, as the papers and references in *Biogeography and Ecology of New Guinea* demonstrate, progressed from mere collecting and simple field observation to an increased emphasis on ecological, biological, and ethological studies, all of which involved a host of specialists and their students.[84]

This great surge was, however, a continuation of a trend begun during World War II when many persons in the services—American, Japanese, and Australian—made collections, some of them substantial. Among these were collections of tree species that provided the nucleus for the herbarium at Lae. Several important publications also resulted. Because these were largely individual undertakings, though, collections and results have become dispersed; no full review is available and thus their historical place cannot yet be assessed.

After the 1960s, the most favorable period for the natural sciences, conditions in Papua New Guinea and the Solomon Islands grew more difficult as funding became harder to obtain and changes took place in the political climate. While budgetary support to Papua New Guinea from Australia continued after independence in 1975, this aid was "untied," that is, none of the grant was earmarked for specific projects or programs. Moreover, approaches to other sources of external aid came to be fairly strictly controlled in accordance with national planning policy, which by and large accorded nonrevenue-raising activities lower priority.[85] In western New Guinea, the transfer of power to Indonesia in 1963 brought about a steep decline in biological fieldwork. Also, the dispersion of results from what few expeditions were mounted increased due to the withdrawal of Dutch scientific efforts from the area and the limited ability of Indonesian scientists to fill the gap. More recently, the area, which in 1969 formally became the Indonesian province of West Irian (later Irian Jaya), has suffered an increase in internal security problems.

The developing educational institutions attempted to counter some of these trends. The new University of Papua New Guinea (UPNG) gradually formed collections of worth under initially difficult circumstances and, more importantly, produced some of the first Melanesians qualified to take part in scientific study. In the late 1970s UPNG established in principle a Natural Sciences Resource Centre, eventually to house collections as well as related activities; funds to erect some of the necessary buildings were granted at the end of 1982. In the same period calls began to be heard for consolidation of the major collection units.[86]

Nevertheless, structural problems remained for the sciences in Papua New Guinea and the Solomon Islands.[87] A scientific society had been organized in the Australian territories after World War II, but, although active for twenty-five years, it did not long survive the end of the colonial period, most likely because of a lack of a sufficiently broad basis and the departure of most of its active membership. Several more specialized societies have partly filled the gap, but the continuing absence of a national academy or council remains a problem. The ad hoc approach to government research that grew up prior to independence also contributed to the fragmentation of the sciences, which in turn has manifested itself at the political level. Only in very recent years have some moves been made to reorganize scientific research into coherent administrative departments.[88] In the Solomon Islands, which gained independence in 1978, scanty resources and an associated concern with immediate survival also limited government work in the natural sciences to essentials.[89]

Legacies and Prospects

The results of over 115 years of continuous study of the natural history of New Guinea and its neighbors have provided a number of legacies for the present and future from which arise certain general questions. These can be grouped as either scientific or structural.

Fundamental to New Guinea's continuing attraction and standing among scientists is its position as the largest tropical island in the world—a miniature continent harboring a high level of diversity in every area of natural science. Its lowland forests are in structure, composition, and dynamics different in many ways from their counterparts in the Sunda Islands and Southeast Asia. Those in the mountains are, as Diels first recognized, central to an understanding of the far-flung, temperate, southern evergreen forests; in the eyes of some, they are the largest surviving component of the old forests of Gondwanaland. New Guinea's alpine zone is the largest in the tropical Pacific basin. An improved perception of the geological instability of most of the region has led in recent years to a dynamic view of the natural vegetation.[90] The biota is to many a puzzle, for it mixes (primarily) Asian and Australian forms; understanding it remains important to all biogeographic research programs. The region is included within the zone wherein flowering plants long were thought to have originated. Finally, Papuasia is "an area . . . that may be the most favorable in the world for the study of speciation."[91]

The task of forming effective syntheses of materials accumulated during the primary phase of inland exploration, which Lam had already indicated as essential, began only in the 1940s. A further stage was reached by the early 1980s, but of necessity, as Gressitt stressed, there is still far to go. Knowledge of the various groups of biota and of the diverse ecosystems, let alone geographical areas, is yet very uneven, as a perusal of the chapters of *Biogeography and Ecology of New Guinea* demonstrates, and in time new syntheses will undoubtedly emerge. As more information is compiled, scientific horizons, research programs, and paradigms will inevitably change.[92]

The level of international scientific activity engendered by the natural world of New Guinea stands in contrast to, and is in part associated with, the comparatively late dates at which a level of infrastructural, economic, and cultural development was reached favorable to the growth and sustenance of substantial scientific institutions or of learned societies. Basic exploration of the kind characteristic of the nineteenth century remained a prime target in the "last unknown" for decades; it is the manner in which this was carried out and the ways biological collections and data were handled under widely varied circumstances that have here been one of my main concerns.

The very size and extent of Papuasia, its rugged inland topography, dense vegetation, and low level of indigenous political organization at first contact were—in contrast to islands or archipelagoes such as New Caledonia, the Philippines, or Madagascar —an obstacle to eventual domination by a single metropolitan power. Rather, its fate was similar to that of Africa: division among the metropolitans to suit their needs, followed by the changes wrought by two world wars. Moreover, the scientific uniqueness of the region and more or less open-door official attitudes attracted investigators from many countries. These factors have resulted in scientific (and cultural) links with a variety of metropolitan countries as large as if Papuasia had been an entire continent.[93]

When effective colonial or imperial control was imposed, it took as many forms as circumstances and interest dictated. But I believe it was the relatively slow and limited development of the territories of Papuasia that left little opportunity for the early formation of local cultural entities, given that, being entirely foreign to local traditions, they were dependent on the representatives of outside powers. It is quite likely that even in the vicinity of Blanche Bay conditions around 1900 would not have been suitable for a relatively advanced undertaking such as the Apia (Samoa) Geophysical Observatory, even had such a site been justified on scientific grounds. No large white-settler community that might press for such institutions as museums and galleries or scientific societies and academies existed before 1942.[94]

The nature and level of government responses thus become of exceptional importance, both on the part of individuals in authority and at the metropolitan level. Sir William MacGregor in British New Guinea was well aware of the importance of collections and scientific documentation, and he and his staff made considerable efforts to gather materials during his ten years as administrator.

His means were, however, very limited, and contemporary Port Moresby was to him scarcely fit for a museum. Efforts toward a botanical garden also failed. The Australian input before World War II in both their territories was minimal and largely utilitarian, probably reflecting attitudes that had developed there as in other parts of the British periphery in the nineteenth century. By contrast, the more largely conceived German effort in the natural sciences in the thirty years prior to 1914 was substantial and has been of lasting importance. Dutch activity was also strong, if late in the day and perhaps reactive.[95]

I believe these contrasting responses are related to basic differences then existing in German and Dutch attitudes as opposed to those of the British (and even more their Australasian dominions). The most extreme discontinuity in Papuasia is provided by a comparison of German and Australian activities in what was German New Guinea. The more limited view of the sciences that in large part gave rise to this discontinuity may, however, to some extent be correlated with a relative quiescence in many disciplines in Australia between World Wars I and II.[96] This view, however, continued to some extent after 1945. Although, as in other local activities undertaken by the territorial administration, much more effort was put into scientific research and collection development, and much was accomplished by dedicated scientists and other staff, the orientation to a large extent remained practical; management continued to be in the form of scattered branches of the public service as had been customary in most British dominions and other territories.[97] Had Australia not been in charge, very possibly research would have been organized in a single branch as was the case in the Philippines from 1906, or as gazetted institutes, considered by some a more satisfactory research environment.[98] I believe that these more sophisticated arrangements would have eased the transition of the sciences in the Papua New Guinea government through independence and beyond, perhaps placing them in a more favorable political position and causing them to be more attractive as a career.[99] What is hard to understand is why the model of CSIRO was not transferred to Papua New Guinea. Would this have been the case had Australia remained the administering power, as was once confidently expected, until the year 2000?

A. B. Katende has argued that in Uganda political independence came well before any real awareness of the sciences. He has reported that the three herbaria in the country existing at independence (1961) all suffered greatly from neglect and/or outright destruction in the ensuing two decades; and he has suggested that consolidation of what remained would be a useful first step toward rebuilding. In Papua New Guinea (and the Solomon Islands) a similar situation appears to exist, with consequences for the good upkeep and effective utilization of scholarly resources such as collections. It was, for example, only through considerable pressure that a potential tragedy with regard to one major collection was recently averted.[100]

The progress of natural history in New Guinea and its neighboring islands presents a case study not only of differing government responses to a difficult challenge, but also of the potential power, however imperfect, of interested private sponsorship. Recent developments also suggest that sound legislative and administrative arrangements for local institutions, a necessary factor in the ethical pursuit of tropical biology, lie in a mix of approaches, whether inherited or not. While it is unfortunate that circumstances (and attitudes) in Papua New Guinea prevented either the establishment of museums during the heyday of natural history or the development of any botanical gardens on the Kew model until well after 1900[101] (the territory was, so to speak, "not good ground"), and that the organization of the scientific resources ultimately inherited from the Australian administration was unsatisfactory, there is scope for change and development that is harder to imagine occurring in Irian Jaya. I would also suggest that it was often fiscal, economic, and practical constraints that guided the ways the sciences developed in dependent territories, although the New Guinea case demonstrates that cultural differences among metropolitan powers as well as the presence of interested officials also played their part.[102]

Notes

I would like to acknowledge the assistance of Peter Stevens of Harvard University and Philip F. Rehbock of the University of Hawaii for substantive comments on this paper, and my sister Joanna H. Frodin of the Federal Reserve Bank in Philadelphia, as well as Roy MacLeod of Sydney University regarding matters of style. I am also very much indebted to Benjamin C. Stone of the Academy of Natural

Sciences of Philadelphia and Garry Trompf, formerly of the University of Papua New Guinea, for many discussions on matters of interest relating to this topic. Thanks are also due to the libraries of the University of Papua New Guinea, the Academy of Natural Sciences of Philadelphia, the American Philosophical Society, and the University of Pennsylvania, as well as the Free Library of Philadelphia for use of their facilities, access to materials, assistance, and loans from other libraries.

1. Lynn Barber, *The Heyday of Natural History, 1820–1870* (Garden City, N.Y.: Doubleday, 1980). Barber argues that after publication of Charles Darwin's *On the Origin of Species,* natural history became increasingly academically oriented, with less of a place for amateurs.

2. A readable introduction to the history of exploration and contact in New Guinea is furnished by Gavin Souter, *New Guinea: The Last Unknown* (Sydney: Angus and Robertson, 1963). An exhaustive survey of all outside contacts and local events through 1902 in New Guinea and nearby islands is given in August Wichmann, "Entdeckungsgeschichte von Neu-Guinea," in *Nova Guinea,* vols. 1–2 (Leiden: Brill, 1909–1912). On New Guinea's famous birds, see E. Thomas Gilliard, *Birds of Paradise and Bower Birds* (London: Wiedenfeld and Nicholson, 1969), chapter 3.

3. Souter, *The Last Unknown.*

4. Bradford Allen Booth, ed., *The Tireless Traveler: Twenty Letters to the Liverpool* Mercury *by Anthony Trollope* (Berkeley and Los Angeles: University of California Press, 1941), 119.

5. The name "Papuasia" was first introduced as a biogeographic term by the German economic botanist Otto Warburg. It encompasses New Guinea, the Bismarck Archipelago, and the Solomon Islands. See Otto Warburg, "Beiträge zur Kenntnis der papuanischen Flora," *Botanische Jahrbücher für Systematik* 13 (1891): 230–455.

6. Lewis Pyenson, "Cultural Imperialism and Exact Sciences: German Expansion Overseas, 1900–1930," *History of Science* 20 (1982): 1–43, esp. 7–9. Pyenson has since expanded this paper into a book of the same title (New York: Peter Lang, 1985).

7. Gilliard, *Birds of Paradise.* A general survey of French voyages is given in John C. Dunmore, *French Explorers in the Pacific,* 2 vols. (Oxford: Oxford University Press, 1965). See also Jacques Brosse, *Great Voyages of Discovery: Circumnavigators and Scientists, 1764–1843,* trans. Stanley Hochman (New York: Facts on File, 1983), 146–151. In this section on the *Coquille,* Brosse symbolizes the importance of Lesson's work with a subheading "Even birds of paradise have feet."

8. I use the term natural history to refer to the study of all forms of biota, although in the last century it has been more often used in a purely zoological context.

9. A concise narrative of the progress of biotic exploration in Papuasia, with selected sources, is given in David G. Frodin and J. Linsley Gressitt, "Biological Exploration of New Guinea," in J. Linsley Gressitt, ed., *Biogeography and Ecology of New Guinea* (The Hague: Junk, 1982), 87–130. Other chapters in this

work also provide exploration chronologies for particular biotic groups. Gilliard *(Birds of Paradise)* gives a gazetteer of collectors and expeditions that have searched for or studied birds of paradise and bower birds.

Other large geographical areas in which natural history exploration enjoyed a prominent early position were Australia and Africa, with its many large mammals. But it may be that the New Guinea pattern compares more closely with the exploration histories of smaller units such as the Galápagos Islands and New Caledonia, where one or two biotic groups of outstanding interest have also attracted great attention.

10. Alfred Russel Wallace, *The Malay Archipelago: The Land of the Orang-utan and the Bird of Paradise* (London: Macmillan, 1869). The striking contrast between the dominant vertebrate life of Borneo and that of New Guinea is further demonstrated by two illustrations from Wallace's *The Geographical Distribution of Animals* (1876), reproduced side by side in Wilma George, "Wallace and His Line," in Timothy C. Whitmore, ed., *Wallace's Line and Plate Tectonics* (Oxford: Oxford University Press, 1981), 3–8.

11. Souter, *The Last Unknown;* J. Goode, *Rape of the Fly* (South Melbourne: Nelson, 1977).

12. De Meneses was the first voyager to arrive from the west in 1526, de Saavedra the first from across the Pacific in 1528, and Mendaña the discoverer of the Solomon Islands in 1567.

13. John Cawte Beaglehole, *The Exploration of the Pacific,* 3d ed. (London: A. and C. Black, 1966). A useful summary of early New Guinea voyages is given in Clements R. Markham, "Progress of Discovery on the Coasts of New Guinea," *Supplementary Papers of the Royal Geographical Society* 1 (1886): 265–284. The Markham River is named after him.

14. Markham, "Progress of Discovery"; P. Smit, "International Influences on the Development of Natural History in the Netherlands and Its East Indian Colonies between 1750 and 1850," *Janus* 65 (1978): 45–65.

15. For a general account of Dampier and his work in Australia, see Colin M. Finney, *To Sail beyond the Sunset: Natural History in Australia, 1699–1829* (Adelaide: Rigby, 1984), 9–13. Information on almost all botanical collectors in Malesia up to 1972 is given in M. J. van Steenis-Kruseman, "Malaysian Plant Collectors and Collections," in Cornelis G. G. J. van Steenis, ed., *Flora Malesiana,* ser. 1, vol. 1 (Jakarta: Noordhoff-Kolff, 1950) and in its two supplements (ibid., vol. 5 [Jakarta, 1958], ccxxxv–cccxlii, and vol. 8 [Leiden: Noordhoff, 1974], [i–iv], i–cxv). A chronological survey of botanical work in the region is in Hendrik C. D. de Wit, "Short History of the Phytography of Malaysian Vascular Plants," in ibid., ser. 1, vol. 4 (Jakarta, 1949): lxx–clxi. Dampier's plant specimens were studied first by John Ray and are now housed in the Sherardian collections of the Oxford University Herbarium. See H. Newman Clokie, *An Account of the Herbaria of the Department of Botany in the University of Oxford* (Oxford: Oxford University Press, 1964).

16. On Rumpf, see van Steenis-Kruseman, "Malaysian Plant Collectors," 452–453; Marius J. Sirks, "Rumphius, the Blind Seer of Amboina," trans. Lily M. Perry, in Pieter Honig and Frans Verdoorn, eds., *Science and Scientists in the Netherlands Indies* (Natuurwetenschappelijk Tijdschrift voor Nederlandsch

Indië, 102, Special Supplement; New York: Board for the Netherlands Indies, Surinam and Curaçao, 1945), 295–308. Rumpf's major works are *D'Amboinsche Rariteitskamer* (Amsterdam, 1705), and *Het Amboinsch Kruidboek/ Herbarium Amboinense,* 7 vols. (Amsterdam: Uytwerf, 1741–1755). The former was in its day a comparative best-seller, and was reissued in 1741. For a collection of extracts from these works, see E. M. Beekman, ed., *The Poison Tree: Selected Writings of Rumphius on the Natural History of the Indies* (Amherst, Mass.: University of Massachusetts Press, 1981).

17. Gilliard, *Birds of Paradise.* Brosse (*Great Voyages,* 149–150) suggests that the myth was finally put to rest only in 1824 when Lesson made his observations at Dorei Bay.

18. Gilliard, *Birds of Paradise.* At this time, Jules Dumont d'Urville, Lesson's colleague on the *Coquille* and later commander of the *Astrolabe* (1826–1829) and *Astrolabe* and *Zélée* (1837–1840) voyages, made the first substantial botanical collections from any part of the mainland. He was to return to Dorei Bay in 1827 with the *Astrolabe,* where for two weeks additional botanical collections were made by Lesson's younger brother Pierre-Adolphe—a year before Zipelius's arrival at Triton Bay.

19. Dunmore *(French Explorers)* is mainly concerned with the voyages themselves and their strategic and political circumstances. Some account of their scientific work, however, is given by Brosse *(Great Voyages).* The strength of the French legacy in the natural sciences, of lasting significance for many parts of the world, was made possible by generous government support for the voyages (and dissemination of their results) and the strong organization and effective research programs of the Muséum National d'Histoire Naturelle in Paris in the period from the Revolution to 1840. See Camille Limoges, "The Development of the Muséum d'Histoire Naturelle of Paris, c. 1800–1914," in Robert Fox and George Weisz, eds., *The Organization of Science and Technology in France, 1808–1914* (Cambridge: Cambridge University Press, 1980), 211–240. Smit ("International Influences," 55) remarks that the zoological results of the French voyages, including their work in the Malay Archipelago and New Guinea, were often quickly worked up and published, further handicapping the Dutch revival. However, some primary studies, for example in phanerogamic botany, were never undertaken or completed owing to a lack of interest (perhaps in part arising from the factors discussed by Limoges) or to the sheer quantity of collections. Even today in the Laboratoire de Phanérogamie of the museum, old collections continue to be found that have never previously been studied or even incorporated (James Mears, personal communication, 21 February 1986).

20. See Alan Frost, "Science for Political Purposes: European Explorations of the Pacific Ocean, 1764–1806," in this volume.

21. Markham, "Progress of Discovery," esp. 283–284; Eduard Servaas de Klerck, *History of the Netherlands East Indies,* 2 vols. (Amsterdam: Brusse, 1938).

22. Smit, "International Influences."

23. Ibid.; Marius Jacob Sirks, *Indisch Natuuronderzoek* (Amsterdam: Koloniaal-Instituut, 1915), 86–140.

24. Summaries appear in Souter, *The Last Unknown,* and Wichmann, "Entdeckungsgeschichte."

25. For Zipelius' work, see van Steenis-Kruseman, "Malaysian Plant Collectors," 592–593. On Müller, see George Gaylord Simpson, "Too Many Lines: The Limits of the Oriental and Australian Zoogeographic Regions," *Proceedings of the American Philosophical Society* 121 (1977): 107–120.

26. Friedrich Anton Wilhelm Miquel, *Flora Indiae batavae/Flora van Nederlandsch Indie,* 4 vols. (Amsterdam: van der Post, 1855–1859). De Wit ("Malaysian Vascular Plants") notes that Miquel was unable to obtain full access to the collections of the Rijksherbarium in Leiden, including much material from the Natural Sciences Commission, during the directorship of Carl Blume (1829–1862).

Heinrich Zollinger, "Über den Begriff and Umfang einer 'Flora Malesiana,' " *Vierteljahrsschrift der Naturforschenden Gesellschaft in Zürich* 2 (1857): 317–349, map. Zollinger considered that the very size of New Guinea might mean the presence of a continental flora as distinct from the predominantly insular flora postulated for Malesia.

27. The *Fly* and *Bramble* survey took place from 1842 to 1846, and that of the *Rattlesnake* from 1846 to 1850. Only a portion of their time was spent in New Guinea waters. Naturalists included John MacGillivray (on both voyages), J. Beete Jukes (on the *Fly*), and the young Thomas Henry Huxley (on the *Rattlesnake*).

28. Pyenson, "Cultural Imperialism," 3.

29. Finney, *Beyond the Sunset,* chap. 10. Local interest in Australia centered on such institutions as the Australian Museum in Sydney, the Botanical Museum of Melbourne (now the National Herbarium of Victoria), and the Queensland Museum in Brisbane, as well as Elizabeth Bay House in Sydney, home of the naturalist Macleay family. Elizabeth Bay House, now a museum, was built in the 1830s for Alexander Macleay, New South Wales colonial secretary. Later it was, successively, the home of his son William S. Macleay and nephew William J. Macleay, the last of whom organized a major New Guinea expedition. On the ground or entrance floor is the Macleays' study. Over a period of some fifty years every visiting naturalist was entertained in this outstanding colonial home.

30. R. C. Thompson, *Australian Imperialism in the Pacific* (Melbourne: Melbourne University Press, 1980). See also C. Harley Grattan, *The Southwest Pacific to 1900* (Ann Arbor: University of Michigan Press, 1963), 491.

31. For recent biographies of d'Albertis and Miklouho-Maclay, see Goode, *Rape of the Fly,* and A. Webster, *The Moon Man* (Melbourne: Melbourne University Press, 1985). The transliteration of Miklouho-Maclay's name adopted here follows Grattan, *Southwest Pacific.*

32. On the arrangements by d'Albertis's sponsors, see Goode, *Rape of the Fly.* A recent biographical account of Beccari and his scientific work in English with a bibliography is by Rodolfo E. G. Pichi-Sermolli and C. G. G. J. van Steenis, "Dedication," in van Steenis, *Flora Malesiana* 9 (1983): 7–44.

33. Van Steenis-Kruseman, "The Collections of the Rijksherbarium," *Blumea* 25 (1979): 29–55, esp. 37. Mission society members (and other travelers and res-

idents) were, however, particularly urged by Ferdinand von Mueller at Melbourne to collect plants; this resulted in the acquisition of thousands of specimens for his herbarium over a twenty-year period from 1875 to 1896. On these was based much of the contents of his major series on the New Guinea flora. See von Mueller, *Descriptive Notes on Papuan Plants,* parts 1–9 (Melbourne: Victorian Government Printer, 1875–1890).

34. Souter, *The Last Unknown;* Grattan, *Southwest Pacific.*

35. Modern Rabaul is situated at the tip of a large peninsula that bears the ship's name, and a range in central New Ireland was named after the commander, later the first administrator of German New Guinea.

36. Goode, *Rape of the Fly.*

37. The year 1875 is also important for Souter *(The Last Unknown).* Grattan *(Southwest Pacific)* has spoken of the mid-1870s as the peak of the so-called fever and associates with it active colonization plans. William J. Macleay himself appears to have been the first prominent Australian to oppose unrestricted outside exploitation. According to Grattan, he argued strongly for preliminary exploration and scientific study under government auspices. This contrasted sharply with John Moresby's optimistic advocacy of New Guinea as a new frontier.

38. Some zoologists would argue, however, that the massive collecting practiced in the nineteenth and early twentieth centuries has provided series of specimens invaluable for the study of variation and for an understanding of species and infraspecific limits. See Miriam Rothschild, *Dear Lord Rothschild* (Philadelphia: ISI Press, 1983), esp. 149–150.

39. Grattan, *Southwest Pacific,* 491. It may be noted that Miklouho-Maclay's third New Guinea visit in 1880–1881 was to the southeastern part, where for a time he was a guest of the Congregational mission at Port Moresby.

40. Von Mueller, *Papuan Plants.* Already in 1876 Rudolph Scheffer at Bogor, in a review based on Teysmann's and earlier published records, would argue that for the flora an Australian relationship did not necessarily exist. See R. H. C. C. Scheffer, "Énumération des plantes de la Nouvelle-Guinée," *Annales du Jardin Botanique de Buitenzorg,* 1 (1876): 1–60. Warburg ("Kenntnis der papuanischen Flora") supported Scheffer's suggestion that, in spite of the Australian element, the flora was predominantly "Asiatic" or "Indian," i.e., Malesian. No definitive resolution of this conundrum, which contributes to the perception of New Guinea as critical from the point of view of floristic and faunistic biogeography, has been achieved within the conventional biogeographic paradigm. This paradigm includes as one principle the recognition of biotic regions; for a review see Gareth Nelson, "From Candolle to Croizat: Comments on the History of Biogeography," *Journal of the History of Biology* 11 (1978): 269–305. Some more recent researchers (below, note 92) have, however, rejected biotic regions. The poverty of dipterocarps was discerned already by Beccari in 1872 and 1875; see Anonymous, "The Dipterocarpaceae of New Guinea," *Gardeners Chronicle,* ser. 2, vol. 9 (1878): 114. That writer, in contrast to Scheffer, boldly went on to conclude that New Guinea vegetation "was not of a markedly Malayan type."

41. In a number of areas of natural history the work of the 1870s was for a century virtually to stand alone. Beccari's work on Papuasian sea grasses and ant-

plants, for example, was not seriously added to until the 1970s, and arachnological studies all but lapsed from 1881 until after World War II; see chapters by Ian Johnstone, Michael Robinson, and Barbara York Main in Gressitt, *Biogeography and Ecology of New Guinea*.

42. On imperial fever in Australia, see Thompson, *Australian Imperialism*, and Grattan, *Southwest Pacific*. On Bismarck and the German colonial empire, see Fritz Stern, *Gold and Iron: Bismarck, Bleichröder, and the Building of the German Empire* (New York: Knopf, 1977), and Mary E. Townsend, *The Rise and Fall of Germany's Colonial Empire, 1884–1918* (1930; New York: Fertig, 1966). Stewart G. Firth, *Germans in Papua New Guinea* (Melbourne: Melbourne University Press, 1983), should be consulted for more specific developments relating to the establishment of German rule in New Guinea.

43. The working-up of the majority of Forbes's botanical collections was delayed for nearly forty years through personal misunderstandings and ill-feelings. It thus fell largely to the Germans and Dutch to make known more fully the nature and diversity of the upland and lower montane vascular flora.

44. This aid not only helped support work in New Guinea but also the last great journeys in the Australian interior and, shortly after, the beginnings of work in Antarctica. Much of it was made possible through the efforts of determined advocates such as Ferdinand von Mueller.

45. Van Steenis-Kruseman, "Malaysian Plant Collectors," 91–92, 360; Arthur Swinson, *Frederick Sander: The Orchid King* (London: Hodder and Stoughton, 1970); Merle A. Reinikka, *A History of the Orchid* (Coral Gables, Fla.: University of Miami Press, 1972). The letters from Micholitz to Sander are now housed in the archives of the Royal Botanic Gardens, Kew. The orchid craze as a phenomenon resembled the fern craze of mid-century described in David E. Allen, *The Victorian Fern Craze* (London: Hutchinson, 1969).

46. Gilliard, *Birds of Paradise*. In the 1880s and 1890s alone, thirty-six of the some ninety currently recognized geographical races of birds of paradise in New Guinea were first described for science, most of them originally as species. Allen *(Victorian Fern Craze)* has described a similar burst of scientific interest aroused by the fern craze, and the same was also true of the orchid craze, which from the 1840s led to the description of myriad species by such authorities as John Lindley in London, Heinrich Gustav Reichenbach in Hamburg, and Robert Allen Rolfe at Kew, and the publication of several authoritative and even sumptuous books.

47. Gilliard, *Birds of Paradise*. Rothschild *(Dear Lord Rothschild)* points out that her uncle, the zoologist Lionel Walter Rothschild, 2d Lord Rothschild, was particularly interested in these birds, and he, along with his Tring Museum curator of vertebrates Ernst Hartert and the Berlin ornithologist Erwin Stresemann, undertook to sponsor Mayr's expedition, the results of which would be embodied in his taxonomic studies, New Guinea bird checklist (below, note 92), and, in turn, his contributions to the mid-twentieth-century evolutionary synthesis (cf. E. Mayr, *Systematics and the Origin of Species* [New York: Columbia, 1942]).

48. Richard Bowdler Sharpe, *Monograph of the Paradiseidae, or Birds of Paradise, and Ptilonorhynchidae, or Bower-Birds,* 2 vols. (London: Sotheran, 1891–1898), v. This was one of the last of the great series of color-plate bird folios initiated in the 1830s by the zoologist and outstanding artist John Gould. Some

of the species treated were based on material collected for Walter Rothschild, who from the 1890s was to become for more than forty years one of the leading sponsors of zoological exploration in New Guinea. Miriam Rothschild *(Dear Lord Rothschild)* provides evidence that the sizeable collections of birds of paradise and bower birds, as well as of other fauna, that Walter Rothschild assembled at Tring aided in his formulation, with Ernst Hartert, of the idea of zoological species as series of one or more geographic races. See also Erwin Stresemann, *Ornithology from Aristotle to the Present* (Cambridge, Mass.: Harvard University Press, 1975), originally published as *Die Entwicklung der Ornithologie von Aristoteles bis zur Gegenwart* (Berlin: Peters, 1951).

49. Pyenson, "Cultural Imperialism."

50. For a concise chronology, see Frodin and Gressitt, "Biological Exploration of New Guinea," or Souter, *The Last Unknown.*

51. Van Steenis-Kruseman ("Malaysian Plant Collectors," Supplement 1, ccxlvii) notes that for the National Herbarium of Victoria in Melbourne "von Mueller had described only a small part of the Papuan material." My investigations in the 1970s and 1980s confirmed that much more was extant than had ever been described or reported in the contemporary literature.

52. Barber, *Heyday of Natural History.*

53. For instance no local natural history journal was founded, nor any learned society. Moreover, there were simply too few scientists and interested persons who could exert pressure for the organization of local museums with a scope including natural history—even when natural history was most in fashion. Cf. Susan Sheets-Pyenson, "Civilizing by Nature's Example: The Development of Colonial Museums of Natural History, 1850–1900," in Nathan Reingold and Marc Rothenberg, eds., *Scientific Imperialism: The American and Australian Experience* (Washington, D.C.: Smithsonian Institution Press, 1987), 351–377. A comparison of New Guinea and Borneo is in this respect of interest. In all Papuasia the sole museum up to 1942 was a twenty-foot-square wooden building in Port Moresby built in 1909, but from the mid-1920s used by government anthropologist Francis Edgar Williams chiefly as an office and as headquarters for his newspaper, the *Papuan Villager.* By contrast, Borneo's first museum, the Sarawak Museum in Kuching, was established in the 1880s due to the efforts of the second Rajah of Sarawak, Sir Charles Brooke, and for decades it was very influential as effectively the only institute of higher learning in that large island. See Jan B. Avé and Victor T. King, *Borneo* (Leiden: National Museum of Ethnology, the Netherlands, 1986), esp. 102, 107–111. Conditions were also adverse to the early establishment of botanical gardens. Ian Stuart, in *Port Moresby: Yesterday and Today* (Sydney: Pacific Publications, 1970), has described how MacGregor's efforts to establish a garden in Port Moresby ended in futility. Not until the development of Rabaul in the first decade of the twentieth century was any garden definitively established in Papuasia. Under German rule it acted purely as a plant introduction and trial station, the precursor of the present Lowlands Agricultural Experiment Station at nearby Kerevat, and only after 1914 was it gradually redeveloped as a garden for both science and pleasure on the Kew model, the trial plots being relocated to Kerevat in 1928. For mainly temporal reasons, New Guinea thus was not involved—or only peripherally so, at a very late stage when

specialization of plant science activities and imperial decentralization were already in full swing—in the kinds of activities, especially economic-plant transfer, and their impact as described by Lucile H. Brockway in her functional if somewhat one-dimensional account of nineteenth century British (particularly Kew) and colonial botanical gardens, *Science and Colonial Expansion: The Role of the British Royal Botanic Gardens* (London: Academic Press, 1979).

54. David G. Frodin, "Herbaria in Papua New Guinea and Nearby Areas: A Review," in Seymour H. Sohmer, ed., *Forum on Systematics Resources in the Pacific* (Honolulu, Hawaii: Bishop Museum Press, 1985), 54–62, esp. 54. MacGregor, however, placed a high value on museums and collections, and with a view to the future arranged for an official New Guinea collection to be formed at the Queensland Museum, then under the direction of the vertebrate zoologist Charles W. de Vis; see Patricia Mather, ed., *A Time for a Museum: The History of the Queensland Museum, 1862–1986,* Memoirs of the Queensland Museum 24 (Brisbane: Queensland Museum, 1986), esp. 202–204. Although ultimately largely ethnographic, the collection by 1898 featured some three thousand zoological specimens, mainly birds.

55. Bailey himself, at age seventy-one, visited the territory some months before MacGregor's departure in 1898, and until 1942 he and his successors acted unofficially as government botanists for British New Guinea. The zoological collections became part of the official collection.

56. Frodin, "Herbaria in Papua New Guinea," 55. The criticism, prepared by Royal Commissioner J. A. Kenneth Mackay, appears in Commonwealth Parliament, "Report of the Royal Commission of Inquiry into the Present Conditions, Including the Method of Government, of the Territory of Papua," *Commonwealth of Australia, Parliamentary Papers* (Melbourne: Government Printer, 1907).

57. Souter, *The Last Unknown;* Stuart, *Port Moresby.* I believe the more than twenty-year rivalry of Lieutenant-Governor Murray and his senior ranking civil servant, Director of Agriculture Miles Staniforth Cater Smith, along with the chronic financial restraints, were the most significant internal factors handicapping government involvement. Murray, however, was able to employ Francis E. Williams as government anthropologist (and curator of what officially was considered a museum) for many years prior to World War II (see n. 53 above).

58. For details, see van Steenis-Kruseman, "Malaysian Plant Collectors," 311, 570–571.

59. Frodin, "Herbaria in Papua New Guinea," 55. Mather *(Time for a Museum)* also notes that discussions and transactions took place from time to time with regard to the ethnographic materials in the MacGregor collection.

60. Cf. Rothschild, *Dear Lord Rothschild,* esp. plate 8.

61. Good general descriptions of the Brandes and Archbold expeditions can be found in James Sinclair, *Wings of Gold* (Sydney: Pacific Publications, 1980).

62. Alex S. George in Bureau of Flora and Fauna, *Flora of Australia,* vol. 1 (Canberra: Australian Government Publishing Service, 1981).

63. On comparative scientific development between Britain and Germany in this period, cf. Pyenson, "Cultural Imperialism," 5.

64. Willem Carel Klein, *Nieuw-Guinée,* 3 vols. (Amsterdam: Molukken-Insti-

tut, 1935–1938). The state of the Australian territories was also examined in some detail in this work, which despite some criticism is a landmark, indicative of a return of substantive interest after the lull of the 1920s.

65. See Lilian Susette Gibbs, *Dutch North West New Guinea: A Contribution to the Phytogeography and Flora and the Arfak Mountains* (London: Taylor and Francis, 1917).

66. Wichmann, "Entdeckungsgeschichte."

67. The zoological syntheses include Max W. C. Weber and Lieven Ferdinand de Beaufort, *The Fishes of the Indo-Australian Archipelago,* 11 vols. (Leiden: Brill, 1911–1962); Nelly de Rooij, *The Reptiles of the Indo-Australian Archipelago,* 2 vols. (Leiden: Brill, 1915–1917); and Pieter N. van Kampen, *The Amphibia of the Indo-Australian Archipelago* (Leiden: Brill, 1923). These were in addition to the reports in *Nova Guinea* and elsewhere. No comparable botanical works covering New Guinea were initiated until the series of family and genus revisions begun at Buitenzorg in the 1920s and the launch of *Flora Malesiana* after World War II. Botanical reports in *Nova Guinea* consisted of lavishly illustrated treatments, family by family, of collections rather than the full regional family revisions sponsored in Germany and published mainly in *Botanische Jahrbücher für Systematik, Pflanzengeschichte und Pflanzengeographie* from 1912 to 1942 as "Beiträge zur Flora von Papuasien" (which often included all available material from Dutch New Guinea, and for which a number of Dutch botanists wrote treatments).

68. De Klerck, *Netherlands East Indies.*

69. Marius Jacobs, *Herman Johannes Lam* (Amsterdam: Rhodopi, 1983).

70. Herman Johannes Lam, "Materials towards a Study of the Flora of the Island of New Guinea," *Blumea* 1 (1935): 115–159, maps. This paper was written in support of a chapter on vegetation in Klein, *Nieuw-Guinée.* It was a primary basis for the later phytogeographical synthesis of Ronald Good.

71. Pyenson, "Cultural Imperialism," 5–12.

72. A notable exception was the English zoologist Arthur Willey, then director of the Colombo Museum in Ceylon (now Sri Lanka), who conducted a two-year survey in the southwestern Pacific in 1895–1897, including stays at Blanche Bay and New Hanover (Lavongai) Island. While in German New Guinea, he conducted some classic studies of the pearly nautilus, *Nautilus pompilius* (published in 1902). Cf. W. Bruce Saunders and Larry E. Davis, "A Preliminary Report on *Nautilus* in Papua New Guinea," *Science in New Guinea* 11 (1985): 60–69.

73. Ludwig Diels, "Die pflanzengeographische Stellung der Gebirgsflora von Neu-Guinea," *Bericht der Freien Vereinigung für Pflanzengeographie und systematische Botanik für das Jahr 1919* (Berlin: Lande, 1921), 45–59. This paper seems, however, to have been overlooked by a number of anglophone writers on New Guinea biogeography. The major series of botanical results, much of it still standard, appeared as Carl Lauterbach and Ludwig Diels, eds., "Beiträge zur Flora von Papuasien," *Botanische Jahrbücher für Systematik* 49–72 (1912–1942).

74. See Mather, *Time for a Museum.*

75. These results appeared primarily in *Brittonia* and the *Journal of the Arnold Arboretum* from 1936 to 1953.

76. Frodin, "Herbaria in Papua New Guinea."

77. Gressitt, *Biogeography and Ecology of New Guinea.*

78. For an introduction, see Frodin, "Herbaria in Papua New Guinea," and Harry Sakulas, "Status and Long Range Goals of Systematics Collections in Papua New Guinea," in Sohmer, *Systematics Resources,* 76–79.

79. These departments were united in 1975 as the Department of Primary Industry, but in 1985 Forests regained its separate identity.

80. Sakulas, "Systematics Collections in Papua New Guinea."

81. David G. Frodin, "Report and Working Paper on Natural History Collections in Papua New Guinea" (Department of Biology, University of Papua New Guinea, 1978, mimeo).

82. Local secondary education in the sciences began only in 1960.

83. Leo D. Brongersma and Gerard F. Venema, *To the Mountains of the Stars,* trans. Alan Readett (London: Hodder and Stoughton, 1962).

84. Gressitt authored a paper demonstrating a zoogeographical discordance of the insect and vertebrate faunas. See J. Linsley Gressitt, *Problems in the Zoogeography of Pacific and Antarctic Insects,* Pacific Insects Monograph 2 (Honolulu, Hawaii: Department of Entomology, Bernice P. Bishop Museum, 1961). He also edited the synthesis *Biogeography and Ecology of New Guinea.*

85. Michael H. Robinson, "The Ecology and Biogeography of Spiders in Papua New Guinea," in Gressitt, *Biogeography and Ecology of New Guinea,* 557–581, esp. 557. This is given as one of two major problems facing systematic biology, the other being neglect by metropolitan governments and academic institutions.

86. A description of the establishment of the center appears in Peter W. Lambley and David G. Frodin, "The Natural Sciences Resource Centre at the University of Papua New Guinea," *Curator* (in press). On consolidation among collections, see Sakulas, "Systematics Collections in Papua New Guinea," esp. 78.

87. Lindsay Farrall, "Science Policy-making in Papua New Guinea," *Science in New Guinea* 3 (1975): 51–54. See also the papers of the 1984 Waigani Seminar at the University of Papua New Guinea: John Pernetta and J. Richard Morton, eds., *The Role of Science and Technology in the Development of Papua New Guinea: The Policy Dimensions,* 3 vols. (Port Moresby: Faculty of Science, University of Papua New Guinea, 1984).

88. Sakulas, "Systematics Collections in Papua New Guinea," 78.

89. R. MacFarlane, "The Insect Collection at Dodo Creek Research Station, Solomon Islands," in Sohmer, *Systematics Resources,* 46–47.

90. Diels, "Gebirgsflora von Neu-Guinea"; Robert J. Johns, "The Instability of the Tropical Ecosystem in New Guinea," *Blumea* 31 (1986): 341–371.

91. Ernst Mayr, "How I Became a Darwinian," in Ernst Mayr and William B. Provine, eds., *The Evolutionary Synthesis: Perspectives on the Unification of Biology* (Cambridge, Mass.: Harvard University Press, 1980), 413–423, esp. 417 (quotation). Mayr credits Ernst Hartert as the source for this opinion. Gressitt (*Biogeography and Ecology of New Guinea,* 897–918) opened his chapter, "Zoogeographical Summary," with the words "New Guinea presents a zoogeographer's puzzle." It would also appear so in phytogeography, according to Daniel I. Axelrod and Peter H. Raven, "Paleobiogeography and the Origin of the New

Guinea Flora," in Gressitt, *Biogeography and Ecology of New Guinea,* 919–941. Earlier, Ernst Mayr had suggested that the construction of combined plant and animal distribution maps was "impractical."

On the biota's importance to fields of study such as orthodox biogeography, panbiogeography, vicariance biogeography, and, more recently, cladistic biogeography, see Axelrod and Raven, "Origin of the New Guinea Flora" (orthodox biogeography); Christopher J. Humphries, "Biogeographical Methods and the Southern Beeches," in Vicki A. Funk and Daniel R. Brooks, eds., *Advances in Cladistics* (New York: New York Botanical Garden, 1981), 177–207 (vicariance biogeography); Léon Croizat, *Panbiogeography* (Caracas: Privately printed, 1958), esp. vol. 2b, fig. 259 (panbiogeography). On the origin of flowering plants, see Albert C. Smith, *The Pacific as a Key to Flowering Plant History,* University of Hawaii Harold L. Lyon Arboretum Lectures 1 (Honolulu: Lyon Arboretum, 1970).

92. Lam, "Flora of New Guinea." Examples of synthesis works are Ernst Mayr, *List of New Guinea Birds* (New York: American Museum of Natural History, 1941); Leonard J. Brass, "The 1938–39 Snow Mountains Expedition," *Journal of the Arnold Arboretum* 22 (1941): 271–342; Elmer D. Merrill, *Plant Life of the Pacific World* (New York: Macmillan, 1945); Ernst Mayr, "Fragments of a Papuan Ornithogeography," in *Proceedings, Seventh Pacific Science Congress* 4 (Wellington: Pacific Science Association, 1954), 11–19; and Ronald d'O. Good, "On the Geographical Relationships of the Angiosperm Flora of New Guinea," *Bulletin of the British Museum (Natural History), Botany* 2 (1960): 203–226.

Gressitt, *Biogeography and Ecology of New Guinea,* chap. 1. Randall T. Schuh and Gary M. Stonedahl ("Historical Biogeography in the Indo-Pacific: A Cladistic Approach," *Cladistics* 2 [1986]: 337–355) suggest that the papers in the Gressitt collection are "virtually devoid of methodological nuance" (p. 339). Changing ideas about the geosphere, such as the formation of mountain systems and island arcs, or the size of the earth at any given period in geological time, may have significant new consequences for our understanding of Papuasian biota. See Robin C. Craw, "Phylogenetics, Areas, Geology and the Biogeography of Croizat: A Radical View," *Systematic Zoology* 31 (1982): 304–316; Hugh G. Owen, *Atlas of Continental Displacement: 200 Million Years to the Present* (Cambridge: Cambridge University Press, 1984); and Warren Hamilton, *Tectonics of the Indonesian Region,* U.S. Geological Survey, Professional Paper 1078 (Washington: U.S. Geological Survey, 1979). Hamilton's work has been instrumental in recent suggestions that the composite nature of the New Guinea biota is related to the island's hybrid origin. See J. P. Duffels, "Biogeography of Indo-Pacific Cicadoidea: A Tentative Recognition of Areas of Endemism," *Cladistics* 2 (1986): 318–336.

93. A parallel may be drawn with Africa. See Edgar B. Worthington, *Science in the Development of Africa* (London: Her Majesty's Stationery Office, 1958), esp. appendix 3.

94. See Worthington, *Development of Africa;* Honig and Verdoorn, *Science and Scientists.* Also relevant is Sheets-Pyenson, "Colonial Museums." The Apia Observatory is reviewed in Pyenson, "Cultural Imperialism," 13–16, and in idem,

"The Limits of Scientific Condominium: Geophysics in Western Samoa, 1914–1940," in Reingold and Rothenberg, *Scientific Imperialism,* 251–295. Only after 1937 was an earth sciences observatory established in the Territory of New Guinea, a response to the volcanic eruptions that in that year had devastated Rabaul. The success of the Apia Observatory also owed much, as Pyenson ("Scientific Condominium," 256) notes, to the positive attitudes shown the Göttingen scientists by the then-Governor of Samoa (and, from 1911, German colonial secretary) Wilhelm Solf.

95. On MacGregor's efforts, see Frodin, "Herbaria in Papua New Guinea," 54. On the Australian input, see Roy MacLeod, "On Visiting the 'Moving Metropolis': Reflections on the Architecture of Imperial Science," in Reingold and Rothenberg, *Scientific Imperialism,* 217–249, esp. 232–234. For Dutch activities, see Smit, "International Influences"; Klein, *Nieuw-Guinée.* I regard the German success as corroborating Fernand Braudel's claim, "He who gives, dominates," as discussed by Pyenson, "Cultural Imperialism," 24–25.

96. For a comparison of German and Australian activities, see Frodin, "Herbaria in Papua New Guinea," 55. The consequences in Samoa of such a discontinuity have been vividly described by Pyenson, "Cultural Imperialism," 15–16, and idem, "The Limits of Scientific Condominium." On Australia between the world wars, see Mather, *Time for a Museum.*

97. Worthington, *Science in the Development of Africa.*

98. The Philippine Bureau of Science is discussed in Dean C. Worcester, *The Philippines, Past and Present,* 2 vols. (New York: Macmillan, 1914), and in Lewis E. Gleeck, *American Institutions in the Philippines (1898–1941)* (Manila: Historical Conservation Society of the Philippines, 1976). Its establishment was largely due to Worcester, a natural scientist who from 1901 to 1913 was secretary of the interior in the Philippines; see Elmer D. Merrill, "Autobiographical: Early Years, the Philippines, California," *Asa Gray Bulletin* 2 (1953): 335–370, esp. 347. An opinion favoring an institute system is advanced in Worthington, *Science in the Development of Africa,* 39; in New Caledonia local scientific research was from the 1960s largely concentrated in a branch of the statutory French metropolitan organization Office de la Recherche Scientifique et Technique d'Outre-Mer (ORSTOM) with, as in Manila, its own "campus."

99. There has been some recognition of this problem in Papua New Guinea in recent years and plans for reorganization of primary industry and forestry research have been advanced. (See Sakulas, "Systematics Collections in Papua New Guinea," 78.) Such steps might help to bring about the development of coherent research programs of potentially wider significance, which also might enhance the status of research workers and how they and their work are perceived. See Limoges, "Muséum d'Histoire Naturelle of Paris," and Kathleen G. Dugan, "The Zoological Exploration of the Australian Region and Its Impact on Biological Theory," in Reingold and Rothenberg, *Scientific Imperialism,* 79–100.

100. A. B. Katende, "Plant Exploration in Uganda," *Bothalia* 14 (1983): 1016–1017; Frodin, "Herbaria in Papua New Guinea," 60.

101. Sheets-Pyenson, "Colonial Museums"; Brockway, *Science and Colonial Expansion.*

102. De Wit, ("Malaysian Vascular Plants," clvi) closes his history with a quo-

tation from Jan Commelijn, a professor of botany and materia medica in late seventeenth-century Amsterdam, which effectively sums up my arguments on the progress of natural history in New Guinea: "It is certain, however, that this science, like all sciences, has flourished sometimes more and sometimes less, all in accordance with the inclination of rulers and the favour of government." The role of personalities also cannot be overlooked (Peter F. Stevens, personal communication).

6

Darwin's Australian Correspondents: Deference and Collaboration in Colonial Science

Barry W. Butcher

ATTEMPTS to construct theoretical models for understanding the spread of Western science from its metropolitan center have attracted considerable attention from historians. Critics of these models have focused their attack on the implicit assumptions that seem to underlie them. George Basalla's three-stage model for the spread and development of Western science has been around for nearly twenty years, and subsequent research has thrown considerable doubt on its usefulness as an explanatory device.[1]

This chapter attempts to sketch an analysis of scientific development in Australia that counters the dismissive attitudes implicit in models of the Basalla type toward the fine texture of science at the colonial "periphery." Between the poles of deference and collaboration in center-periphery relationships, there exists a field for historical enquiry that encompasses both local and global questions, but in a way that recognizes the coherence and legitimacy of science at the periphery. The chapter's argument depends on recognition of the fact that no single set of historical materials or conditions represents the true state of science in Australia at any one time. It follows, therefore, that analyses based on single areas such as the institutional growth of science, or the process of professionalization in science, will give at best a limited view of scientific development, and at worst an erroneous one.

The reception of Darwin's work in Australia in the years following the publication of the *Origin of Species* in 1859 provides an interesting subject for a historical analysis that takes account of ideas as components in the mechanism of scientific development. Darwinism, as Robert Young and others have shown, embraces a host of doctrines, attitudes, and disputes that lift it from its somewhat narrow scientific base into a wider realm of cultural history. Darwinism constitutes at once an example of a new understanding of the biological sciences emerging from a series of debates undertaken between 1830 and 1870, and a crucial component of those debates.[2] Put simply, the change in perception of what biology was taken to be involved an epistemological shift from a "creationist" stance to a "naturalistic" one. Neil Gillespie has defined the creationist position as being predicated on the belief that "the world and its contents and processes were a direct or indirect result of divine activity." In the naturalistic approach, scientific knowledge (and specifically in this instance, biological knowledge) was limited to the laws of nature and to processes explicable by reference to secondary or natural causes.[3] In Australia debate upon the scientific validity of Darwinism took place against a background of colonial science that must be understood on several levels, including one that involves this changing view of science.

Scientific knowledge in Australia in the nineteenth century was constructed in Europe, by Europeans, within a European tradition, and with constraints imposed by that tradition. The creation of scientific societies in each of the Australian colonies, the setting up of government-supported geological surveys and botanical gardens, and finally the establishment of the first universities in Sydney and Melbourne ensured that the European domination of Australian science became entrenched and institutionalized. Colonial culture, derived as it was from an essentially British background, reinforced that Eurocentricity still further. Scientific societies were based on British models, produced journals along the lines of their British counterparts, and investigated problems on the agenda of British scientists. Scientific departments were staffed in the main from Britain, by Britons, and on the recommendation of fellow Britons. At Melbourne, for example, Frederick McCoy was given the chair of natural science on the recommendation of a London-based committee that included John Herschel and George Airy, while George Britton Halford became the first professor of medicine on the strength of recommendations from Richard Owen and James Paget.[4] Owen was the foremost anatomist of his day and the head of the British Natural History

Museum for thirty years. Through a network of correspondence he dominated Australian zoology and paleontology for four decades. Paget was a major figure in British medicine, for many years surgeon to Queen Victoria and a president of the Royal College of Surgeons.

Thus the institutional and to some extent the professional growth of science between 1830 and 1870 in the Australian colonies contributed to a commitment to a British structure of science. But, more importantly, it contributed to the entrenchment of a particular vision of the scientific enterprise, namely, a creationist vision. Hence, in the latter half of the nineteenth century there developed a tension in the history of Australian science—and specifically, though not exclusively, affecting biology. For, at a time when naturalism was rising to dominance in Britain in the hands of Thomas Henry Huxley and friends, an older scientific tradition was becoming institutionalized in Australia. McCoy and Halford in Melbourne, along with William Sharpe Macleay in Sydney, shaped the public image of the biological sciences well into the 1870s, and they shared the creationism of the men who had appointed them, or to whom they looked at the metropolitan center for intellectual approval.[5] It is this type of institutionalized science that provides the norm against which models of scientific development at the periphery are invariably assessed. Yet, however much it dominated Australian perceptions, it did not prevent the emergence of a heterodox tradition. This tradition was grounded in a naturalistic approach to the biological sciences and grew in large part out of the Darwinian view of the natural world, thereby gaining a certain legitimacy at the metropolitan center, along with a research program distinguishing it from its institutional rival.

Some of the work produced within that program will be discussed here, but first it is useful to examine the manner in which Charles Darwin collected and used Australian material prior to the publication of the *Origin of Species,* and how he employed the imperial scientific networks to obtain correspondents once that work had been made public. This digression serves to provide a contrast between relationships essentially based on deferential colonial positions and those based on a recognition of mutual needs and interests. It is the former that have attracted the attention of historians taking the Basalla approach to scientific develop-

ment; the latter have yet to be fully understood by historians of
Australian science.

Darwin and Australia: The Deferential Element

In the years preceding the appearance of the *Origin,* Darwin relied
heavily on published sources for any material he required on Australia. The exploration journals of Thomas Mitchell, Charles
Sturt, and George Grey, along with the natural history works of
John Gould and George Bennett, provided the bulk of that material.[6] There were occasional personal contacts—for example with
Mitchell at the Geographical Society in London in 1837 and with
the pastoralist William Macarthur at Down House in 1856—and,
though rarely, some direct correspondence. The directors of the
Sydney and Melbourne botanical gardens, Charles Moore and
Ferdinand Mueller, responded to Darwin's requests for information in this period but had no significant contact with him thereafter.[7]

After the publication of the *Origin,* the number of Darwin's
Australian correspondents increased as he pursued material favorable to his ideas. Darwin was never a patron of science in the sense
that Joseph Banks and Richard Owen were, but his friendship
with Joseph Hooker enabled him to make contact with overseas
naturalists through the imperial network centered at Kew. Six
months after the publication of the *Origin,* Darwin used this channel to obtain information from James Drummond in Western Australia. A professional collector for nearly thirty years and a correspondent of William and Joseph Hooker, Drummond provided
collections of Western Australian plants to Kew and supplied commercial outlets in Britain with Australian seeds.[8]

In January 1861 Darwin reported in the *Gardener's Chronicle*
on his success in cultivating plants of the Australian composite
Pumilio in the hothouse at Down House, using seeds sent by
Drummond. *Pumilio* has a number of peculiar contrivances
"designed" to assist its survival in the arid environment of Western
Australia, and Darwin made much of these apparently adaptive
structures as support for his ideas on natural selection.[9]

Drummond's greatest contribution to Darwin's work came
through his observations on another Australian plant, *Leschenaultia formosa.* Initially, he was unable to find any evidence support-

ing Darwin's belief that insects played a crucial role in the fertilization of this group. But, urged on by Darwin, he continued his observations and late in 1860 reported that he had seen small bees extracting pollen from the indusium of *Leschenaultia*. In May 1861 Darwin contributed a paper to the *Journal of Horticulture* describing his own and others' experiments with *Leschenaultia*, including those communicated by Drummond.[10]

Ten years later, and eight years after Drummond's death, Darwin published a second paper explaining his interest in *Leschenaultia* in the broader context of his evolutionary ideas. Contrary to some opinions, these plants were not forced by "inevitable contingency" to undertake self-fertilization. For Darwin, cross-fertilization was a crucial component in his explanation of survival strategies among plants and animals; it provided more vigorous offspring, and its remixing of the (then unknown) hereditary material increased the likelihood of favorable variations emerging upon which natural selection could work.[11] By 1876, when he published his ideas on this subject in book form, Darwin had accumulated a large body of information from botanists around the world and direct reference to Drummond's work was omitted, although the 1871 paper received passing mention.[12] Darwin's relationship with Drummond, albeit short-lived, fits the classic pattern of the metropolitan theorist drawing upon data obtained from the colonial fact-gatherer. Drummond himself seems to have been happy with this relationship, for he "treasured Darwin's letters, placing them carefully with the bundles of letters received from Hooker and others."[13]

The acceptance of this unequal division of labor as the norm is strongly embedded in the writing of the history of Australian science, and while this may reflect the reality of the situation in cases such as Drummond's, it might be argued that in many instances it serves only to obscure the issues under discussion. It has certainly skewed the interpretation of Australia's scientific traditions, while contributing to a now outmoded historiographical approach to the history of science generally. Australians have outgrown the crudely formulated "great man" syndrome, but as James Secord has recently pointed out, we continue to view nineteenth-century science from the perspective of the hagiographers who bequeathed to us a daunting array of multivolume biographies of the most prominent figures in the major debates.[14]

In Australia, geographical isolation coupled with what is seen as an intellectual isolation ensures that colonial scientists are viewed as "bit" players in the drama of science and its spread and development. This has made it possible for Australian historians to accept simplistic, generalized models for the development of colonial science that promote the view that science flows outward from the metropolitan center according to fixed rules.[15] In this approach, it is assumed that science in the colonies is backward: geographical peripherality implies intellectual peripherality.

The reality is of course quite different. Science does not develop in a social vacuum according to its own internal evolutionary processes but, rather, in particular sociocultural settings that often determine the role, structure, and form of science. Science in nineteenth-century Australia was the product of many factors, but the peculiarities of the colonization process and the timing of key events must be allotted a significant role in its development. As an illustration of this, consider the creation of Australia's first universities in the period between 1850 and 1860. If conservative social forces in colonial Australian society had succeeded in postponing this development for twenty years, then appointments to the senior positions within those institutions would have been made by committees of a very different composition from those that appointed McCoy and Halford. While still metropolitan in orientation, the result might well have been the institutionalization of a very different view of biology, one that in the event received "official" recognition only with the replacement of these earlier appointees in the 1880s.[16] Ironically, the progressive move to develop universities at so early a period in Australia's history—itself a product of socioeconomic factors such as the discovery of gold—led to the entrenchment in the discipline's official structures of a regressive epistemology. It would be hard to see this pattern of development being repeated outside of Australia in just this way, and equally difficult to see how it might be fitted into any model of the Basalla type. The advantage of the type of analysis sketched here, which takes account of a wide range of sociocultural factors within a given society, is that it throws light not only upon the way the structures of science develop, but also upon the type of science that is undertaken and the philosophical framework that underpins it.

With this in mind, we can turn our attention to the work of individuals whose approach set them apart from the school of thought that dominated the official structures of Australian science. In most cases this meant that they worked literally outside of those structures, as "amateurs," but in one prominent case this was not so, and the tensions engendered by that individual's attachment to an institution under the control of men committed to a view of science radically different from his own are an interesting topic for discussion.

Three Australian Darwinians: Gerard Krefft, Alfred Howitt, and Robert Fitzgerald

The surviving correspondence between Darwin and Gerard Krefft amounts to some fifteen items dating from 1872 to 1876. During most of this period Krefft, a German, was curator of the Australian Museum in Sydney, but his term there was clouded by the hostility between himself and the trustees of the museum. Krefft claimed that he had been converted to Darwinism after reading the *Origin,* but there is little evidence that he incorporated any evolutionary doctrine into his work before 1870. Only after that date did he become an active and aggressive supporter of Darwin, especially in the popular press where he used his regular column in the *Sydney Mail* to air discussion of evolutionary topics.[17]

Krefft's first letter to Darwin arose as part of a campaign to rally support for his own view that the fossil marsupial *Thylacaleo* had been herbivorous and not—as another of his correspondents, Richard Owen, had claimed—carnivorous. There is some evidence to support the view that part of the reason for Krefft's acceptance of Darwinism lay in his continuing uneasy relationship with Owen.[18] But to this can be added his independence from strong religious and scientific commitments. Krefft was a late starter in what he termed natural history, beginning serious study at the age of twenty-five. He arrived in Australia from Germany in 1852 after a short stay in America, and worked on the Victorian goldfields before taking up employment with the National Museum of Victoria. There, working under its director, Frederick McCoy, he cataloged the large natural history collection that he himself had donated to the museum. He returned briefly to Germany in 1858, but came back to Australia in 1860 when he was appointed assistant curator of the Australian Museum in Sydney.

Four years later he was made curator, a position he held until his enforced departure in 1874.[19]

We do not know whether Krefft's brief trip home brought him into contact with the evolutionary and materialist doctrines then being discussed in the work of Jakob Moleschott, Ludwig Buchner, and Carl Vogt. Nevertheless, he returned to Australia with a full knowledge of the new approaches to the role and purpose of museums being adopted in Europe. But any hopes he may have had of introducing such innovations in Sydney's premier museum were severely hampered by the trustees and their colleagues. The Australian Museum was both the creation and the property of the Sydney scientific elite, led by William Sharpe Macleay, and it tended to reflect their interests in collecting and classifying natural history specimens.[20] Krefft did little to disguise his contempt for these activities, at least in letters to his overseas correspondents. Darwinism was just one of the many issues that separated him from the men he described as "collectors of specimens and accumulators of hard names," but it loomed sufficiently large for him to complain to Darwin that one of the reasons for his eventual removal from the museum was his rejection of the "God of Moses" as the creator and his acceptance of "the theory of development."[21]

Krefft's letters to Darwin reveal how deeply he was impressed by the explanatory power of what was termed the development theory. He was especially struck by Darwin's *The Expression of the Emotions* (1872), and as corroborative evidence for some of Darwin's claims, sent him anecdotes of a monkey at the museum that exhibited passions of rage and jealousy by hurling stones and sardine cans. Stories of intelligent pigs and horses followed, along with photographs of Australian aboriginal skulls, which Darwin passed to George Busk in London. But Krefft was not averse to offering critical comment when necessary. He was quick to point out that Darwin had been wrong in his claim that Australia's native inhabitants were unable to count beyond the number four; they had in fact a complex system of counting in multiples, which according to Krefft, were distinguished by differing vocal sounds. Through Darwin he attempted to interest Huxley in the bipedal tendencies of the Australian frilled lizard, which he believed had great evolutionary significance in the light of Huxley's suggestion that birds were probably descended from dinosaurs.[22]

This, together with the material sent to Darwin, shows the

extent to which Krefft observed through Darwinian eyes, a habit that often brought tensions into his working relationships. As a regular contributor to the *Sydney Mail,* he occasionally fell foul of its proprietor, John Fairfax. In Krefft's view, Fairfax was "rather a thorough believer in revealed religion, though he allows me to give an opinion now and then as long as I do not come it strong." Fairfax censored Krefft's column on at least one occasion in order to remove favorable references to Darwin.[23]

As a scientist Krefft occupied a position far removed from that of the typical collector at the periphery. He was a theoretically sophisticated naturalist whose contribution to the zoological literature of Australia was substantial and of lasting value. His letters to Darwin were those of a colleague and fellow scientist rather than a mere informant, and he took advantage of the existing networks of correspondence in furthering both his own career and the cause of science in the Australian colonies generally. Against the odds he remained vocal in championing new doctrines. As a result he won an international reputation outside Australia, but he was ultimately brought down by the entrenched interests of those he was committed to opposing. In a letter to Richard Lydekker in London, written six years after his forcible removal from the museum, he complained bitterly and with some truth, "here in Australia you must follow the footprints of those ancient gentlemen who still follow Cuvier." That comment is significant, for it shows that in the common perception Richard Owen's grip on Australian natural history had not yet loosened.[24]

Krefft's acceptance of Darwinism had led to problems that in combination with other factors brought about his downfall. By contrast, others working outside the physical architecture of colonial science were able to employ evolutionary theory to produce important work in the natural sciences. Two men who like Krefft achieved international reputations by doing so were the anthropologist Alfred Howitt and the botanist Robert David Fitzgerald.

Throughout Darwin's early notebooks are numerous references to anthropological topics, and Australian material is frequently cited. In 1867, while gathering material for his two major anthropological works, Darwin used the colonial networks to circulate a questionnaire eliciting information on "primitive" populations from missionaries and government officials that would support his case for an evolutionary history of man. Thirteen sets of replies to this questionnaire were returned from Australia, and these he used extensively in *The Expression of the Emotions*.[25]

With the publication of this book, Darwin's anthropological work came to an end. Thus when Alfred Howitt wrote in 1874 offering his services as an observer of the Australian Aborigines in the Gippsland district of Victoria, his offer was politely declined. Darwin urged Howitt to continue his observations, however, making the prescient comment that in doing so he might accumulate sufficient material to "write a very valuable memoir or book" on the subject.[26] Six years later Howitt and the missionary cum anthropologist Lorimer Fison fulfilled that prediction when they published their researches on Aboriginal society under the title *Kamilaroi and Kurnai*. Darwin's earlier response, and the divergence of the two men's interests, had nipped their correspondence in the bud, and Howitt and Fison turned instead for advice to the American Lewis Henry Morgan, whose evolutionary view of society was then the subject of controversy in Europe. Morgan responded with more enthusiasm than Darwin had done and thereby initiated a correspondence lasting some seven years, during which Howitt and Fison provided him with ethnological material that he incorporated into his later work.[27]

The reception of Howitt and Fison's work in Britain was mixed; J. F. McLennan and John Lubbock were critical, opposing the Australian's use of Morgan's system of kinship analysis, but Edward Tylor and James Fraser were more enthusiastic. In Europe, Howitt's work was later to provide much of the empirical data for the cognitive anthropology of Emile Durkheim and Marcel Mauss.[28]

Howitt's career suggests analogies with the classic patron-client relationship—the collector at the periphery working with the assistance of powerful associates at the center. Tylor, for example, provided material assistance by ensuring publication of Howitt's work in the *Journal of the Anthropological Institute*. Closer inspection, however, reveals a different picture, one that gives Howitt a greater role and considerably more autonomy than the patron-client relationship generally permitted. He appears in this view as a primary contributor to the so-called new anthropology emerging post-Darwin. Along with later researchers such as Baldwin Spencer and Frank Gillen, Howitt and Fison provided the Australian material, and to some extent the analysis of that material, that Morgan, Tylor, Frazer, Durkheim, and others would incorporate into their own evolutionary studies of society. *Kamilaroi and Kurnai* became a standard text both for the new material that it contained and for its acceptance and development of Morgan's theoretical concerns. When in 1904 Cambridge University conferred upon Howitt the degree of Doctor of Science, in Baldwin Spencer's words it "fully recognised the primary importance of his work."[29]

Howitt's admiration for Darwin's ideas was clearly the starting point for his anthropological work. In a letter to his sister in England in July 1874, he complained that the conservative nature of the churches and their "stubborn" clinging to dogmas were increasingly isolating them "from the intellect of the country." Turning specifically to Darwin's theories he added, "I take a very great interest in them, and feel satisfied of the main truth of the evolutionary hypothesis." To his father at the same time he wrote, "you and I need not enter into any discussion of Darwin's hypothesis—we might differ and after all, as I said, it is of no consequence. But I think you will agree with me (if I can manage to work it out properly) that the enquiry into the kinship system of the Aborigines clearly proves a great advance upon a former social condition."[30] In Howitt's view, social evolution was merely an extension of biological evolution—indeed it flowed as an inevitable consequence from it. At times, his descriptions of the destruction of Aboriginal society echo the worst excesses of the social Darwinists, taking for granted the inevitability of progress in the face of an encroaching "superior" civilization.

Darwinism provided Howitt with a philosophical framework for an evolutionary understanding of society. Within that overall scheme, Morgan offered his support, and this combination allowed Howitt to move beyond the position of client-collector. At a time when the new anthropology was emerging, post-Darwin, in Europe and America, he was working at the periphery as an investigator of equal status (and in many ways a better-equipped one) into the "primitive condition of mankind." Imbued with contemporary theories of biological and social evolution, Howitt differed notably from his colonial predecessors—the missionaries and government officials who provided Darwin with responses to his questionnaire, for example. Unattached to any scientific institution, he was equally unattached to any creationist program of sci-

ence. His work placed him firmly in the vanguard of the new naturalistic program of science and in a position at center stage in the
new anthropology.

Robert David Fitzgerald, the son of a banker, was born in
County Kerry, Ireland, in 1830. After studying engineering at
Queens College, Cork, he emigrated to New South Wales in 1856,
joining the Department of Lands, where he became deputy surveyor general in 1873. His interest in the natural sciences extended
back to his youth in Ireland, where he had contributed articles on
local birdlife to the newspapers. But if ornithology provided his
entrée into the study of natural history, it was as a botanist that he
achieved lasting renown. His lavishly illustrated work on the Australian orchids, published serially between 1875 and 1882, quickly became recognized as a major contribution to the orchid literature and established him as the first authority on the subject in
Australia. It also secured him an introduction to Darwin, to whom
he sent part one of the work in 1875 and further parts as they
became available, until Darwin's death in 1882.[31]

In the second edition of his own work on orchid fertilization,
published in 1877, Darwin incorporated many of Fitzgerald's
observations, testifying to his high regard for the colonial botanist.[32] The first edition, published in 1862, contained Darwin's
arguments for the powerful effects of insect agency in pollination.
Orchids were an ideal vehicle for study as they exhibited a staggeringly complex range of apparently adaptive structures. The second edition was much enlarged through the addition of material
sent to Darwin by botanists around the world in the intervening
years.

Fitzgerald's detailed observations relating to pollination greatly
interested Darwin, although he was initially skeptical of his claim
that many Australian orchids were self-fertilized. Years later, however, he conceded that in consequence of Fitzgerald's investigations, "It is . . . now evident that there is more self-fertilisation
with the *Orchidaceae* than I supposed." In his first communication
with Fitzgerald, Darwin followed his usual practice by outlining a
number of problems he wished his correspondent to investigate.
Did Fitzgerald, for example, "think it possible that *calli* on the
labellum are gnawed or sucked by insects?" A reference in
Darwin's book makes clear that Fitzgerald duly researched the
problem and answered in the negative. However, Fitzgerald was
not simply another minor contributor to Darwin's developing evo-

lutionary corpus. His own monograph was described by Joseph
Hooker as "a work which would be an honour to any country and
to any botanist," while Darwin himself expressed astonishment
"that such a work could have been prepared at Sydney."[33]

Fitzgerald's acceptance of Darwin's theory, made easier by his
early rejection of all religious doctrines and by his lack of alle-
giance to any scientific institution (and by extension, therefore, to
any institutional scientific program), plunged him into the naturalistic program without the often associated traumas of conversion.
Yet it was not an unqualified Darwinism that emerged from his
own book. Investigation convinced him that cross-fertilization
was not universal and that the "beautiful contrivances" displayed
by the *Orchidaceae* were not always to be explained in adaptive
terms. Although the great majority of Australian orchids "appear
to be frequently impregnated by pollen brought from other
flowers . . . they are also frequently fertilised by their own and
again there are others always self-impregnated."[34]

Fitzgerald's response to this apparently non-Darwinian finding
was not to seek for extra Darwinian mechanisms, but to utilize the
Darwinian principle of fitness itself for an answer:

> observing that the orchids which were self-fertilised produced a
> much greater quantity of seed than those most dependent upon
> insects and therefore most likely to be fertilised by the pollen of
> other individuals, it seemed to me that the "good" derived was
> increased fertility in the seed itself, thereby making the smaller pro-
> portion produced by crossed species of more avail than the larger
> quantity from species always reproduced from themselves.[35]

The "beautiful contrivances" that Darwin was so concerned to
show as adaptations useful for the purpose of fertilization might,
in reality, have no adaptive significance. They could be "modifica-
tions of parts which *may* have been once of use, and all the more
likely to occur in exaggerated forms where there has been much
disturbance by hybridisation. . . . There seem to be no reason
why they should not be continued in varying forms unless they
happen to become so detrimental as to cause extinction." Even
Darwin, Fitzgerald concluded, "speaks of contrivances and the
purpose of an organ, whereas the determination not to expect or
look for any object or purpose enables us to accept without difficulty such transitions as are to be found in the labellum of ptero-

stylis, to find special utility for which might well puzzle any naturalist." Fitzgerald had paved the way for this conclusion in his introduction, where he criticized the accepted view that elaborate contrivance implied design, an integral component of the arguments to be found in natural theology and thus of all those committed to a creationist program of biology. According to Fitzgerald, design might just as well be seen as adaptation in some cases, and as due to inheritance in others where similar contrivances are extended to closely related species and genera without palpable benefit to the organism.[36]

Darwinism proved to be an effective research program for Fitzgerald. Species in the genus *Caladenia* are so similar and resemble each other so closely that "the distinction between species and varieties has been very much at the caprice of botanists." This was of course precisely the argument Darwin had proposed in the *Origin* and Fitzgerald pursued it vigorously. Orchids that generally resemble each other often differ on some specific point: if these differences can be shown to be hereditary, then the term "variety" becomes superfluous unless the specific description is extended, "which is nothing more than begging the question." "The submergence of possibly constant forms, under the head of varieties, induces a brevity and laxity in their descriptions that embarrasses the student, and prevents that close investigation into their stability become so necessary at present, when science demands the determination of the great question of mutability."[37]

Fitzgerald had earlier nailed his Darwinian colors firmly to the mast and did not shirk the philosophical implications they presented.

> Supposing that species are but more persistent varieties, and that genera are but species cut asunder by the destruction of the intermediate forms or species, how overwhelming the contemplation becomes of the vastness of the time required, with the means before us, to bring about such a divergence with yet a retention of a trace of common origin and how vast and relentless must have been the sweeping away of all the strange forms that must have connected them . . . how insignificant, for what it has accomplished, all time short of eternity appears to be.[38]

Prepared to challenge even "the greatest naturalist" when circumstances required it, Fitzgerald was none the less happy to add "a

single stone to the very great pile constructed by the boldest specu-
lator of the age."[39] While he showed all due deference to Darwin,
it was collaboration, with each using the other's data and theory,
that signified the true meaning of the relationship.

Conclusion

In this chapter I have tried to show a pattern of colonial science
that does not fit easily within well-known models of scientific
development. The evidence suggests a deviant tradition in Australian science in the second half of the nineteenth century, running
contemporaneously with an orthodox tradition represented by
institutional and personal commitments to a dominant scientific
tradition that can be broadly termed creationist. Those who were
uncommitted to this dominant tradition tended also to be uncommitted to the institutional bases of science and were therefore free
to pursue their scientific interests outside of the constraints
imposed by those two factors. This is not altogether true of
Gerard Krefft, and his controversial career and spectacular downfall may have been due in part to the tensions engendered by his
scientific heterodoxy, as he appears to have recognized.

The term heterodox should not be taken to imply that the work
of these men failed to gain the respect of those opposed to the philosophy within which it was undertaken. On the contrary, it was
often greatly admired, a fact pointing up the difficulty of recreat-
ing the social context in which scientific controversy takes place.
Opposing positions are not necessarily destructive of dialogue.[40]
This is especially true in the case of Fitzgerald, whose work illus-
trates clearly the distinction between the waning creationist program of science and the waxing naturalistic program. Fitzgerald
had a good grasp of the Darwinian theory and understood clearly
both its possibilities as a research program and its radically different philosophical stance from the creationism of the majority of
his colleagues, and by extension the broader implications that
could be drawn from it. In all these areas he stood outside the
mainstream of the science of his day, but he succeeded nonetheless
in maintaining close friendships with men who strongly repu-
diated the program of science he was committed to pursuing.

Roy MacLeod has recently revived interest in understanding the development of science at the periphery through an analysis that embeds it in the broader framework of British imperial ambitions. In doing so, he has once again drawn attention to the role played by power brokers at the metropolis in the development of colonial science. At the same time he has hinted at the shifting of power from the hands of men like Richard Owen, who pursued science within a creationist framework, to those like T. H. Huxley, who led "the advancing forces of scientific naturalism."[41] That shift in power was reflected in Australia by the involvement of men like Krefft, Howitt, and Fitzgerald in the program of naturalism as it applied to the biological sciences. The colonial institutions that represented the public face of science became committed to naturalism only in the last two decades of the century. In the 1880s the power to make appointments to Australian scientific institutions still resided at the metropolitan center, though by then it was in the hands of men with a radically different view of science. The new men who came to take up institutional positions at the outpost of empire brought with them a background in the biological sciences that grounded them firmly in the naturalists' camp. They were not, however, the first colonial scientists to embrace the doctrines of naturalism, as this chapter has shown.

Those who seek to understand the spread and development of Western science in terms of the apparent sophistication of a given period and place need to recognize that there may often be a heterodox tradition at work alongside the orthodoxy represented by the governing personalities and institutions of the day. Given that fact it will no longer be a surprise to find that there are men like the colonial-based Krefft, whose view of science makes him more "advanced" than the metropolitan-based Owen; anthropologists like Howitt who are more sophisticated scientists than members of the London Anthropological Institute; and amateurs like Fitzgerald who are more "progressive" than some professional botanists. Seen in this light, the relationship between center and periphery may become even more interesting.

Notes

I would like to thank Anthea Hyslop, Rod Home, Rita Hutchison, Monica Mac-Callum, and Judy Sammons for their assistance with this paper. Roy MacLeod

and Fritz Rehbock showed great patience and provided much help in their deal-
ings with me. Peter Gautrey and Anne Secord at the Cambridge University
Library Manuscript Room provided invaluable help in locating much of the relevant correspondence, as did the staff at the Mitchell Library in Sydney and the
National Library of Victoria.

1. George Basalla, "The Spread of Western Science," *Science* 156 (5 May
1967): 611–622. Roy MacLeod has reviewed the Basalla paper and some of the
more trenchant criticisms made of it in his paper "On Visiting the 'Moving
Metropolis': Reflections on the Architecture of Imperial Science," *Historical
Records of Australian Science* 5, no. 3 (1982): 1–16.

2. Robert Young, *Darwin's Metaphor—Nature's Place in Victorian Culture*
(Cambridge: Cambridge University Press, 1985).

3. Neal C. Gillespie, *Charles Darwin and the Problem of Creation* (Chicago:
University of Chicago Press, 1979), 3. See chap. 1, "Positivism and Creationism:
Two Epistemes," for a discussion of the subject.

4. Ernest Scott, *A History of the University of Melbourne* (Melbourne: Melbourne University Press, 1936), 20–24.

5. The scientific careers of McCoy, Halford, and Macleay are discussed in
Ann Moyal, *Scientists in Nineteenth Century Australia* (New South Wales: Cas-
sell Australia, 1976).

6. Thomas Mitchell, *Three Expeditions into the Interior of Eastern Australia*
(London: T. and W. Bone, 1838); Charles Sturt, *Two Expeditions into the Interior of Southern Australia* (London: Smith, Elder and Co., 1833); George Grey,
Two Expeditions of Discovery in the North-West and Western Australia (London: T. and W. Bone, 1841); G. Bennett, *Wanderings in New South Wales* (London: Richard Bentley, 1834). Gould almost certainly provided Darwin with
information firsthand. His numerous publications on the Australian fauna are
listed in his entry in *The Australian Dictionary of Biography,* vol. 1 (Melbourne:
Melbourne University Press, 1966), 465–467. References to all these authors and
their works are found scattered throughout "Charles Darwin's Notebooks on
Transmutation of Species," ed. Gavin de Beer, 6 vols., published as *Bulletin of the
British Museum (Natural History)* Historical Series, vol. 2, nos. 2–6 (1960–
1961).

7. Moore to Darwin, 11 August 1858, Dar. 171, Cambridge University
Library. Von Mueller's correspondence with Darwin is lost. In a letter dated 6
December 1957, Hooker suggested that Darwin write to Moore and von Mueller
for information about the distribution of Australian plants (Dar. 104). Copies of
all correspondence cited in this paper are now held in the Cambridge University
Library and are listed in Frederick Burkhardt and Sydney Smith, eds., *A Calendar
of the Correspondence of Charles Darwin, 1821–1882* (New York: Garland Publishing, 1985).

8. The extent of the Kew Network has been discussed in Lucille Brockway,
Science and Colonial Expansion: The Role of the British Royal Botanic Gardens
(New York: Academic Press, 1979). Drummond's career is covered extensively in
Rica Erickson, *The Drummonds of Hawthornden* (Western Australia: Lamb Pat-
terson, 1969).

9. Charles Darwin, "Note on the Achenia of Pumilio Argyrolepis," *Gardeners' Chronicle and Agricultural Gazette,* no. 1 (5 January 1861): 4–5, reprinted in Paul H. Barrett, *The Collected Papers of Charles Darwin* (Chicago: University of Chicago Press, 1977), vol. 2: 36–38.

10. Drummond to Darwin, 17 September 1860 (letter has been lost, but Darwin refers to it in his reply of 22 November 1860, original in the Battye Library, Perth, Acc. 2275A); Drummond to Darwin, 8 October 1860, Dar. 162; Charles Darwin, "Cross Breeding in Plants: Fertilisation of Leschenaultia Formosa," *Journal of Horticulture and Cottage Gardener,* n.s. 1 (28 May 1861): 151, reprinted in Barrett, *Collected Papers* 2:42–43.

11. Charles Darwin, "Fertilisation of Leschenaultia," *Gardeners' Chronicle and Agricultural Gazette,* no. 36 (9 September 1871), 1166, reprinted in Barrett, *Collected Papers* 2:162–165.

12. Charles Darwin, *The Effects of Cross and Self-Fertilisation in the Vegetable Kingdom* (London: John Murray, 1876).

13. Erickson, *The Drummonds,* 154.

14. James A. Secord, "John W. Salter: The Rise and Fall of a Victorian Palaeontological Career," in *From Linnaeus to Darwin: Commentaries on the History of Biology and Geology,* ed. Alwyne Wheeler and James H. Price (London: Society for History of Natural History, 1985).

15. The Basalla model is used explicitly in this way by Ann Moyal, *Scientists.*

16. At the University of Sydney, William Haswell, a former student of Huxley, became Challis Professor of Biology in 1889, but he had been teaching Darwinism for some years prior to that date. At Melbourne Darwinism became part of the biology syllabus after the appointment of Walter Baldwin Spencer to the chair of biology in 1888. For Haswell, see Moyal, *Scientists,* chaps. 9 and 10. For Spencer, see John Mulvanney and John Calaby, *So Much That is New— Baldwin Spencer 1860–1929* (Melbourne: Melbourne University Press, 1985).

17. See Krefft's entry in the *Australian Dictionary of Biography,* vol. 5 (Melbourne: Melbourne University Press, 1914), 42–44; see also Gerald Whitley, "Gerard Krefft (1830–1851) and His Bibliography," in *Proceedings of the Royal Society of New South Wales,* 1967–1968 (1969), 38–42.

18. Krefft to Darwin, 15 May 1872, Dar. 169.

19. *Australian Dictionary of Biography,* vol. 5, "Gerard Krefft."

20. Ibid.

21. Krefft to Darwin, 22 October 1874, Dar. 169.

22. Krefft to Darwin, 30 December 1872, Dar. 169; Darwin to Krefft, 17 February 1873, Mitchell Library, Sydney, Ref. No. Ad. 1. Krefft to Darwin, 3 May 1873, Dar. 169; Darwin to Krefft, 12 July 1873, Mitchell Library Ref. No. Ad. 1. According to Darwin, Huxley was then too ill to respond to Krefft's information.

23. Krefft to Darwin, 8 August 1873 and July-August (?) 1873, Dar. 169.

24. Krefft to Richard Lydekker, 18 December 1880, Mitchell Library Ref. No. A262. For Richard Owen's influence on Australian science, see Ann Moyal, "Richard Owen and His Influence on Australian Zoological and Palaeontological Science," *Records of the Australian Academy of Science* 3, no. 2 (1975): 41–56.

25. See Richard Broke Freeman and Peter Gautrey, "Charles Darwin's Queries

about Expression," *Bulletin of the British Museum (Natural History) Historical Series* 4, no. 3 (London, 1972), for a discussion of this material.

26. Quoted in Mary Howitt Walker, *Come Wind, Come Weather—A Biography of Alfred Howitt* (Melbourne: Melbourne University Press, 1971), 221. This letter is not listed in Burkhardt and Smith, *Correspondence.*

27. Much of the Fison-Howitt-Morgan correspondence is reproduced with discussion by Bernhard J. Stern in "Selections from the Letters of Lorimer Fison and Alfred Howitt to Lewis Henry Morgan," *American Anthropologist,* n.s., 32 (1930): 257–279, 419–453.

28. McLennan appears to have been referred to Howitt and Fison's work by Darwin himself; see McLennan to Darwin, 30 November 1880, Dar. 171. Lubbock's antagonism to their work is documented in later editions of his book, *The Origin of Civilisation and the Primitive Condition of Man* (first published by Longmans, Green, and Co., London, 1870). See, for example, the preface to the seventh edition of 1912. Tylor frequently refers to *Kamilaroi and Kurnai* in his book, *Anthropology* (London: MacMillan, 1911). Durkheim and Mauss base their chapter "The Australian Type of Classification" in *Primitive Classification* (1903; English translation by Rodney Needham, London: Cohen and West, 1963) almost entirely on the investigation of Howitt and Fison.

29. Walter Baldwin Spencer, "Alfred Howitt," *The Victorian Naturalist* (April 1908): 181–189.

30. Howitt to Anna May Watts, July 1874 (original in the La Trobe Library, Melbourne, Box No. 1047/3A); Howitt to William Howitt, 7 July 1874, La Trobe Library, Box No. 1047/3A.

31. "Robert David Fitzgerald," in *Australian Dictionary of Biography,* vol. 4.

32. Charles Darwin, *The Various Contrivances by Which Orchids Are Fertilised by Insects* (1862; London: John Murray, 1877), 89–91, 114–115, 127, 279–281.

33. Darwin to Fitzgerald, 9 February 1881 (original in the Mitchell Library, Ref. No. A2546); Darwin to Fitzgerald, 15 July 1875, Mitchell Library Ref. No. A2546; C. Darwin, *Orchids,* 89. The comment by Hooker is found in Fitzgerald's entry, *Australian Dictionary;* Darwin's comment is in Darwin to Fitzgerald, 16 July 1875, Mitchell Library Ref. No. A2546.

34. Robert David Fitzgerald, *Australian Orchids,* vol. 1, part 1, July 1875, no pagination.

35. Ibid., "Introduction," 4.

36. Ibid., vol. 1, part 2, March 1876; ibid., "Introduction," 2.

37. Ibid., vol. 1, parts 1 and 2.

38. Ibid., vol. 1, "Introduction," 5.

39. Ibid., vol. 1, "Introduction," 1.

40. One of Fitzgerald's closest botanical associates, and a staunch opponent of Darwin, was the Reverend William Woolls. Woolls wrote a poetic eulogy for Fitzgerald on his death in 1892. See Fitzgerald's entry, *Australian Dictionary.*

41. Roy MacLeod, *Moving Metropolis,* 10.

7

Imperial Reflections in the Southern Seas: The Funafuti Expeditions, 1896–1904

ROY MACLEOD

*T*HE last decade has seen a growing interest in the role of science in the history of imperial expansion. This has reflected both a renewed interest in the imperial relations of metropolitan science, and a concern with the ways in which science, as instrument and ideology, served as a "tool of empire," securing for the metropolis regions hitherto unknown to Europe or unclaimed by Europeans. At the same time, studies of colonial science, once fashionable in America, are now enjoying a wider vogue as historians review the nature of colonial endeavor as seen from the academies of Europe and from the "frontier." Prevailing mythologies concerning so-called characteristic features of colonial science—observational, rather than theoretical; fact-gathering, not fundamental; derivative of metropolitan intellectual "maps" and institutions—are being more closely examined and correctives applied. More recently, interest has turned to the place of science in colonial nationalism, and to the role played by science in consolidating empire loyalties.[1]

As I have suggested elsewhere, "imperial science" and "colonial science" have different connotations when viewed from the metropolis and the periphery. In the British context, we frequently see the discourse of science invoked with the metaphors of familial responsibility and obligation,[2] and in many respects, the interests of British and colonial science were similar, if not identical.[3] By the close of the nineteenth century, however, the ambitions of the settler colonies had disturbed the tranquil assumptions of metropolitan superiority. These early impulses toward independence were infrequent, and their significance should not be exaggerated; they were founded upon a deep commitment to empire, and to Britain's own interests. But at least in the Australian colonies, the points at issue would be construed as important both to the celebration of Australians as scientific equals, and to the recognition of colonial governments as vigorous patrons of the advancement of science.

One of the most significant encounters between the interests of British and colonial Australian science occurred among the coral atolls of the South Pacific between 1896 and 1902. Of all the mysteries of the Pacific, none was more provocative than the history of what the Elizabethans called the "low islands," dotted over 117 million square kilometers of sea and bristling with danger to the mariner. Atolls were a puzzle equally to the naturalist and geologist. Their interpretation highlighted one goal of late Victorian geologists—to wrest, for Britain, the secrets of the last remaining unexplored areas on earth.[4] By the last quarter of the nineteenth century, the "coral atoll question" had reawakened public interest in a long-standing geological and personal controversy. At the same time, and quite by chance, it revealed certain ambitions awakening within colonial science, and demonstrated the skill of British geologists in containing these ambitions in the interests of empire. At the center of this gentlemanly tempest was Funafuti, an atoll that, between 1896 and 1904, became perhaps the most important field laboratory in British geology.

The Coral Reef Problem

"A singular degree of obscurity," wrote James Dana in 1872, "has possessed the popular mind with regard to the growth of corals and coral reefs, in consequence of the readiness with which speculations have been suggested and accepted in place of facts; and to the present day the subject is seldom mentioned without the gratifying adjective *mysterious* expressed or understood."[5] Almost immediately following Cook's voyages, the coral atolls of the southern oceans attracted keen interest. By the early nineteenth century, European scholars had established the biology of coral polyps and knew that coral reefs were built on volcanic rock in shallow waters. The way in which they were formed, however, remained unknown. Hypotheses abounded. Most, following Adelbert Cha-

misso, Jean Quoy, and Joseph Gaimard of France,[6] depended
upon observations of shallow reefs growing on submarine mountains.[7] Explanations were deductive, inferential, and highly controversial. But all were united by an epistemological commitment
to the permanence of continental areas and ocean basins; that is,
to the "immutability of oceans."

In 1836, during the *Beagle*'s long stay in South America,
Darwin devoted many months to speculation about the relative
nature of geological change.[8] Charles Lyell's *Principles of Geology*
(1830–1833) had posited the action of gradual processes at work
in the present, as in the geological past.[9] In his travels, Darwin had
observed mountain building and upheaval in the Andes, and from
this, he deduced that the earth's crust could sink as well as rise. If
this were so, coral reefs were simply an expression of a larger fact:
that atolls were formed by the *subsidence* of the volcanic islands
on which corals grew. That is, they grew upwards and outwards,
first forming a barrier, then a ring with no intervening islands at
all. To Darwin, reefs represented different stages in a continuous
process of evolution as significant to geology as was the origin of
new species to biology.[10]

Between 1837 and 1842, Darwin published what became
known as the "subsidence theory" in his *Structure and Distribution of Coral Reefs*. This was his first great work, and, with his
studies of volcanic islands (1844) and South America (1846), comprised the "*Beagle* trilogy."[11] To Darwin, the subsidence theory
represented the ultimate appeal of geology, offering, in his words,
"the same grand ideas respecting the world which Astronomy does
for the Universe."[12] The simplicity of his scheme so greatly
appealed that for many years no other explanation seemed necessary. In particular, Darwin's theory won the enthusiastic support
of the American naturalist James Dana, who served on the U.S.
Exploring (Wilkes) Expedition (1838–1842), and apparently encountered a report of Darwin's views during a visit to Sydney.[13]
Nevertheless, Darwin's views were not without difficulties. They
implied, for example, the sinking of submarine mountain chains
on a vast scale across the central Pacific, a third of the earth's surface. What would have produced this? Was it still happening?
Were *all* reefs and atolls formed in the same way? And, if subsidence were in fact the dominant process in their formation, what
was the cause of that process?

Between 1863 and 1870, geologists across Europe and America took up Darwin's geological problem, recognizing in it an issue that was a key to geomorphology. In Germany, Carl Semper and Johannes Rein, considering reefs in other parts of the world, discounted the likelihood of subsidence, preferring to believe in *rising* volcanic foundations on *stable* mountains on which coral shelves grew by deposition.[14] But the greatest threat to Darwin's view came in 1880, when John (later Sir John) Murray, a veteran of the *Challenger* expedition (1872–1876), introduced at the Royal Society of Edinburgh an opposing interpretation. Offering, from his *Challenger* years, empirical information Darwin did not have— that submarine banks do actually exist in the ocean—Murray argued that corals grew on stable islands, sometimes of volcanic origin.[15] Atolls, he argued, were formed when corals grew along the edges of these islands. Debris from the islands then gathered below the surface, while within the edges of the reef the island material was dissolved chemically by the corrosive action of sea water. As the "island" grew smaller, the reef encircled it, ultimately forming a lagoon. If this interpretation were true, the immutability of the oceans was preserved.[16]

Hearing of Murray's challenge, Darwin appealed in a letter to the American naturalist Alexander Agassiz for a "doubly rich millionaire [to] have borings made in the Pacific, and [to] bring home cores for slicing from a depth of 500 to 600 ft" to determine an atoll's foundations and how deep they lay.[17] Observation alone would determine the correct interpretation. If Darwin were correct, a bore would pass through a great thickness of reef limestone, deeper than the shallow layers of reef coral formed during the supposed period of subsidence. Below that, at great depth, there should be volcanic rock. According to Murray's theory, on the other hand, there should be a shallow cap of coral reef limestone, and a boring should soon pierce through to the original platform of plankton skeletons and other debris, then to volcanic rock (fig. 4).

The lines of debate were drawn, but nothing was done immediately. Darwin died in 1882 and the issue rested for five years. In 1887, however, atolls again became an issue when the Duke of Argyll, a well-known critic of Darwinian theory, accused geologists of a "conspiracy of silence" in overlooking difficulties in the subsidence theory out of deference to Darwin. Argyll claimed that

DARWIN   MURRAY

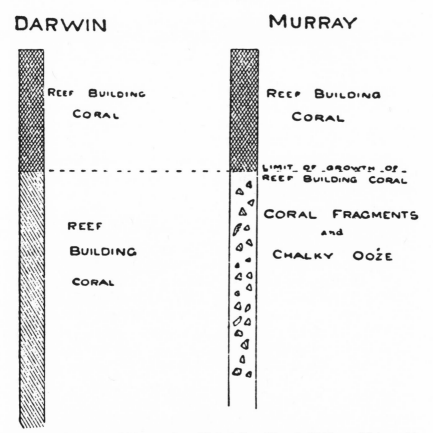

Figure 4. Darwin and Murray, from W. J. Sollas, "Funafuti," *Natural Science* 14 (1899): 24.

Murray had been advised to delay publication of his views for two years, even though they were supported by the *Challenger* data. Had Darwin, Argyll thundered, established a dogmatic "reign of terror," abandoning clear and certain reasonings for apparent simplicity?[18] By 1890 the solution to the atoll question had ceased to be merely a scientific problem; it had become a philosophical battlefield as well. Soon, it would also acquire a political dimension wholly unforeseen by its protagonists.

The last decades of the century witnessed many attempts to interpret the origins of species, to determine the mechanisms of natural selection, and to extend the metaphors of Darwinism to social and political spheres.[19] Few contemporaries, however, could seize upon an *experimentum crucis* to demonstrate Darwinism in action. Fortunately for geologists, the atoll question offered Darwinists, and champions of uniformitarianism, a chance to establish beyond reasonable doubt the merits of a single explanation of a given set of natural phenomena, which, by analogy with biological evolution, would be incontestably clear to the world at large.

This promise of supplying an evidential basis to an ontological preference had enormous appeal, and not least to three men in Britain: Thomas G. Bonney (1833–1923), Fellow of St. John's, Cambridge, and professor of geology at University College, London—an Anglican priest, but a steadfast Lyellian; William J. Sollas (1849–1936), formerly an undergraduate pupil of Bonney, at this time professor of geology at Trinity College, Dublin; and the young T. W. Edgeworth (later Sir Edgeworth) David (1858–1934), Welsh-born Oxford classicist turned mining geologist, who had emigrated to Sydney in 1882 as a field surveyor for the colonial government of New South Wales.[20] As Homeric heroes the three could not have been more charismatic; as geologists they were exemplary. Bonney, one of England's leading geologists, had written an appendix to the third edition of Darwin's *Coral Reefs* in 1889, summarizing the arguments for and against subsidence. Sollas, a brilliant naturalist and ethnologist (and a Fellow of the Royal Society since 1889), had long recognized the intellectual importance of the atoll question. The issue transcended science, schools, and generations. Both Sollas and Edgeworth David were former students of the Royal School of Mines and could claim practical expertise; both were Darwinians by inclination. In 1893, Bonney was sixty years old, Sollas was forty-four, and Edgeworth David was thirty-five.

From unpublished letters, it appears that in 1891 Sollas requested Bonney, then assistant general secretary of the British Association for the Advancement of Science (BA), to form a committee to consider ways of finding Darwin's "millionaire."[21] Three years and much discussion later, Bonney and the BA took the problem to the Royal Society, requesting assistance from the Government Grant Committee and from the Admiralty.

In November 1895, following conventional procedure, a "Coral Reef Committee" (CRC) was established by the society to oversee the project.[22] Michael (later Sir Michael) Foster, the distinguished Cambridge physiologist, then biological secretary of the

Royal Society, strongly supported the experimental venture and the imperial connection it implied.[23] He also backed the new CRC, of which Sollas and W. W. Watts (then of the Geological Survey, later of Imperial College) were joint secretaries. To ensure impartiality, Murray was added to the committee, which eventually, and with unintended symbolism, numbered twelve men. Murray had helped explode the "Bathybian myth" in 1874; might he explode another convenient hypothesis? After all, he had the support of Alexander Agassiz of Harvard.[24]

Where could the tournament be held? Admiral (later Sir) William Wharton, FRS, hydrographer to the Admiralty, suggested the atoll of Funafuti in the Ellice Islands (now Tuvalu). In January 1896, Edgeworth David (then visiting London) was appointed to the local Sydney committee, together with Professor Thomas P. Anderson Stuart, dean of medicine at Sydney University and a trustee of the Australian Museum. The local committee was to provide a base and hospitality for the British expedition, to which the Royal Society gave a grant of eight hundred pounds. By the northern spring of 1896, the committee was ready to begin work.[25]

The Promise of Funafuti

Funafuti lies in the middle of a chain of nine atolls comprising twenty-four square kilometers, and scattered over six hundred kilometers of the Pacific just below the equator (fig. 5). European mariners first discovered these islands between 1764 and 1824; by the mid-nineteenth century their Polynesian population had been plundered by the "blackbirding" of South American slaves, and Christianised by the Protestant London Missionary Society.[26] The Ellice Islands were brought under the High Commissioner for the Western Pacific in 1877. In 1892, in the face of energetic American traders, Captain H. M. Davis in HMS *Royalist* showed the flag through the islands, and they were subsequently declared a British Protectorate. A British Resident was established in Fiji.[27] The islands were peaceful, and Funafuti especially so. Precisely why Funafuti was chosen for the Royal Society expedition is not clear. Geologically, it was a typical atoll; and the Ellice Archipelago bor-

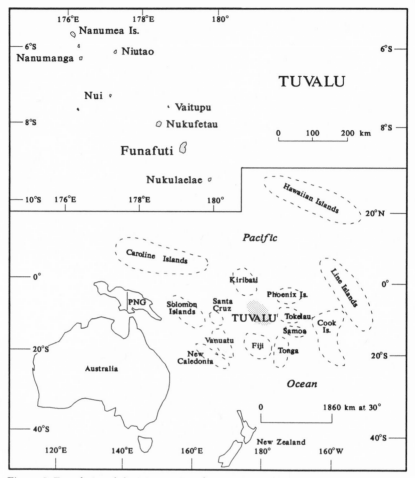

Figure 5. Funafuti and the Western Pacific.

dered one of the deep open basins of the Pacific. Arguably, results
from borings here could be applied by analogy to other island
chains and to submarine ridges forming the Melanesian plateau.

For the Royal Society to conduct such an expedition, ships and
machinery were needed. The first, the Admiralty was willing to
supply, with the cooperation of the Colonial Office. The second
was forthcoming from the ambitious colony of New South Wales.
Anderson Stuart secured the use of a diamond drill and a drilling
foreman from the colonial government, and local advice was
offered by Edgeworth David, who in 1894, in an unprecedented

upset of conventional practice, had outbid Sollas for the chair of geology at Sydney University.[28] This was the first time in the university's fifty-year history that an Australian candidate had been chosen over the recommendation of the London Committee. The success of the expedition depended on securing Anglo-Australian cooperation at all levels. How would the Royal Society proceed?

By the early 1890s, emerging from two generations of vigorous internal reform, secure in its international reputation and gifted in its relations with government, the Royal Society was to all appearances enjoying the fruits of a *pax scientifica*. Yet, its internal affairs were far from serene. In 1894 the superficial calm of the preceding decade was rudely shattered by a series of published attacks on election practices, favoritism, inefficiency, and the alleged influence of cliques within the council. The society, shocked by the publicity given these disclosures and cautious of its good name, resisted further public exposure wherever possible. The need for neutrality and freedom from controversy was underlined by the society's position as Britain's de facto "Department of Science" at home and proconsular representative abroad. Years of empire building—from the Americas to Africa, India to Australasia, and from pole to pole—had also imbued the society with a deep sense of its obligations toward "imperial management." Even more than in the days of Huxley, Hooker, and other "expeditioners" of the early Victorian period, the Royal Society's view of the world was now imperiously "metropolitan." Scientific voyages to the Pacific had been successfully coordinated by the society since 1768; a century or more later, no one would expect less. As events revealed, Funafuti would put all these considerations to the test.[29]

The Admiralty's cooperation, customary on such occasions, had in this case the special interest of Admiral Wharton. He, in turn, had added reasons for securing deep-sea soundings in parts of the Pacific that could be of importance to imperial communications. Following the Imperial Colonial Conference of 1887, there were repeated attempts to establish an imperial submarine telegraph linking British North America and Australia across the Pacific. Eventually, a more geographically convenient, northern Pacific route, via Japan, was abandoned for strategic reasons, and in 1896 plans were made for a link across the southern ocean.[30] By

1898 the southern route was still undecided. Partly for this purpose, the Admiralty kept at least two ships for hydrographic work
in Pacific waters. It was, however, highly selective in their deployment.[31] Indeed, in July 1894 the Admiralty (and the Colonial
Office) had turned down a request from the Royal Society, backed
by Lord Kelvin and Lord Rayleigh, for naval help with an Antarctic expedition.[32] But with the growing adventurism of American
merchants and German men-of-war in southern waters, the Colonial Office (if not yet the Admiralty) had reason to be concerned.

The intercolonial Conference of Australian Premiers held at
Hobart in February 1895 reminded Britain that this concern had
been shared by the colonies of Australia since at least 1883. At
that time, Britain had been urged to proclaim a Monroe Doctrine
for the South Pacific. The government of New South Wales, in
particular, had urged the importance of improving colonial defense, and had adopted a vigorous colonial foreign policy following the annexation of Papua New Guinea, and during the Sudan
conflict in 1885.[33] Subsequently, New South Wales appeared willing to cooperate with loyal expressions that would commit Britain
and her navy more fully to the region. In 1896 it could do so by
expressing its support of Britain's scientific interests overseas.
Funafuti thus became a symbol of geopolitical, as of geological,
importance, a manifestation of colonial nationalism, and a colonial reassertion of imperial unity.

The Expeditions

The three ensuing expeditions can be briefly summarized. The
first, under the leadership of Sollas, embarked from London in
March 1896 and from Sydney in May of that year, on the gunboat
HMS *Penguin* under Captain Mostyn Field, FRS, the hydrographer. Edgeworth David left the expedition unequivocally to Sollas.
With Sollas went H. J. Slee, chief inspector of mines for the New
South Wales government; Charles Hedley, curator of molluscs at
the Australian Museum; and J. Stanley Gardiner, Fellow of Caius
College, Cambridge.[34] David was anxious that Australian inter-
ests be recognized, but to propitiate London, he agreed that all
core samples obtained from drilling would be sent first to the

Royal Society, which, when it chose, would then return half to Sydney.[35]

Sollas's mission was twofold: as Bonney put it, to bring back safely his crew and "a chunk of coral rock from a depth of 100 fathoms." Committed to the project, and to its "favorable outcome," Bonney dreaded the possibility of Sollas finding "only a thinnish cap of coral with the volcanic rock or some such rubbish below." Sollas put down two bores, the greater to a depth of 105 feet. But within weeks disaster struck. By August, untrained in island morphology and facing unexpected slides of sand and boulders, the drillers and their machinery came to a halt. Systematic cores were impossible to obtain. In dismay, Sollas stayed on the atoll eleven weeks, then ordered the expedition home.[36]

Returning to Dublin in October, Sollas admitted failure. The expedition had been in vain. "It is very unfortunate," Norman Lockyer, editor of *Nature* mused, "that the . . . liberal aid of the Admiralty and of friends and authorities in Sydney, should be so ill-rewarded."[37] Still, as Bonney consoled, "it is not in mortals to command success." As far as they went, the borings did reveal depths at which coral could be found; and thanks to Captain Field, the floor of the lagoon had been mapped with great accuracy. To mitigate criticism of the Royal Society, Bonney urged Sollas to "lie as low" as possible. On theoretical issues, he was, moreover, not to "wave the red flag," but merely to report the facts with, if necessary, his personal view that they "appear to support" Darwin's theory. "Depend upon it," Bonney warned, "John Murray will say they do nothing of the kind."[38]

In his report to the Royal Society in February 1897, Sollas followed Bonney's advice. The expedition was over, the funds were spent, and so the affair might have ended.[39] But it did not. Wharton advanced a new theory; *Nature* received a series of letters and articles; and growing sentiment favored a retrial.[40] The Darwinians were anxious to see the case proved. "A little fighting," Bonney added, "will do no harm and keep the ball rolling."[41] When the Royal Society, its funds gone, hesitated to reopen the matter, Bonney seized the initiative, and in a preface to the report on the first expedition appealed to colonial pride to sustain a second. "The attempt can be much more easily made, and with a far greater probability of success," he argued, "if Australia, instead of England be the base of operations."[42] When Agassiz proposed an Anglo-American expedition, sharing costs, Bonney quickly disagreed: "A dispute with Australians is at any rate domestic," he said, "with Americans it would have a different character."[43]

For some months in early 1897, however, these domestic relations were ruffled when Charles Hedley published in Sydney biological data from the expedition. The British accused the Australians of a serious breach of scientific protocol.[44] But with *Nature's* help, these irritations were eventually set aside. Bonney acknowledged Australian loyalties, and sent David an invitation to lead a second expedition. David immediately agreed to organize a fresh expedition and set about raising funds from Sydney benefactors. David's concern was quickened by the belief that if nothing more were done, blame would be laid "on the conduct of that part of the expedition for which New South Wales was responsible, viz, the arrangements for carrying out the boring operations."[45] His sense of obligation was matched by colonial pride. "New South Wales," he informed Sydney University, "is probably in a better position than any other English-speaking community to undertake this work and bring it to a successful issue." For this purpose, he must lead the expedition himself; his chancellor agreed. He urged in particular the Royal Geographical Society of Australasia to contribute funds "for a work which, if successful, would win renown for this country amongst men of science throughout the world."[46]

The second expedition, under David's leadership, sailed from Sydney in June 1897. David brought the best Australian mining and surveying expertise, together with the latest diamond drilling technology. (For his model of the atoll, see fig. 6.) With characteristic energy and charm, David mobilized the help of private individuals, the colonial government of New South Wales, and the resident commissioner in Fiji, and secured transport from Fiji to Funafuti through the London Missionary Society. By September, the expedition had put down bores to a depth of 557 feet (fig. 7).[47] David then returned to his lecture room in Sydney, where he was "greeted with ringing cheers";[48] the drilling continued, following his instructions, to a depth of 698 feet. Several fresh cores were sent for examination to David's former teacher, Professor J. W. Judd at the Royal College of Science in London.[49] Surely now the question would be settled?

News of David's success in reaching such unprecedented depths

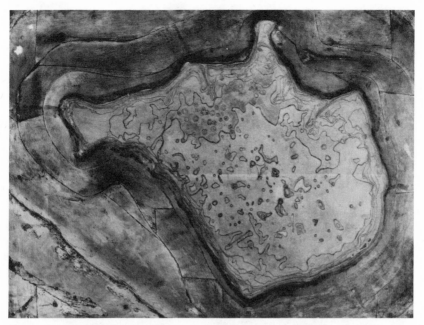

Figure 6. Model of Funafuti, photographed by Kate Lowe. (Courtesy of the Australian Museum, Sydney)

met a rapturous response in Australia. The Melbourne correspondent of the *Times* reported the event in language that recalled William Caldwell's announcement of the oviparous nature of the platypus to the BA in Montreal thirteen years before. That event had attracted enormous attention to Australia. The experience of seeing a key discovery in Australian zoology aired to the world overseas, without a prior Australian announcement, prompted the governments of Victoria and New South Wales to invite the BA to hold a future meeting in Australia, and contributed to the new federal spirit animating the founders of the Australasian Association for the Advancement of Science (AAAS) in 1888.[50] This time, the discoveries at Funafuti would be claimed and described in Australia. Thus, the Melbourne correspondent reported with pride: "The scientific expedition . . . under Professor David has confirmed Darwin's theory"; though, he added at a distance, "a final judgement depends upon microscopic examination of the drill cores."[51]

Not surprisingly, it was this note of caution that appealed to the Royal Society. In December, *Nature* carried news of David's report to the CRC. Bonney, however, limited himself to praising the oper-

Figure 7. David's bore, from the Edgeworth David Papers. (Courtesy of University of Sydney Archives)

Figure 8. "Success," from the Edgeworth David Papers. (Courtesy of University of Sydney Archives)

ation and its success in gathering specimens. Judd declined to comment publicly. Universally the cores were thought to be promising. But promising of what? The evidence, if not convincing, could split the community of British geologists, reopen old controversies, and embarrass the Royal Society. In February 1898 Gardiner told the Cambridge Philosophical Society that nothing could be learned from the expedition save that the subsidence theory was unlikely—a view he repeated before the International Congress of Zoologists in Cambridge later that year. A month before, David had given a more optimistic account to the AAAS Congress at Sydney. He admitted that a deeper bore was necessary; as far as he had gone; the core obtained might even weaken the subsidence theory. Was a third expedition necessary? And if so, in order to prove the point objectively, or to find "enough" evidence to support Darwin?[52]

The question soon became not whether there should be another voyage, but rather when, and at whose cost. Thanks to David, an Australian push was on. The Royal Society this time granted David five hundred pounds directly and the Admiralty deployed

HMS *Porpoise* to help with drilling the lagoon floor.[53] Conveyed to Funafuti from Fiji again by the LMS ship, this third expedition was led by Edgeworth David's student, A. E. Finckh, who, with a team of six, stayed on the atoll from June to September and finally returned to Sydney in January 1899. Using heavy diamond drills and sand pumps, the Sydney team reached a depth of over eleven hundred feet and produced a vast amount of new information. In the meantime, as fresh intelligence reached Sydney, David quickly had it published.[54] News was relayed in November to Sydney's *Daily Telegraph,* then to *Nature* and the scientific world at large. "The results, so far obtained," *Nature* trumpeted, "are very satisfactory." Certainly they were to the scientists of New South Wales. Whatever the conclusions, "the results," observed Bonney in *Nature,* "are most interesting, and our friends in Sydney may be congratulated on [their] success." On New Year's Eve 1898, the London *Standard,* summing up the year's scientific achievements, made special reference to the energy of David and Stuart and the aid of the New South Wales government.[55] In November 1898, David was nominated for the Fellowship of the Royal Society, an honor that eventually came to him in 1900. In January 1899, David was among the first Australians to win the Bigsby Medal of the Geological Society of London.[56] Australia, it was said, had redeemed Britain's failure. In the meantime, Darwinists could rejoice: the borings, when analyzed, promised to be fatal to Murray's heresy.

By early 1899 the adventures of Australians at war in South Africa had replaced Funafuti in the Sydney newspapers. The final cores of the third expedition were sent to Judd in April 1899, and for the next five years the results were painstakingly assembled. David's wife recounted her journey in a popular book,[57] and David's international reputation soared. The story was the stuff of imperial opera: the understudy who had overtaken the feted diva; the young "scientific soldier," who won instant heroism by deeds of derring-do. In 1926, when Cambridge University awarded him an honorary D.Sc., the Public Orator spoke of David's "achieving what our countrymen had attempted in vain . . . , boring through the coral, almost to the world below."[58] Sollas, brooding in the cold corridors of Oxford's University Museum, wrote a generous tribute to David in *Natural Science* in January 1899 and quit the

Figure 9. "My hut in centre," from Mrs. Edgeworth David, *Funafuti or Three Months on a Coral Island* (London: Sir Isaac Pitman, 1913).

field of his missed opportunity. Sollas received the Royal Medal in 1914 for his work, but never forgot his failure.[59] Funafuti had changed the balance of power in the geological Pacific, and given both David and Australian geology an enormous fillip.

Interpreting the Results

In 1904 the Royal Society received a final report on the expeditions—a volume of nearly four hundred pages, edited by Bonney but published under the name of the CRC. The press spoke respectfully of the story told, of "cylinders, under-reamers, lining pipes, gearing-wheels and all the technicalities of the diamond drill." Indeed, the way in which difficulties were overcome during six years' investigation added a new chapter to the annals of scientific pluck and pride and what the *Times Literary Supplement (TLS)*, embracing Australia into the colonial fold, called "British perseverance, thoroughness, ingenuity and adaptability to circum-

Figure 10. The Expedition Group (clockwise from top left: G. Sweet, Foreman Burns, W. Poole, Mrs. David, Professor David, W. Woolnough, B.A., Foreman Dent), from Mrs. Edgeworth David, *Funafuti or Three Months on a Coral Island* (London: Sir Isaac Pitman, 1913).

stances, qualities which we are told too often are forsaking our race at the present day."[60]

What proof was there of Darwin's hypothesis of sixty years before? Had the expeditions determined whether, in Sollas's hyperbole, the typical atoll was a "garland laid by the hands of Nature on the tomb of a sunken island" or "a wreath of victory crowning a youthful summit on its first conquest of the main?"[61] The Royal Society's report was noncommital. Judd's analysis demonstrated both possibilities, or neither, according to persuasion. Even at such unprecedented depths, the bores had failed to reach a foundation in the island's volcanic rock. Still, the deeper limestones recovered did contain fossils of organisms that lived only in shallow water, and this, subsidence alone could explain. With this knowledge, Darwinists were content. Murray, however, was unconvinced, maintaining that the reef had simply grown out over its own waste, and that it was this waste, the talus, that the boreholes had disclosed. There might be subsidence, but the evidence gave no confirmation that "here a mountain reared its head, round which the coral necklace was hung."[62]

The *TLS* put on a brave face: although the report "nowhere drew conclusions," it gave a "mass of solid fact upon which opposing philosophers will long be able to quarry material for their fascinating theories."[63] Many of the observations supported Murray's theory: the action of the sea indisputably affected the shape of the atoll. However, Murray's "fairy-ring" hypothesis depended upon its corollary, expansion by corrosion within the lagoon; and as the borings in this particular lagoon contained no evidence of corrosion, the initial hypothesis was probably unfounded. In reading the Book of Nature, Darwin might be wrong, but Murray could not be right.

Resolution Postponed

"When the history of nineteenth century science is written, the Coral Reef chapter will not be in all respects flattering to the acumen of many who contributed to it." Writing in 1928, William Davis, the distinguished Harvard geologist, thus summarized what had been one of the most passionate geological controversies of his time. Why had the CRC been reluctant to pronounce a ver-

dict? Ernest Skeat, one of Judd's assistants in London, wrote his
D.Sc. on data from the Funafuti expedition. In 1919 he announced that the Royal Society had itself decided that "the experts
to whom the material was submitted should . . . draw no conclusions from the facts as to the mode of formation of the atoll."[64] In
Skeat's view, the mass of solid fact "supported Darwin," but no one
would publicly say so. Davis observed that the Royal Society's
decision "rendered those best qualified to express opinions on the
main questions at issue—namely, the inferred processes of the past
which would most competently explain the observed facts of the
present"—no opportunity to do so.[65] Why this was so remains
unexplained. It may be that the society, now under the presidency
of Sir William Huggins, was seeking new objectives and had no
wish to reopen old wounds. We know for certain only that Bonney, the editor of the report, wished to close the debate and avoid
further controversy. Perhaps there were deeper fears of personal
animus implicit in his advice to Sollas that it was "no use shouting
till we are out of the woods."[66]

In Sydney, Edgeworth David made clear his conviction that the
evidence pointed to subsidence. To his mind, Darwin's dying wish
had been granted and his theory confirmed.[67] But Sir Archibald
Geikie's 1909 Rede Lecture at Cambridge honoring Darwin's cen-
tennial left the verdict open. And the following year, Frederick
Wood-Jones, writing for both British and Australian readers, concluded that "the warfare of rival explanations cannot be said to
have yet ceased."[68]

In the meantime, American and European geologists were shifting the focus of coral atoll investigations away from Funafuti. In
1910 Reginald Daly of Harvard proposed what has since become
known as the "glacial control theory" of oceanic submergence, a
proposition that offered a plausible alternative, or at least a complement, to Darwin's theory. Daly argued that Darwin's theory did
not take into account fluctuations in sea level produced by continental glaciers in the Pleistocene.[69] But Daly also made a deductive
inference lacking irrefutable empirical evidence. In particular,
three questions remained unresolved: (1) On what structure did
corals first build? (2) What accounted for the regularity of the
atoll's circular shape? (3) Could explanations of atoll formation
apply to other coral formations, including fringing and barrier
reefs?

For another forty years these questions remained unanswered. Finally, in 1952, American military-sponsored drilling operations at the atoll of Eniwetok in the Marshall Islands reached depths of over four thousand feet and at last confirmed the central outlines of Darwin's theory—at least in the Pacific. Ironically, the "millionaire" who obliged Darwin was neither British nor Australian, but the U.S. Atomic Energy Commission.[70]

Today, Darwin's theory, "subordinately modified," as Davis put it, is considered at least part of the correct explanation. H. W. Menard announced in 1964 that Darwin's hypothesis of the association of atolls with regional subsidence was no longer "open to dispute."[71] In fact, however, the question of cause remains unanswered. Subsidence changes are now explained by thermal contractions of the ocean floor, but we still do not know why ocean crust descends—whether it is pushed, pulled, or merely falls. Moreover, difficulties persist in using coral reefs as direct evidence for ocean subsidence, as their geology is not directly coupled with their immediate ocean surroundings. For this reason, the atoll question retains an air of mystery. In Rosen's words, "we can observe [coral reefs] directly underwater, drill into them, take portions back to laboratories for further studies, fly over them with satellite sensors, and conduct on-the-reef experiments, and yet we still feel that we do not adequately understand reef processes."[72]

Imperial Implications

Nearly a century later, the coral reef question recalls the glacial theory debates and the great Devonian controversies of the 1840s.[73] Funafuti remains part of the mythology of late-Victorian, "monotheistic" Darwinism, enshrined in the archives of the Royal Society of London, the University Museum at Oxford, and the Australian Museum in Sydney. In retrospect, the philosophical and political lessons of the expeditions far outweigh their contributions to theory. At Funafuti, imperial science passed from a descriptive phase, characterized by expeditions from Cook to *Challenger,* and entered one of experiment and investigation. In this case, however, geologists were faced by the necessity of accepting a conceptual pluralism. No single explanation accounted for every phenomenon. In all likelihood, more than one factor was at work, and the principal rival theories were neither wholly right nor wholly wrong.

For Darwin, as David Stoddart has argued, theory took precedence over fact.[74] Darwin's bias was intuitional, not inductive. Even if his coral reef theory could not be proved right or wrong, it still had enormous explanatory value, and in that lay its importance—a point easily obscured by the contemporary friction of politics and personalities. As with many Victorian controversies— glacial action and spontaneous generation are other spectacular examples—the coral reef question involved competing paradigms that were in fact incommensurable; and in the absence of a conclusive, critical experiment, evaluative theories would merely reflect epistemological preferences.

Behind it all lay the impassive impartiality of the Royal Society. Officially obeying Newton's dictum, the CRC "framed no hypotheses." In a 1910 address, Bonney may have explained his own reasoning for not casting a deciding vote. He spoke of glacial theories, but his conclusions spoke to Funafuti as well: "there are stages in the development of a scientific idea when the best service we can do it is by attempting to separate facts from fantasies . . . and by remembering that if hypotheses yet on their trial are treated as axioms, the result will often bring disaster, like building a tower on a foundation of sand."[75]

The political lessons of the expeditions were less equivocal. The coral reef controversy celebrated a victory for Australian geology, and Australian colonial nationalism in science.[76] But, by keeping the peace among rival theoretical camps, the Royal Society also preserved the unifying spirit of imperial science, strengthening, rather than weakening, the ties between Oxford and Dublin, London and Sydney. To southern eyes, there was glory in David's success—a story taken up by both the British and Australian popular press.[77] In retrospect, Funafuti was among the first major imperial geological expeditions led by Australian scientists and the forerunner of many others.[78] The "spirit of Funafuti" infused David's journeys to Mount Erebus and the south magnetic pole during Shackleton's Antarctic expedition of 1907–1908, and his geological work with the Australian Mining and Tunnelling Companies on the western front in 1916–1918. This tradition of imperial unity and cooperation would survive well after the war—thanks largely to David's superb diplomacy and technical skill—giving a new dimension to the legend of "bush endurance" and Australian enterprise. The reality of this legend—self-help, unending energy, and local support from colonial Australians loyally committed to an imperial cause—was to be the hallmark of Australian science for decades to come.

Notes

The author wishes to express his particular thanks to the librarian of the Royal Society of London for assistance with committee reports; to H. P. Powell, assistant curator, University Museum, Oxford, for access to the correspondence of W. J. Sollas; to Graeme Powell of the Australian Joint Copying Project for information concerning Admiralty papers; to Gwen Baker-Lowry and Carol Cantrell of the Australian Museum, Sydney, for access to museum archives; to Brian Rosen of the British Museum (Natural History) for his generous advice on atoll matters, and for giving me the use of unpublished exhibition material cited herein; to Christa Ludlow, for invaluable help with locating sources; and to Ken Smith of the University Archives, Sydney University, for access to the Edgeworth David Papers. These papers are cited with his permission.

1. Daniel Headrick, *The Tools of Empire: Technology and European Imperialism in the Nineteenth Century* (New York: Oxford University Press, 1981); Ian Inkster, "Scientific Enterprise and the Colonial Model," *Social Studies of Science* 15 (1985): 677–704; Roy MacLeod, ed., *The Commonwealth of Science* (Melbourne: Oxford University Press, 1988).

2. Roy MacLeod, "On Visiting the 'Moving Metropolis': Reflections on the Architecture of Imperial Science," *Historical Records of Australian Science* 5 (1982): 1–16; reprinted in Nathan Reingold and Marc Rothenberg, eds., *Scientific Colonialism: A Cross-Cultural Comparison* (Washington, D.C.: Smithsonian Institution Press, 1987), 217–249.

3. See, inter alia, J. C. Beaglehole, *The Exploration of the Pacific* (1934; London: S. and C. Black, 1966); Jacques Brosse, *Great Voyages of Exploration* (New York: Doubleday, 1983); David Mackay, *In the Wake of Cook* (Wellington: Victoria University Press, 1985); William Stanton, *The Great United States Exploring Expedition* (Berkeley and Los Angeles: University of California Press, 1975); Erik Linklater, *The Voyage of the Challenger* (London: John Murray, 1972).

4. Herman Friis, *The Pacific Basin: A History of Its Geographical Exploration* (New York: American Geographical Society, 1967), esp. chaps. 11–13.

5. James Dana, *Corals and Coral Islands* (1872; New York: Dodd and Mead, 1890), 11.

6. Dorothea Rudnik, "Chamisso, Adelbert von," *Dictionary of Scientific Biography* 15, supplement 1 (New York: Charles Scribner, 1978), 81–83; Toby A. Appel, "Quoy, Jean Rene Constant," ibid. 11 (1975): 242–244; and William Coleman, "Gaimard, Joseph Paul," ibid. 5 (1972): 224–225.

7. For early accounts and a useful survey, see W. M. Davis, *The Coral Reef Problem* (New York: American Geographical Society, 1928). For a definitive account of successive theories, evidence, and their implications for contemporary geomorphology, see J. A. Steers and D. R. Stoddart, "The Origin of Fringing Reefs, Barrier Reefs and Atolls," *Biology and Geology of Coral Reefs* 4 (1977): 21–57.

8. Steers and Stoddart, "Origin of Fringing Reefs," 23–25; D. R. Stoddart, " 'Grandeur in This View of Life': Darwin and the Ocean World," *Bulletin of Marine Science* 33 (1983): 521–527; Brian Rosen, "Darwin, Coral Reefs, and Global Geology," *Bioscience* 32 (1982): 519–525.

9. Charles Lyell, *Principles of Geology* (London: John Murray, 1830–1833); D. R. Stoddart, "Darwin, Lyell & the Geological Significance of Coral Reefs," *British Journal of the History of Science* 9 (1976): 199–218.

10. Brian Rosen, *Coral Reefs* (an exhibition text commemorating the voyage of HMS *Challenger*) (London: British Museum [Natural History], 1983), f. 2.

11. Charles Darwin, *The Structure and Distribution of Coral Reefs (Being the First Part of the Geology of the Voyage of the Beagle . . . , 1832–1836)* (London: Smith, Elder, 1842); idem, *Geological Observations on the Volcanic Islands Visited during the Voyage of HMS Beagle . . .* (London: Smith, Elder, 1844); idem, *Geological Observations on South America (Being the Third Part of the Geology of the Voyage of the Beagle . . .)* (London: Smith, Elder, 1846). The first work went into a second edition in 1844, a third in 1889, and a fourth (edition by J. W. Judd) in 1890.

12. Darwin quoted in J. W. Judd, "Critical Introduction," to Charles Darwin, *On the Structure and Distribution of Coral Reefs . . .* (London: Ward Lock, 1890), 159.

13. Dana, *Corals and Coral Islands,* 7. See also W. M. Davis, "Dana's Confirmation of Darwin's Theory of Coral Reefs," *American Journal of Science* 35 (1913): 182; James Dana, *On Coral Reefs and Islands* (New York: G. P. Putnam, 1853), 118–119; and idem, *Corals and Coral Islands.*

14. On the subsidence issue, see Rosen, *Coral Reefs,* f. 3; Steers and Stoddart, "Origin of Fringing Reefs," 30. For Carl Gottfried Semper, see *Dictionary of Scientific Biography* 12 (1975): 299; for Johannes Rein, J. C., see *Biographisch—Literarisches Handwörterbuch* 6 (Berlin: Verlag Chemie, 1930), 2147.

15. For Murray's views, see John Murray, ed., *Reports on the Scientific Results of the Voyage of HMS Challenger* (1880–1895); John Murray, "The Structure and Origin of Coral Reefs and Islands," *Proceedings of the Royal Society of Edinburgh* 10 (1880): 505; cf. his later *Deep Sea Depositions of the Atlantic Ocean* (London: Macmillan, 1912); also Margaret Deacon, *Scientists and the Sea, 1650–1900: A Study of Marine Science* (New York: Academic Press, 1971), 383–385. Murray (1841–1914) was elected an FRS in 1896 and knighted (KCB) in 1898. See A. E. Shipley, "Sir John Murray: A Great Oceanographer," *Cornhill Magazine* 36 (May 1914): 3–12.

16. Steers and Stoddart ("Origin of Fringing Reefs," 31) observe that the idea of lagoon formation by solution, held by Murray, and by Gardner until the 1930s, was disproved by the demonstration that typical seawater cannot chemically dissolve limestone on the required scale; and that lagoons are sites of sedimentation, not erosion. See J. S. Gardiner, *Coral Reefs and Atolls* (New York:

Macmillan, 1931); Preston E. Cloud, Jr., "Carbonate Precipitation and Dissolution in the Marine Environment," in J. P. Riley and G. Skirrow, eds., *Chemical Oceanography* (New York: Wiley, 1965), 2:127–158.

17. Francis Darwin, ed., *Life and Letters of Charles Darwin* (London: Macmillan, 1887), 3:183–184.

18. George Campbell, Eighth Duke of Argyll, "A Great Lesson," *Nineteenth Century* 127 (1887): 307. Argyll denied that Darwin's subsidence theory had any special connection with the "hypothesis of Evolution"; but by scorning the prospect that "the apparent sufficiency of an explanation may be any proof whatever of its truth" (ibid., 308–309), by implication associated the two. Argyll's sentiments met a spirited response from T. H. Huxley in "Science and the Bishops," *Nineteenth Century* 122 (November 1887): 636. See Bonney's defensive review, "A Conspiracy of Silence," *Nature* 37 (10 November 1887): 25–26, and Argyll's angry reply, *Nature* 37 (17 November 1887): 53–54.

19. See J. D. Y. Peel, *Herbert Spencer: The Evolution of a Sociologist* (London: Heinemann, 1971); James Moore, *The Post Darwinian Controversies* (Cambridge: Cambridge University Press, 1979); David Hull, *Darwin and His Critics: The Reception of Darwin's Theory of Evolution by the Scientific Community* (Cambridge, Mass.: Harvard University Press, 1973); Frank Turner, *Between Science and Religion: The Reaction to Scientific Naturalism in Late Victorian England* (New Haven, Conn.: Yale University Press, 1974).

20. For Bonney, see especially "Eminent Living Geologists," *Geological Magazine* 19 (September 1901): 385–400. For Sollas, see *Obituary Notices of Fellows of the Royal Society* (1936–1938) (London: Royal Society, 1939), 2:266–281. For Edgeworth David, see *Obituary Notices* (1932–1935) (London: Royal Society, 1936), 1:494–501. Sollas's obituary was written by A. Smith Woodward and W. W. Watts (the latter, secretary to the Coral Reef Committee). Edgeworth David's was written by Douglas Mawson, who sailed to the Antarctic with David, but who had no personal experience of the coral atoll question.

21. Bonney to Sollas, January–December 1891, Sollas Papers, University Museum, Oxford.

22. *Coral Reef Committee,* 14 November 1895–16 December 1902, Archives of the Royal Society.

23. Foster was an important advocate of imperial scientific cooperation and a particular friend to Australian scientists. In this he followed his teacher, T. H. Huxley. He was elected an honorary member of the Royal Society of New South Wales in May 1887. See Foster to Liversidge, 1 July 1887, *Journal and Proceedings of the Royal Society of New South Wales* 21 (1887): 216.

24. On the Bathybian myth, see Philip F. Rehbock, "Huxley, Haeckel, and the Oceanographers: The Case of *Bathybius Haeckelii,*" *Isis* 66 (1975): 529–530; cf. John Murray, "Preliminary Report to Professor Wyville Thomson, FRS, . . . On Work Done on Board the *Challenger,*" *Proceedings of the Royal Society of London* 24 (1876): 471–543. For Agassiz's role in the controversy, see Davis, *Coral Reef Problem,* and idem, "Dana's Confirmation," 184; also Agassiz's reports of his observations on the *Albatross* (1899–1900), especially in *Bulletin of the Museum of Comparative Zoology* 26 (1902–1911): 37–43; and "The Coral Reefs of the Tropical Pacific," ibid. 28 (1903): 1–410.

25. Wharton had become hydrographer in 1884 at the age of only forty-one.

He was elected to the Royal Society in 1886, promoted to Admiral and knighted (KCB) in 1897. He was particularly knowledgeable about the Pacific, and in 1893 edited the journal of Cook's first voyage. He was also well known for his influential *Hydrographical Surveying* (1882). See Vice Admiral Sir Archibald Day, *The Admiralty Hydrographical Service, 1795–1919* (London: Her Majesty's Stationery Office, 1967); also G. S. Ritchie, *The Admiralty Chart: British Naval Hydrography in the Nineteenth Century* (New York: Elsevier, 1967), chap. 22, "Wharton and Scientific Surveying." For a description of the financial arrangements, see Watts to Sir John Evans, 13 March 1896, *Royal Society Archives,* MC.16.297.

26. Barrie Macdonald, *Cinderellas of the Empire: Towards a History of Kiribati and Tuvalu* (Canberra: Australian National University Press, 1982), 14–16, 29; R. G. Roberts, "Te atu Tuvalu: A Short History of the Ellice Islands," *Journal of the Polynesian Society* 67 (1958): 394–397.

27. *Records of the Colonial and Dominions Office* (London: Her Majesty's Stationery Office, 1964). For the steps by which Britain reluctantly acquired administration of the islands, see Macdonald, *Cinderellas of the Empire,* 68–69. In 1882 the population of Funafuti was 250 and subsisted mainly on breadfruit, bananas, and fish. The islands became a colony in 1916 and served as forward bases for U.S. attacks on the Japanese-held Gilbert Islands in 1942–1943. They became independent in 1978. Today, Funafuti is the capital of Tuvalu, known as "the smallest, least favoured, least known independent country in the world" (*Bulletin,* 28 August 1984, p. 122). In his Independence Day address the prime minister proclaimed, "All we have is sunshine, wind and a portion of the Pacific Ocean" (ibid.). The population of the islands is around 8,700 (1984). The unit of currency is the Australian dollar.

28. Breaking with convention, the university appointed Edgeworth David on the recommendation of the local (Sydney) committee, in recognition of his knowledge of Australian geology. The London committee comprised Sir Saul Samuel (agent general of New South Wales), Sir Charles Nicolson (one of the founders of the University of Sydney, then resident in England), Professor J. Judd (Royal School of Mines), Professor Boyd Dawkins (Owens College, Manchester), and Sir Archibald Geikie (director general, Geological Survey). The affair provoked some sharp words between London and Sydney. See University of Sydney, *Reports of the Senate for 1891,* 395.

29. On the controversy during the 1890s, see Lord Rayleigh, *John William Strutt—Third Baron Rayleigh* (London: Edward Arnold, 1924), 173; *Times* (London), 1 December 1893; Foster to Huxley, 2 December 1893, Huxley Papers, Imperial College London, 4, f. 369; *Times,* 1 December 1894; cf. Roy MacLeod and Sophie Forgan, "Cliques, Conflicts & Consensus: The Royal Society in the late-19th Century" (forthcoming). For the Society as "Department of Science," see Roy MacLeod, "Science and the Treasury: Principles, Personalities and Policies, 1870–1885," in G. L. E. Turner, ed., *The Patronage of Science* (Leyden: Noordhoff, 1976), 115–172. For the Royal Society's metropolitan worldview, see Roy MacLeod, "Advice for British India: Imperial Perceptions and Administrative Goals, 1898–1923," *Modern Asian Studies* 9 (1975): 343–384; M. Boas Hall, *All Scientists Now: The Royal Society in the Nineteenth Century* (Cambridge: Cambridge University Press, 1984), 162–181, 199–216.

30. See George Johnson's classic, *The All-Red Line* (Ottawa: J. Hope and Sons, 1903). For the arrival of the first telegraph from England in 1872 via the Middle East and Java, see K. Inglis, "The Imperial Connection: Telegraphic Communication between England and Australia, 1872–1902," in A. F. Madden and W. H. Morris-Jones, eds., *Australia and Britain: Studies in a Changing Relationship* (Sydney: University of Sydney Press, 1980), 21–38. The southern link did not materialize until 1902. See "Pacific Cable," *Australian Encyclopedia* (Sydney: Grolier Society, n.d.), 6:435–436.

31. Day, *Admiralty Hydrographical Service*, 142.

32. Correspondence with Royal Society and Royal Geographical Society, July 1894, Adm 1/7212, Public Record Office. Cf. also Day, ibid., 119. In 1888 an Australian request for a British expedition to Antarctica was similarly declined. However, the Admiralty later supported Scott in the British National Antarctic Expedition (1901–1904).

33. Roger C. Thompson, *Australian Imperialism in the Pacific* (Melbourne: Melbourne University Press, 1980), chaps. 4 and 5. For contemporary comment, see Arthur White, "Australia as a Strategic Base," *Nineteenth Century* 34 (1896): 457–464; *Report of the Intercolonial Conference of 1883*, 8, cited in Stephen P. Shortus, " 'Colonial Nationalism': New South Welsh Identity in the Mid-1880s," *Journal of the Royal Australian Historical Society* 59 (1973): 32, 37, 47–49.

34. Correspondence with the Colonial Office and the Royal Society, August 1895–February 1896, Adm 1/7265. Wharton was instrumental in obtaining the surveying vessel and virtually drafted Admiralty policy on the expedition, specifically diverting the *Penguin* from competing telegraph cable work (Wharton to Admiralty, minuting letter to Colonial Office, 17 September 1895). Of the six vessels the navy had available for survey work, the *Penguin* had severe limitations, but she was the right size (1,130 tons, crew of 117) and in the right place (see Vice Admiral Boyle Somerville, *The Chart Makers* [Edinburgh: Blackwood, 1928]). Captain Field (1855–1950) ultimately succeeded Wharton as hydrographer in 1904, became an FRS in 1905, and was promoted to rear admiral in 1906. During the 1914–1918 war, Slee served in the AIF's Tunnelling Corps. J. S. Gardiner (1872–1946) became an FRS in 1908 and later professor of zoology at Cambridge. Charles Hedley became a principal keeper in the Australian Museum.

35. David Papers, box 1, p. 11, Sydney University Archives. The scientific papers began a running commentary on what had become the subject of the season. Cf. *Nature* 53 (9 January 1876): 225. As W. W. Watts observed, "The necessity for an investigation into the submarine structure of a coral reef is so well known to the readers of *Nature,* that it is unnecessary to enter into any minute particulars," ("Boring a Coral Reef at Funafuti," *Nature* 54 [July 1896]: 201–202).

36. Bonney to Sollas, 10 December 1896, 14 June 1896, Sollas Papers. Sollas thought the expedition's failure would end his chances of appointment to the recently vacated chair of geology at Oxford. But Bonney counseled patience: "though the first game has been lost there is still time to win the rubber!" (Bonney to Mrs. Sollas, 26 August 1896, Sollas Papers).

37. David called the expedition a "complete failure" in "all but its main object, the boring." In view of the expense, he added, "it seems a thousand pities that this

work should not be brought to successful issue by the completion of the boring"
(David to Chancellor, 2 February 1897, David Papers). For Lockyer's comment,
see *Nature* 54 (24 September 1896): 517. An interim report by Bonney's committee announced the failure to the British Association at Liverpool in September
1896; at the same time Bonney praised the assistance of the Australians, who
provided the boring tools and workmen (*Report of the 66th Meeting of the British Association for the Advancement of Science, Liverpool (1896)*, 31–41). For
Bonney's comments, see Bonney to Sollas, 23 September 1896, Sollas Papers.
"You had skilled men," he added, "and if they could not succeed who can blame
you?"

38. Bonney to Sollas, 10 December 1896, Sollas Papers. Lockyer in the meantime urged a full report on the successful collecting aspect of the expedition. See
Nature 55 (5 November 1896): 12.

39. W. J. Sollas, "Report . . . ," *Proceedings of the Royal Society* 60 (1896–
1897): 502–512. A version of Sollas's formal report to the Royal Society
appeared in *Nature* on 18 February (*Nature* 55 [1897]: 373–374). However, a
popular account by Sollas, which pleasantly softened the ground, had appeared a
week earlier ("The Legendary History of Funafuti, Ellice Group," *Nature* 55
[1897]: 353–355). In March 1897, Sollas was elected to the chair of geology at
Oxford and moved to the University Museum. Bonney wished him good luck in
the uphill struggle to establish scientific geology at Oxford. "You have felt Dublin
is enervating," he warned, "the town on the Isis is the same" (Bonney to Sollas, 21
March 1897, Sollas Papers).

40. Wharton seized upon Field's hydrographic data to argue that neither Murray's theory of solution nor Darwin's theory of subsidence were necessary, where
the evidence suggested simply that atolls were created by the wearing away of
volcanic islands by waves and currents ("Foundations of Coral Atolls," *Nature* 55
[25 February 1897]: 390–393).

41. Bonney to Sollas, 9 March 1897, Sollas Papers, summarizing correspondence between Sollas and Bonney between 1 February and 6 March 1897.

42. Bonney, Prefatory Note to "Report . . . ," *Proceedings of the Royal Society* 60 (1896–1897): 503. "I think the position of the controlling authority may
make all the difference," he confided. "Suppose the R.S. had been at Sydney
instead of in London. When the first boring failed you . . . would have gone
back and discussed the matter with the purse bearer—a thing of that kind could
not be done by telegraph without ruinous expense. You would have returned
(probably) with new machinery and instruments to stay another month . . ."
(Bonney to Sollas, 24 January 1897, Sollas Papers). The Royal Society, he
pointed out (20 January 1897) had now come to accept that Britain was too distant; and that the project could succeed only if the "Sydney people undertook the
charge and we cooperated by giving some money help." However, if the society
did this, they could "hardly demand to nominate the leader" (24 January 1897).

43. On Agassiz's proposal, see Bonney to Sollas, 6 March 1897, Sollas Papers.
Earlier, Bonney counselled: "Between different nationalities, anything of that
kind is apt to be a difficult and delicate matter . . ." (28 January 1897). Infor-
mally he had reservations about the "scientific courtesy" of Australians that
scarcely do credit to his public responses.

44. In December 1896 and February 1897, owing to what appeared to be con-

flicting instructions, Charles Hedley had published his data in two parts through the Australian Museum, thereby breaking the convention that guaranteed the Royal Society right of prior publication. Sollas was outraged, and Michael Foster threatened a cessation of relations. When it was revealed that Sollas was at least in part to blame, the breach was repaired by Anderson Stuart with the help of Edgeworth David, and Foster agreed to withdraw British objections (Correspondence, 11 March–30 July 1897, Australian Museum Archives, R.15/97). Hedley's work eventually appeared in four parts as: *The Atoll of Funafuti, Ellice Group: Its Zoology, Botany, Ethnology and General Structure* (Sydney: Australian Museum), Memoir 3, 1896–1900. It was reviewed in *Nature* 58 (1896): 221–222.

45. For David's comments, see David to Chancellor, 2 February 1897, David Papers, box 2. Virtually every fortnight from March to June 1897, *Nature* published letters and articles on Funafuti, the expedition, and the atoll question. Bonney's invitation to the Australians was conveyed by Archibald Liversidge, Sydney University's professor of chemistry and archbroker of imperial science. Liversidge, as trustee of the Australian Museum, acted as Sydney's representative during his study leave in England in 1896. When he returned to Australia in January 1897 he continued in this capacity—approving, for example, the correspondence concluding Sydney's "case" versus the Royal Society in the Hedley affair (Liversidge Minute, 2 September 1897, Australian Museum Archives, R.37/97). The mediating influence of such men forms a vital, if neglected, chapter in Anglo-Australian scientific relations.

46. David to Chancellor, 2 February 1897, David Papers, box 2.

47. Under David's instruction, a special boring rig was devised weighing twenty-five tons and capable of boring to a depth of one thousand feet. His equipment included duplicate parts, and his team was double the number needed to work the drills in nontropical climates. The expedition sailed in the SS *Tavuni* to Suva, thence by the sloop *Maori* to Funafuti. With David went his wife, George Sweet, FGS, of Melbourne, and two students—W. Poole and W. G. Woolnough, of Sydney. The LMS schooner *John Williams* brought the Davids home in September. David secured £800 from private sources. The Walker and Abercromby families of Sydney contributed £500, the Royal Society contributed a further £200, and David himself contributed £100 to cover his own expenses and his replacement teaching at the university. The government of New South Wales contributed £400 to cover the wages of the drilling foremen, and the minister of mines granted the use of a diamond drill. The Admiralty agreed to assist with the return voyage in September (David to G. H. Reid, Premier of NSW, 15 March 1897, David Papers). The Davids' skill in both rescuing the operation and winning the cordial assistance of native chiefs and workers is sensitively treated in their daughter's account of the expedition: *Professor David: The Life of Sir Edgeworth David* (London: Edward Arnold, 1937), chap. 4, "Funafuti."

48. *Hermes* 3 (28 October 1897): 5–6.

49. Judd was the "analytical" member of the Coral Reef Committee; whether he was uniquely equipped to assess the samples, given the existence of Sydney's new School of Mines, is open to question. Almost certainly, his participation was considered necessary as a neutral referee.

50. *Hermes* 3 (30 November 1897): 8–11; ibid. 4 (29 October 1898): 8–11.

See M. Hoare, "The Intercolonial Science Movement in Australia, 1870–1890," *Records of the Australian Academy of Science* 3, no. 2 (1976): 22–23; R. Mac-Leod, "The Organization of Science under the Southern Cross," in MacLeod, *The Commonwealth of Science.*

51. *Times,* 4 October 1897; *Nature* 56 (7 October 1897): 549. The *Daily Telegraph* (4 October 1897) contrasted the failure of Sollas with David's Australian success and described in detail the case attending the expedition, its choice of seasons, and its desire to build on the work of the earlier expedition. David's team managed to go through the sand and drift that had stopped Sollas (*Daily Telegraph,* 15 October 1897).

52. Bonney, as vice chairman of the Coral Reef Committee, communicated David's report to the Royal Society, 25 November 1897. See "Coral Boring at Funafuti," *Nature* 55 (9 December 1897): 137–138. Bonney sent a similar caveat to the British Association in Bristol. See *Report of the 68th Meeting, British Association for the Advancement of Science* (Bristol, 1898), 886–887. For Bonney's response, see Bonney to Sollas, 30 November 1897, Sollas Papers. He described David as "the most industrious of men" and was glad Sollas had "kept silence." Gardiner's view was reported in *Nature* 57 (24 March 1898): 502; cf. "Fourth International Congress of Zoologists," *Nature* 58 (1 September 1898). Bonney thought this hypothesis would "take a good deal of proving," and hoped Gardiner's zeal for publicity would give way to "silence . . . for the future" (Bonney to Sollas, 28 March 1898, Sollas Papers). For David's account, see address to Section C, *Report AAAS* (Sydney, 1898), reprinted in "The Australasian Association," *Nature* 57 (24 March 1898): 495: "Opinions amongst scientific men in Great Britain as to the conclusions to be drawn from the Funafuti bores were at present divided. While the advocates of the Darwinian theory were inclined to congratulate themselves upon the results, Dr. Murray's supporters say that the evidence substantiates their views."

53. Third Coral Boring Expedition, 1897, David Papers, box 2.

54. David Papers, box 1. Finckh's party was conveyed to Samoa by the SS *Ovalan,* and from Apia to Funafuti by the *John Williams.* Bores were taken both on land and in the lagoon. HMS *Porpoise,* under Captain Sturdee, succeeded in mooring so that the boring pipes could descend to unprecedented depths. In the meantime, E. C. Andrews and B. Sawyer of Sydney University were exploring the raised coral reefs of Fiji on behalf of Agassiz of Harvard. Both reported to David. The *Daily Telegraph* (Sydney) closely monitored dispatches from the expedition, as did the British scientific press. See "News," *Natural Science* 13 (July 1898): 68, 71.

55. The boring had at this time reached a depth of 987 feet on land and 144 feet (245 feet below sea level) in the lagoon ("Recent Coral Boring Operations at Funafuti," *Nature* 59 [3 November 1898]: 22–23). When Bonney received information from David on 6 September, borings were continuing. "But what has been already accomplished," Bonney wrote, "will be an immense addition to our knowledge of atolls" (*Nature* 59 [10 November 1898]: 29). According to the *Standard,* "The result is of great importance; for it seems fatal to the hypothesis that the lagoon is enlarged by the corrosive action of the water on the calcareous material of the reef [Murray's view]" (31 December 1898, p. 6). This entry may

have been written by Bonney, who was earning extra money by writing for the *Standard* at the time. See Bonney to Sollas, 29 September 1897, Sollas Papers.

56. David's nomination stated that he "superintended and conducted to a successful issue" the Funafuti expeditions. See Royal Society Candidates' Book (1900). Cf. Mawson's account in *Obituary Notices of Fellows of the Royal Society of London* 1 (1932–1935): 495. Sollas won the Bigsby Medal in 1891.

57. Mrs. Edgeworth David, *Funafuti, or Three Months on a Coral Island: An Unscientific Account of a Scientific Expedition* (London: John Murray, 1899). Her ethnography of the islands and the islanders was rather patronizingly reviewed by Bonney in *Nature* 59 (13 April 1899): 554–555; but a highly successful second edition, "abridged for scholars," was published by Pitman and Sons in 1913.

58. Quoted in "Sir Edgeworth David," *The Union Recorder* 6 (8 April 1926): 23.

59. W. J. Sollas, "Funafuti: The Study of a Coral Atoll," *Natural Science* 14 (January 1899): 17–37. Sollas delivered this paper as an evening discourse to the British Association at Bristol in September 1898. As president of Section C (Geology) of the BA at Bradford in 1904, he referred to the wider geological significance of ocean borings. Cf. W. J. Sollas, *The Age of the Earth* (London: Fisher Unwin, 1905). *Nature* (94 [3 December 1914]: 368) reported Sollas's Royal Medal. Twenty-five years later, nearly a page of his official obituary was devoted to the Funafuti expedition, in which his failure seemed acutely observed by contrast with the "enterprise and enthusiasm of . . . David and his colleagues, [who] organized a new expedition which, prepared with machinery and methods to deal with the difficulties, returned to the island, carried the main boring into the atoll over a thousand feet, and put down a subsidiary boring under the water of the lagoon" (A. Smith Woodward and W. Watt, "W. J. Sollas," *Obituary Notices of Fellows of the Royal Society of London* [1936–1938] [London: Royal Society, 1939], 2:270).

60. For the final report, see Coral Reef Committee, *The Atoll of Funafuti: Borings into a Coral Reef and the Results* (London: Royal Society, 1904); cf. "The Secret of the Atolls," *Times Literary Supplement,* 22 April 1904 (quotations); "Borings into a Coral Reef," *Nature* 69 (1904): 582–585. Bonney called it a "heavy job," and left for a Mediterranean cruise. "I am curious to know how the Murray School will deal with it," he confided (Bonney to Sollas, 29 February 1904, Sollas Papers). Cf. C. Hedley, "The Formation of Coral Reefs," *Nature* 70 (1904): 391.

61. Sollas, "Funafuti," 37.

62. Ibid. An anonymous reviewer in *Nature* (69 [1904]: 582, 585) observed that "little modern scientific work shows a better record of determination and thoroughness than this," and summarized the biological as well as the geological data derived. But he went no further than to say that the report "adds immensely to our knowledge of the possible means of the formation of coral reefs, and shows that subsidence may have at any rate played a dominant part in the formation of Funafuti."

63. *TLS,* 22 April 1904. The report ably summarized Bonney's philosophy of "judicial fairness" (see "Eminent Living Geologists: The Rev. T. G. Bonney,"

Geological Magazine, n.s. 8 [September 1901], 343), but it said nothing to advance the position Bonney had stated in his appendix to the third (1889) edition of Darwin's *Coral Reefs*. The *Geological Magazine* spoke of Bonney's earlier refusal to accept uncritically arguments advanced for glacier action by the "so-called Uniformitarian School" (391), which "in its neglect of quantitative reasoning was content for the most part to discover tendencies, without proceeding to inquire whether these were sufficient or continued far enough to produce the effect they were supposed to explain." His biographer records, however, that Bonney never shrank from controversy, and had "but little reason to regret it" (393).

64. Davis, *Coral Reef Problem*, 75; E. W. Skeats, "The Coral-Reef Problem and the Evidence of the Funafuti Borings," *American Journal of Science*, 4th ser., vol. 45 (February 1918): 82. Davis believed it unfortunate that the British and Australian borings had been made on the atoll reef where the supposed volcanic foundation was deepest, instead of "on a shoal near the lagoon centre, below which the foundation probably lies nearer the sea surface" (Davis, *Coral Reef Problem*, 514).

65. Davis, *Coral Reef Problem*, 514.

66. Bonney to Sollas, 28 March 1898, Sollas Papers.

67. See David's lecture to the Sydney Technical College Association, "Coral Islands and the Recent Expedition to Funifuti [sic]," *Australian Technical Journal* 4 (30 November 1900): 294–297.

68. Archibald Geikie, "Charles Darwin as Geologist," *Rede Lecture*, 24 June 1909 (Cambridge: Cambridge University Press, 1909); Frederic Wood-Jones, *Corals and Atolls* (London: Reeve, 1910), 212. At the time, Bonney suggested that Geikie could have at least shown how the final borings and Judd's results were "fatal" to Agassiz and Murray (Bonney to Sollas, 9 July 1909, Sollas Papers). Arguably, he had only himself to blame, for reserving judgment in the Royal Society Report five years earlier.

69. See Reginald A. Daly, "Pleistocene Glaciation and the Coral Reef Problem," *American Journal of Science* 30 (1910): 297–338; Daly, "Problems of the Pacific Islands," ibid. 41 (1916): 153–186; Daly, *The Changing World of the Ice Age* (New Haven, Conn.: Yale University Press, 1934); Steers and Stoddart, "Origin of Fringing Reefs," 31–37. For further theoretical developments, including the "antecedent platform theory" proposed by J. E. Hoffmeister and H. S. Ladd in the 1930s, and for difficulties in reaching an integrated theory, see Steers and Stoddart, "Origin of Fringing Reefs," 37–54.

70. Rosen, *Coral Reefs*, 5.

71. W. M. Davis, "The Small Islands of Almost-Atolls," *Nature* 105 (6 May 1920): 293; H. W. Menard, "Foreward," in C. Darwin, *The Structure and Distribution of Coral Reefs* (Reprint, Berkeley and Los Angeles: University of California Press, 1962), ix. For a sympathetic contemporary assessment, see Sir Gavin de Beer's *Charles Darwin* (London: Thomas Nelson, 1963), chap. 4: "Geological Results of the Voyage of the *Beagle*," 74–75.

72. Rosen, *Coral Reefs*, 521 (quotation), 524.

73. See Martin Rudwick, "The Glacial Theory," *History of Science* 8 (1969): 136–157; and idem, *The Great Devonian Controversy* (Chicago: University of Chicago Press, 1985).

74. Stoddart, "This View of Life," 526.

75. T. G. Bonney, "Presidential Address, Section C," *British Association for the Advancement of Science* (Sheffield, 1910), 34.

76. For its place in the history of imperial science, cf. Roy MacLeod, "Moving Metropolis."

77. See W. M. Davis, *Coral Reef Problem*. At the Pan-Pacific Science Congress held at Sydney in 1923, Edgeworth David met several participants in the controversy, and spoke on coral reefs and submerged platforms. Daly agreed that the glacial control and submerged platform hypotheses were consistent, and Darwin's theory could not easily be accommodated with both. In any case, all reefs could not be explained by one hypothesis alone; an integrated theory was still needed. See *Proceedings* 2 (1923): 1128–1134; cf. D. R. Stoddart, "Coral Reefs: The Last Two Million Years," *Geography* 58 (November 1973): 320–323. The question continues to be of interest: see the provisional program for the Sixteenth Pacific Science Congress, to be held at Seoul in August 1987.

78. The Funafuti expedition was followed by the Australasian Antarctic expedition, 1911–1914; and the BANZARE and imperial geophysical expeditions of the 1920s and 1930s. See Douglas Mawson, "The Unveiling of Australia," *Report of the Australian and New Zealand Association for the Advancement of Science* 22 (Melbourne, 1935): 1–37; B. Butcher, "Science and the Imperial Vision: The Imperial Geophysical Experimental Survey, 1928–1930," *Historical Records of Australian Science* 6 (1984): 31–44. The point is made by C. M. Yonge, "The Royal Society and the Study of Coral Reefs," in M. Sears and D. Merriman, eds., *Oceanography: The Past* (New York: Springer-Verlag, 1981). On David's later journeys, see M. E. David, *Professor David* (London: Edward Arnold, 1932). Edgeworth David received honorary doctorates from Oxford in 1911, Manchester in 1919, and Wales in 1921. During the war, he was mentioned in dispatches, promoted to lieutenant-colonel, and awarded the DSO. He was knighted (KBE) in 1920.

PART III
PACIFIC SCIENCE
IN THE MAKING

8

Organizing Pacific Science:
Local and International Origins of
the Pacific Science Association

PHILIP F. REHBOCK

*I*N August 1920, less than two years after the close of World War
I, Honolulu played host to the First Pan-Pacific Science Conference. One hundred and three participants, from as far away as
New England, New Zealand, the Philippines, and the United
Kingdom, assembled for three weeks of papers, field excursions,
and camaraderie. The first conference was so successful that its
organizers resolved to hold a second within three year's time. Melbourne and Sydney were chosen as joint sites for the Second Pan-
Pacific Science Congress, held in August 1923. The number of
participants had grown to 580, and the countries represented
increased to sixteen.[1]

With a pattern of success now emerging, congress advocates
began to think that a modest but permanent institutional structure
was necessary to ensure efficient congress planning. A constitution
was drafted calling for an association of member countries, each
represented by its national academy, research council, or other scientific institution of recognized national stature. With the approval of this constitution at the third congress in Tokyo (1926), the
Pacific Science Association (hereafter PSA) was born.

PSA is now entering its third generation, and its congresses have
been among the most prominent scientific events in the Pacific
region for sixty-five years. Sixty-five may be a common retirement
age for individuals, but PSA, now planning a return to Honolulu
in 1991 for its seventeenth congress shows no signs of senility. The
present volume seems an opportune occasion for examining the

early history of PSA, with a view to determining more precisely the local, national, and international circumstances that brought it into existence, and why, when so many other international and Pan-Pacific schemes of the post–World War I era failed to survive, PSA continues to thrive.

International congresses have been an increasingly prevalent phenomenon in the lives of scientists and other professionals since their inception in the late nineteenth century.[2] For the rest of the world, such events may be a context for intrigue and defection, as purveyed in television thrillers and occasionally in novels; one thinks of Arthur Koestler's *The Call Girls,* for example, in which a neurotic collection of scientists meet at Schneedorf, Switzerland, to discuss "Approaches to Survival."[3] From the viewpoint of the organizers and participants, however, international congresses serve a multitude of perhaps less dramatic but serious purposes. Generally, the overt aims of the participant are to report on new research and solicit advice and criticism prior to formal publication; to learn of developments at the leading edge of one's discipline, or to acquire more general knowledge of peripheral areas (especially for those who are geographically distant or intellectually isolated); and to discuss directions for future research. Other objectives less often mentioned are frequently more prominent. Congresses give opportunities to claim priority in discovery; to reduce unnecessary duplication in research effort; to establish new contacts outside the meeting rooms in the informal networks of the congress;[4] and to surmount the national considerations that surround intellectual work.[5] Finally, they enable scientists to interact as peers with scientists of international stature; and they provide the excitement of travel to a foreign country and escape, if only momentary, from the frustrations of domestic institutions.

It is likely that the participants of the early Pacific science congresses recognized most if not all of these objectives. Later, I will describe some additional motivations—relating especially to the financial support of science—expressed at the first congress. For the moment, however, it is worth noting that from the outset PSA organizers stressed the importance of the congress as a vehicle for addressing the problems of Pacific Islanders, and for promoting peace among Pacific peoples.[6] The political benefits of international scientific cooperation, a common theme of the cold war era and epitomized in the Pugwash Movement,[7] were, in the 1920s, first voiced in the Atlantic community. That these motivations surfaced so early in the Pacific context as well was clearly the result of the unique circumstances that brought about the first congress.

Science and Internationalism Following World War I

One of the well-known legacies of the 1914–1918 war was the fervent hope that new instruments of international cooperation might be forged that would deal peacefully with political and economic disputes and thus prevent future wars. Woodrow Wilson's League of Nations was the most visible, but certainly not the only postwar organization to proclaim the furtherance of international brotherhood among its primary goals. A wave of internationalist sentiment swept the globe and, as we shall see, had an impact in the Pacific as well as the Atlantic. Probably the best known scientific institution to emerge from this era was the International Research Council (predecessor of the International Council of Scientific Unions, hereafter IRC), established in 1919 to promote worldwide cooperation in scientific endeavors. Lingering chauvinism prevented the full realization of the internationalist ideal, however, even among scientists: the Central Powers were prevented from becoming members of the IRC until 1926.[8]

International cooperation in science in the Pacific became an increasingly prominent theme even during the war years. At the Australia meeting of the British Association in 1914, the advantages of a coordinated approach to Pacific research were touted by the prominent Harvard geographer-geomorphologist William Morris Davis (1850–1934).[9] Two years later, in the middle of the war, Davis arranged a "Symposium on Pacific Exploration" at the annual meeting of the U.S. National Academy of Sciences. Davis argued that the eighteenth-century voyages of discovery had employed a "discontinuous and local" method of scientific exploration, while nineteenth-century research in the Pacific had been "continuous and linear." The time had now come for a survey that would be continuous both temporally and geographically: "Discontinuous, local or linear, individual work, economically conducted, cannot, however excellent, compass the immense extent and the infinite variety of that great water hemisphere. Thoroughgoing Pacific exploration will demand most munificent support."[10]

From this symposium emerged the Committee on Pacific Exploration, appointed by the National Academy. After the war, this committee—led by the Berkeley paleontologist John Campbell Merriam (1869–1945), later president of the Carnegie Institution —was tranferred to the newly established National Research Council and its Division of Foreign Relations, and given the new title "Committee on Pacific Investigations." This committee would become one of the leading agencies in the organization of PSA.

Meanwhile, several West Coast exhibitions and conferences were focusing fresh attention on the Pacific region. The opening of the Panama Canal in 1914 was the stimulus for the Panama-Pacific International Exposition in San Francisco the following year. In conjunction with the exposition, historians led by H. Morse Stephens, professor of Pacific history at the University of California, Berkeley, held a Panama-Pacific Historical Congress in San Francisco, Berkeley, and Palo Alto. In his presidential address, Stephens argued that the opening of the canal had begun a major new chapter in Pacific history.[11] Concurrently, at the American Association for the Advancement of Science (AAAS) meeting in San Francisco, Reginald A. Daly (1871–1957), Davis's geological successor at Harvard, delivered a lengthy address on "Problems of the Pacific Islands," with suggestions for new exploration.[12] Geologists were clearly among the most vocal advocates of Pacific science in these years.

Pacific issues continued prominent in California at the 1918 Conference on International Relations (part of the University of California's fiftieth anniversary celebrations), and in 1919 at the new Pacific Division of the AAAS, meeting that year in Pasadena. A major event in Pasadena was a symposium on "The Exploration of the North Pacific Ocean," organized by William E. Ritter, then director of Scripps Institution for Biological Research. Ritter called for an extensive program of research on economic aspects of the biology, oceanography, and meteorology of the North Pacific as the only means of mitigating what he saw as the major problem of the Pacific, namely the inevitable diffusion of Asians across the Pacific to the Americas—the latest chapter in the history of the "yellow peril."[13] Both Ritter and his successor at Scripps, T. Wayland Vaughn, were to be key figures on the Committee on Pacific Investigations and at the early Pacific science congresses, although it would be the topic of Pacific Island depopulation far more than Pacific rim migration that would exercise the congress.

The quickening of Pacific science on the American West Coast during the early decades of this century should also be seen as a stage in the progressive evolution of American science. The American scientific community in the East had reached maturity and increasingly saw itself as equal in energy and intellect, and more than equal in numbers, to its European counterpart.[14] And as this eastern node gained recognition, wealthy patrons aided eager scientists to establish cultural bearings in the Far West. The steadily growing list of scientific institutions on the West Coast—from the Lick Observatory in 1888 and the Mount Wilson Observatory in 1904, to the Scripps Institution in 1912, the Pacific Division of the AAAS in 1914, and the Throop Polytechnic (becoming the California Institute of Technology in 1920)—were symbols of this new western dynamism. Looking even further west, however, we find an even stronger enthusiasm for an international assault on Pacific science in the United States' recently acquired territory of Hawaii.

The circumstances surrounding the First Pan-Pacific Science Conference were decisively shaped by movements for internationalism and science in Honolulu, beginning shortly after the turn of the century. From the 1880s, King Kalakaua and his chief minister, Walter Murray Gibson, had advocated internationalist ventures that would assure the Hawaiian monarchy a central role in the political affairs of the remaining independent native peoples of Polynesia, if not of the entire Pacific, and would, at the same time, rejuvenate the Hawaiians' self-esteem and pride in their own cultural traditions. Moreover, the enduring social myth of Hawaii—the land of paradisal beauty and multicultural harmony—had by this time already taken hold, providing activists with ample rationale for promoting the Islands as, simultaneously, an ideal tourist destination, a logical entrepot of trans-Pacific commercial and naval activities, and the supreme example of racial cooperation to all Pacific nations.[15]

Kalakaua's actions were confined to friendly personal diplomacy with Pacific leaders, but the flamboyant Gibson went so far as to issue a "Monroe Doctrine of the Pacific" in 1883—protesting the annexation of Pacific islands by European powers—and to advocate a federation of Polynesia led from Hawaii.[16] Though Gibson's efforts were unsuccessful, he gave enduring credence to the belief that Hawaii was destined, even obligated, to become involved in affairs far beyond its own shores. These dreams were temporarily forgotten with the ouster of Gibson in 1887 and the demise of the Hawaiian monarchy in 1893, and they gave way to the larger considerations of internal political and economic policy when the Hawaiian republic became a U.S. territory in 1898. But in the next decade, internationalist sentiments reappeared. The leader of this second wave of Hawaiian internationalism, beginning around 1910, was not a veteran of the earlier turbulent years but a newly arrived devotee of island culture and a fresh convert to Hawaii-Pacific internationalist causes.

Alexander Hume Ford (1868–1945) seemed an unlikely candidate to become one of the most colorful and energetic figures of early twentieth-century Hawaiian history. A native of South Carolina, Ford left his parents' rice plantation in 1886 for New York and a career in journalism. The offer of a position with the construction of the Trans-Siberian railway, plus writing assignments for *Harpers* and several other magazines, took him to Siberia in 1899, with a one-day stopover in Hawaii. Anxious to experience the islands at greater length, Ford returned as journalist with a congressional fact-finding party in May 1907, and from then until 1935 Honolulu remained his home base.[17]

At first, Ford occupied himself principally with efforts to expand Hawaii's young tourist industry, but tourism gradually merged with schemes to increase social contact among Hawaii's many racial groups and at the same time promote interracial harmony on a Pacific-wide basis. In 1908 Ford was appointed to the governor's Territorial Transportation Committee to effect tourism arrangements with Australia and New Zealand. In 1911 this committee evolved into a luncheon group, the Hands-Around-the-Pacific Club, following Honolulu's first Pan-Pacific conference (which dealt with tourism, commerce, and immigration).[18] The club became the Pan-Pacific Union in 1917, the most powerful and enduring of Ford's innovations.

Modeled consciously upon, and with assistance from, the Pan-American Union, the Pan-Pacific Union took as its charge the improvement of relations among the peoples of the countries within and bordering on the Pacific. Ford conjured up a seemingly endless agenda for the union: bureaus of information to distribute educational materials in each Pacific country; large dioramas to depict Pacific culture; a Pan-Pacific exposition and other, local fairs to exhibit native products and handicrafts; a Pan-Pacific Commercial Museum and Art Gallery in Honolulu; even a permanent college for "training men in [the] commercial knowledge of Pacific lands."[19] Ford hoped, in his own words, to see created a true "Patriotism of the Pacific" in this "Great Theater of the World's Commerce."[20] And Hawaii was to provide both leadership and example.

The course of Ford's various ventures was well documented in his monthly journal, *Mid-Pacific Magazine*. Begun in 1910, *Mid-Pacific* was at first largely a travel guide, its articles celebrating the enchanting physical beauties of Hawaii and other Pacific tourist destinations. By 1915, however, Ford's increasing activities in international relations had transformed the magazine. It now emphasized Hawaii's centrality in the political and commercial affairs of the Pacific, with a rationale based not merely on geographic location but on its rich racial and cultural blend. If, as Ford argued, harmony among the races could exist in Hawaii, the microcosm, could it not exist among the peoples of the entire Pacific region? The best insurance for peace in the Pacific community was, he thought, cross-cultural understanding: every country, every people, must become acquainted with the customs and objectives of every other.[21]

The keystone, and in the end the most successful, of the Pan-Pacific Union's plans was a series of international conferences intended to bring together delegates from all Pacific nations, generally to be held in Honolulu, the "cross-roads of the Pacific," as Ford loved to call it. The first of these conferences was none other than our First Pan-Pacific Science Conference of 1920.[22]

The Pacific Scientific Institution

Ford's 1920 conference was not the first attempt to launch a coordinated research effort in Pacific science from a Hawaiian base. That prize must go to the elusive and ill-fated Pacific Scientific Institution (PSI), incorporated in Honolulu in 1907. Although Ford arrived in Hawaii that year, he seems to have had no direct connection with PSI, the brainchild of William Alanson Bryan, Jr. (1875–1942), ornithological curator of Honolulu's Bernice P. Bishop Museum, and of the museum's first director, William T. Brigham (1841–1926). At the age of twenty-four, Bryan had been sent to Hawaii to survey the Hawaiian fauna for the U.S. Department of Agriculture. Possibly as early as 1905 he had became convinced of the necessity for a major survey of all the Pacific islands, to include ethnography and geology as well as zoology and botany.[23]

At first Bryan worked closely on the survey plan with Brigham —in fact, much of the original concept may have been Brigham's. He wrote a paper entitled "Shall We Explore the Pacific Islands Now?" which he evidently intended to deliver at the inaugural meeting of the American Association of Museums, held in New York in May 1906.[24] But finding himself unable to attend the meeting, Brigham sent Bryan to read the paper and at the same time forwarded advance copies to a number of influential colleagues, requesting that their reactions be sent to Bryan in New York. Responses to the Bryan-Brigham plan were highly supportive, and Bryan went ahead with the drafting of a charter, naming himself president of PSI with Brigham as honorary or consulting director. Several additional organizations were proposed to support the survey: a marine biological laboratory, a zoological garden and aviary, and a "garden of acclimatization." Financial support soon began to arrive. In June 1906 C. M. Cooke of Castle and Cooke, one of Hawaii's "Big Five" sugar entrepreneurs, promised sugar bonds worth possibly one hundred thousand dollars, the interest from which was to finance the biological laboratory. Support for other projects followed.[25]

By November, however, relations between Bryan and Brigham had deteriorated. The precise cause is unknown, but the two seem to have been at odds over both the scale and focus of the intended survey. Brigham was concerned that ethnographic data be collected before it was too late, whereas Bryan envisaged a much broader program, one of natural history investigation. Moreover, Bryan, the aggressive thirty-one-year-old curator, had apparently become an annoyance to his sixty-six-year-old superior, who was irritated by Bryan's assumption of the leading role in PSI.[26] On 6 November Brigham advised Bryan (in an interview the substance of which was later contested) that the Bishop Museum could not assume support of the survey, nor would he (Brigham) allow himself to be designated honorary director. The following summer Bryan's contract as curator at the museum was not renewed. The museum trustees thanked him cordially for his services but gave no explanation for terminating his employment.

Over the next two years Bryan devoted much of his time to the promotion of PSI and its survey. By late 1907 the institution was formally incorporated in accordance with the laws of Hawaii, and a board of trustees was assembled consisting of Bryan and fourteen of Hawaii's most prominent business and judicial leaders. At the end of the year Bryan read a paper outlining the aims of PSI before the zoological section of the AAAS at its meeting in Chicago. The exploring expedition was to be the centerpiece of PSI's program:

> The present plan for field work [Bryan explained] is to acquire an especially equipped yacht of from five to seven hundred tons capacity, which will be provided with sails as well as oil-burning engines, and fitted with the necessary accommodations for fifteen scientific men, including laboratories, field library, storage tanks, etc. This vessel, using Honolulu as a base, and establishing secondary focal points from which to carry on its work, will make cruises to the various groups of islands in the Pacific region. The voyages can be so arranged that the entire ocean, with its more than two thousand islands, may be thoroughly covered in about fifteen excursions. Thus the vast region would be worked over, group by group, with a fully equipped corps of especially trained field scientists; the time required to complete the work, of course, varying with the number and size of the parties in the field. In this way the work and publication on any group as for example on the Society Islands, would be uniform and complete; every department of ethnology and natural history will be treated, both in the field and in the subsequent publication, by a specialist. By reason of a carefully prearranged plan, the study of each island will be made with an understanding of the great ultimate object, namely, knowledge of the Pacific Ocean as a whole. The data thus gathered will always be even and of a comparable character.[27]

Bryan corresponded widely with scientific leaders, from anthropologist E. B. Tylor at Oxford to Stanford University president David Starr Jordan, and by the end of 1908 a thick file of testimonials in support of the program was on hand. One of Bryan's typescripts of this period even refers to the survey as the "James J. Hill Pacific Exploring Expedition," suggesting that he had hopes for financing from the Great Northern Railway magnate. But no further publications were issued, and no additional financing was

forthcoming. Cooke's contribution of sugar bonds had been con-
ditional upon Bryan's finding other funds to support the main survey. In 1909 Bryan accepted an appointment as professor of zoology and geology at the newly established College of Hawaii.
Perhaps these new duties prevented his continued advancement of
PSI; perhaps he had expectations that the college would eventually
take on the institution's mission; or perhaps Brigham convinced
PSI trustees that Bryan's scheme was too grandiose to be managed
and that the Bishop Museum would accomplish many of the same
objectives, given time. In any case, nothing further was heard
of PSI.[28]

Ironically, just as Bryan's dreams of a Pacific-wide research program were fading, Alexander Hume Ford was beginning to con-
ceive his schemes for international brotherhood that would lead to
the Pan-Pacific science conference. Although scientific research
was not initially among Ford's schemes, the notion of promoting
Pacific science through international conferences was certainly in
his mind by 1917 when the Pan-Pacific Union (PPU) was formally
organized. There is unfortunately no known surviving correspondence between Bryan and Ford, but certainly their paths crossed
frequently: Bryan was corresponding secretary of Ford's Hands-
Around-the-Pacific Club in 1912, and he was on hand for the congress in 1920.[29] Moreover, several of the trustees of PSI were
among the founding trustees of Ford's Pan-Pacific Union. Thus it
seems likely that Bryan's focusing of attention on the need for
Hawaii to take the lead in organizing a vigorous and extensive
program of science in the Pacific gave Ford's scientific promotions
a ring of familiarity and helped lubricate the legislative process
when public funds were eventually sought.

The Pan-Pacific Science Conference

From its establishment in 1917, the Pan-Pacific Union's foremost
priority was the arrangement of international conferences in
Hawaii.[30] As World War I ended, PPU was proposing that a Pan-
Pacific commercial and educational congress be held in Honolulu
in two or three years' time. By April 1919 the territorial legislature
had voted ten thousand dollars for this proposal, with the proviso
that at least three other Pacific countries appropriated funds to

send delegates. To plan the conference, Governor Charles J. McCarthy appointed a committee chaired by George P. Denison, general manager of Oahu Railway Company and a founding trustee of the PPU. Denison's committee made the pivotal decision in July that the subject of the first commercial and educational congress should in fact be Pacific science.[31] According to the official call for the conference, "The purpose of the conference is to outline scientific problems of the Pacific Ocean region, and to suggest methods for their solution."[32] This seemingly minor decision on the part of the Denison committee was in reality the germination of the Pacific science congresses and thus of PSA itself. Unfortunately, records do not relate how this decision was reached, nor who among the committee members might have proposed or supported it. Interestingly, however, three of the committee members, former Governor Walter F. Frear, Castle and Cooke director F. C. Atherton, and Bishop Museum trustee Richard H. Trent, had also been trustees of Bryan's Pacific Scientific Institution.[33] Bryan's aspirations had, it seems, not been entirely forgotten.

With the subject for the first Pan-Pacific congress set, Ford traveled to the east coast to win government and philanthropic support for the Pan-Pacific Union's activities. In January 1920 he and other PPU officials convened a meeting in Washington with numerous ministers and trade commissioners of Pacific countries, along with representatives of the Pan-American Union. Among these dignitaries, Dr. Paul Reinsch, the pioneer in international organization and ex-U.S. minister to China (1913–1919), emerged as one of the most vocal advocates of Honolulu-based Pan-Pacific conferences. He was confident that China would support such a movement. He also gave strong backing to one of Ford's long-standing (but ill-starred) objectives: the eventual assumption of control of PPU by the nations of the Pacific.[34]

Ford's east coast junket was successful in at least two respects. Senator Henry Cabot Lodge's Committee on Foreign Relations saw to it that nine thousand dollars was appropriated for Pan-Pacific conferences. And in New Haven, Ford became better acquainted with Herbert E. Gregory, the Yale geologist who would become presiding officer of the Pan-Pacific Scientific Conference, and who would eventually be regarded as the founder of PSA. Gregory (1869–1952) was the eleventh of thirteen children of a modest mid-western family. He took both B.S. and B.A.

degrees from Gates College in Nebraska, tried teaching briefly, then went on to Yale for graduate study in geology. Receiving the doctorate in 1899, Gregory taught at Yale from then until 1920, holding the Silliman chair of geology from 1904 until retirement in 1936.[35]

When William Brigham retired from the Bishop Museum directorship in 1918, the museum trustees asked Gregory to take over the post. Gregory came to Hawaii as acting director in 1919 and surveyed the situation. He was skeptical of giving up his responsibilities in the east and hesitant to abandon his beloved research, the geology of the southwestern states.[36] But his appetite for the Pacific had been whetted in 1915 by a trip to Australia and New Zealand; and on the return voyage he had visited Hawaii, where a group of former Yale students impressed upon him the great potential for significant scientific research in the Pacific. It was decided that he would teach at Yale during the fall term, then go to Hawaii to direct activities at the Bishop Museum from January until the summer, returning to the east by way of his research sites in Utah and Colorado.

Gregory quickly became one of the most eloquent advocates of coordinated, cooperative research in the Pacific. He had been active in the establishment of the National Research Council (NRC) in 1916, and was chairman of its Committee on Pacific Investigations by 1919, a position he held until 1946. The committee had been anxious to arrange an international gathering of Pacific scientists, with the purpose of establishing a priority listing of research problems in the region. When in June 1919 the Denison committee was formed to lay plans for the first educational and commercial congress, Gregory's name immediately appeared on the list of committee members. It is entirely possible, therefore, that Gregory prevailed upon the Denison committee to make the first Pan-Pacific congress a scientific one. Direct evidence of his influence is lacking, but the circumstances suggest that the new director of the Bishop Museum would have had an active voice on the committee. Once the committee agreed that science would be the focus, they requested (through the museum trustees) that Gregory take charge of organizing the congress.[37]

With the advice of the NRC Committee on Pacific Investigations, whose members then included Davis and Daly of Harvard and Ritter of Scripps,[38] Gregory assembled a program and a list of scientists to be invited. Additional financial support was contributed by Australia and New Zealand ($3000), and China ($1000), bringing the total governmental allocations for the conference to twenty-three thousand dollars.

Ford and the Pan-Pacific Union were delighted to have Gregory take the lead in organizing the conference. To Ford it signaled that the ideals of his Pan-Pacific movement had been acknowledged by scientists of national stature. In January 1920 Ford wrote to Governor McCarthy from Washington where he was lobbying for additional conference support: "Until Dr. Gregory came into the movement I have never had the cooperation of any really big man who would give his time to the work. Dr. Gregory is a wonder, it is a supreme privilege to work with such a man. I believe he is a firm friend and a believer in my methods of work, he taking up where I leave off. . . ."[39] Arrangements for the congress proceeded smoothly, with one exception. In May, just three months before the congress was to open, the U.S. State Department informed Ford that it had received no official invitation, and thus the United States could not recognize the existence of the congress nor appoint delegates to it—an embarrassing situation, especially if the organizing chairman, Gregory, was himself to be a delegate from the United States. Eventually the muddle was clarified by having the Pan-Pacific Union issue the formal call for the conference while Gregory forwarded to Washington the proposed list of U.S. delegates to be invited by the State Department.[40]

That such a situation could arise, however, suggests that there may well have been a void, in communication if not in understanding, at the point where the ever-optimistic visions of Ford were translated into the practical organizing functions of Gregory. Ford's modus operandi was that of the conceptualizer, not the administrator; he was constantly creating a new scheme, then trying to place it in the hands of others for execution so that he could be free to move on to the next scheme. After all the effort he had invested in bringing about the first scientific congress, he had little interest in attending it himself. When the congress got underway in August, Ford was conducting a congressional tour through the Orient.

There are few hints indicating how Ford and Gregory, the two most important figures behind the congress, got on in later years, but what evidence there is suggests that relations were not always cordial. In 1921 Ford created the Pan-Pacific Research Council, with William Brigham as its chairman,[41] to discuss possible projects in applied science, especially agriculture. The council evolved, in 1924, into the more viable Pan-Pacific Research Institute, a mini–think tank and gathering place for visiting scientists and students, with an oceanographic focus.[42] Ford had little interest in scientific knowledge, however, except that which might be immediately applied to human problems in the Pacific. In 1925 he asked Gregory for assistance should matters of pure science come before the Pan-Pacific Union: "we may [Ford wrote] be dragged into pure science once in awhile when it is our desire not to delve deeper than economic science."[43] But later the same year the two became embroiled briefly in a battle over who should take the credit for organizing the 1920 conference.[44] One suspects their strong, divergent personalities led them to respect but avoid one another.

The 1920 congress may have been the smallest of the Pacific science congresses,[45] but in terms of scientific content and resolutions, cooperative spirit, pageantry, and camaraderie, it lacked nothing. Scientific sessions concentrated on ocean currents, Hawaiian flora and fauna, race relations, animal distribution in the Pacific, geographical and geological mapping, seismology and volcanology, the training of scientists for work in the Pacific, and scientific institutions around the Pacific and their history. Among the participants, curiously, were our two earlier antagonists, Bryan and Brigham. Bryan, now living in Los Angeles and soon to become director of the Los Angeles County Museum, had just returned from explorations along the Central and South American coasts to Easter and Juan Fernandez islands; he spoke on the origins of the Hawaiian flora and fauna. Brigham gave one of the opening-day addresses, on Hawaiian anthropology; and in a later anthropological section meeting, harking back to those PSI hopes of 1906 he spoke on "plans for an extended exploration of the Pacific."[46]

With a view to imparting a distinct impetus to future Pacific research, the congress passed some thirty-nine resolutions. These resolutions specified that, inter alia, governments be urged to support survey ships for Pacific exploration; geological surveys be conducted of Easter Island, the Hawaiian Islands, and islands of eastern Fiji; the Pacific Ocean bottom be mapped more accurately and magnetic surveys underway be completed; new permanent volcano observatories be set up around the Pacific and a meteorological station for upper air studies be erected on Mauna Loa; a comprehensive survey of Pacific fisheries be instigated; surveys of fauna and flora be conducted, especially on small islands where extinction might be imminent and in areas where there had recently been volcanic activity; the origins of Pacific Island peoples, especially the Polynesians, be pursued; and, finally, that the governor of Hawaii take action to create a permanent organization for the advancement of Pacific science.[47] Four years later, when the second congress had concluded and plans were being laid for a third, Gregory proudly reported: "The resolutions adopted are not generalized statements of obvious possibilities in the advancement of science; they relate to urgent, well-defined pieces of work within the scope and means of the institutions and government bureaus concerned. Most of the investigations called for by the Honolulu Conference have been completed or are in progress. . . ."[48]

The first congress had moments of majesty and mirth. Plenary sessions were held in the throne room and executive chamber of Iolani Palace (the Executive Office Building since the overthrow of the monarchy). During the second week the congress party moved to the island of Hawaii where delegates made the trek to Kilauea volcano, fortunately active. Strictly social activities included a dinner at the venerable Moana Hotel hosted by Governor McCarthy, and an after-dinner one-act play in four "scenes": Eocene, Miocene, Pliocene, and Obscene—demonstrating once again that the geologists were in control of things.

The spirit of the first congress was probably best preserved in the following poem, read at the congress after the delegates' visit to the volcano district of Kilauea. Apparently penned by Henry S. Washington, geologist of the Carnegie Institute, it is entitled "Pele to the Pan-Pacifics" (a reply from the volcano goddess Pele to her visitors).

> I've heard of many a conference in my day,
>   Aloha to the first upon this spot.
> All delegates are queer—I've heard men say—
>   But these must be the queerest of the lot.
> They raise the ocean floor from 'neath its ooze
>   To make a bridge for slimy snails to tread;
> Eat poi, and drink okolehao booze;
>   Or snatch the very hair from off my head.

They are botanists, zoologists, or wuss;
    They're bald, or bear long, shaggy, silver hair;
They speak in words more syllabled than Russ;
    Of everything on earth, in sea or air.

They're flirting with my shy endemic plants;
    Or hunting fierce achatinellid snails;
There's one who can the hula hula dance,
    One looks for blue-green algae 'long the trails.
Some chase the corals o'er the craggy reefs
    Where "papa hee nalus" dot the foam;
They argue whether Melanesian chiefs
    In Mayflower-laden boats came to my home.
Pan-Pacific is a versatile old boy—
    He'll talk on anything you wish,
From plankton to the ropy pa hoehoe;
    From Polynesian races down to fish.

There's one who is the only man who kens
    How pahoehoe is different from aa;
Another, by the zigzags of some pens,
    Can spot a typhoon leagues outside the bar.
There's one who says his prayers in pure Fiji,
    Another writes on "Useful Pants of Guam,"
A third just longs for sweet tranquilitee,
    A fourth drives off leaf hoppers from the farm.
Anthropologist, geodesist, or such,
    You've trod my lumpy aa lava plain,
You've felt my liquid sunshine's gentle touch—
    We kamaainas know you'll come again.

Hawaii Nei's done her trade-wind freshened best
    To make your stay a dream of sheer delight—
A red-stoned, golden-lettered, spell of rest
    Along your path of learning all in sight.
So here's to you, Pan-Pacific,
    As you leave my fair Hawaii—
Though your pidgin's scientific
    I sure hate to say good-bye
Aloha! Pan-Pacific!
    As you sail across the blue,
From the islands beatific
    Pele's best regards to you.[49]

Figure 11. "Giving Hawaii the Scientific Once Over," newspaper cartoon, 20 August 1920. (Courtesy of Bishop Museum, Pacific Science Congress Scrapbook)

In the final days of the congress, symposia were conducted on "Means and Methods of Cooperation" and "Training Scientists for Pacific Work." Remarks made by participants in these symposia demonstrate that they valued the congress for reasons that go well beyond those outlined at the beginning of this chapter. First, here was the hope that the work of the congress would persuade scientists' home governments to take a more serious interest in the support of science. For example, John Henderson, zoologist for the U.S. National Museum of Natural History, advocated the passage of a resolution that would aid the museum in obtaining funding from Congress to work up existing Pacific collections. Similarly, Henry C. Richards, professor of geology at the University of Queensland, argued that the influence of Australian universities had not been sufficient to persuade the government to establish fellowships for research in Pacific islands. But "if we can go home from the Conference and absolutely convince the Commonwealth government that it is their job to carry out this work, it will be of considerable help." Josephine Tilden, professor of botany at the University of Minnesota, hoped that the congress would recommend to universities that fellowships for study in the Pacific be established in scientific departments. And J. Allan Thomson, geologist and director of the Dominion Museum, Wellington, complained that "a prophet has no honor in his own country. . . . We find it sometimes very hard, although we make out a very good case, to get the Government to act, and for that reason we always welcome any external pressure. For instance, if any suggestion comes from official circles in London it is acted upon at once, whereas we may have been advocating the same thing for years without the least response."[50]

Sometimes the problem was not the allocation of new funds to science but a reprogramming of existing funds. C. M. Fraser, director of the biological station at Nanaimo, British Columbia, pointed out that the emphasis in Canadian scientific funding was toward the Atlantic; and until there was a reorientation toward the Pacific, the institutions on the west coast would have to provide assistance to each other and solicit the cooperation of their counterparts around the Pacific. Another proposal came from T. C. Frye of the Puget Sound Biological Station, who asked that the congress recommend to the governments concerned that fares for shipboard travel in the Pacific be reduced for scientists en route to and from research sites.[51]

Finally, participants spoke repeatedly of the value of the congress in facilitating cooperation among individual scientists, a factor especially crucial in Pacific research. Herbert Gregory summed this up well, emphasizing that Pacific problems are often too large and entail too many specialties to be effectively treated by scientists working independently.

> Discussions during this Conference have shown clearly that the scientific problems of the Pacific are not one-man jobs. They are either too complex to be grasped by one mind or require masses of data impossible to be obtained even by a Methuselah. Such problems as we have discussed here can be successfully attacked only by cooperative effort and that on a generous scale. Whether or not we like the feeling, we might as well humbly recognize that problems whose significance justify a lifetime of devoted effort, are too big for one man or for one institution.[52]

Pacific science was, from the outset, Big Science.

From Congress to Association

As the congress drew to a close, arrangements were made with the Bishop Museum to publish the proceedings and to act as an interim representative of the delegates until the next congress. A committee of six, chaired by Gregory, was appointed to make preparations for a second Pan-Pacific congress. The committee itself was not funded or formally empowered to call a second meeting, but the members of the committee could exert influence on their respective governments and national academies of science. This strategy proved its soundness when committee member E. C. Andrews, chief of the New South Wales Geological Survey, convinced geologist Sir Edgeworth David and chemist Sir David Orme Masson that the second congress should be held in Australia. Masson, then president of the Australian National Research Council, presided over the second Congress, held in Melbourne and Sydney in August and September 1923.

During the general meeting at Sydney, a permanent organization was proposed and an international organization committee representing each of the participating countries was formed to draw up a constitution. The resulting document was approved with minimal changes at the third congress (Tokyo) on 11 November 1926, marking the official beginning of the Pacific Science Association.[53]

Whereas the first congress had depended heavily on personal contacts and had a very local, unofficial flavor, the second and subsequent congresses had their basis in government agencies and formal scientific institutions.[54] Scientific cooperation was increasingly seen as a vehicle for improving international relations and preserving peace in the Pacific region. This became evident in the opening addresses of the Australia meeting and was formalized in article 2 of the constitution: "The main object of the Association shall be . . . to strengthen the bonds of peace among Pacific peoples by promoting a feeling of brotherhood among the scientists of all the Pacific countries."[55]

The formal establishment of PSA was not seen as a license to set up a large administrative structure. In fact, Gregory and others insisted that the burden of administration be assumed by the nation (and especially its national research council) hosting the next congress. The only standing body was to be the Pacific Sci-

Figure 12. Sir Edgeworth David and Australian fauna greet delegates to the Second Pan-Pacific Science Congress, Australia, August 1923. Cartoon by Hal Eyre Sen, in the *Daily Telegraph,* Sydney. (Courtesy of University of Sydney Archives, M. 123)

ence Council, composed of representatives from the ten to fifteen most active nations. Two decades later, Gregory could still proclaim happily that the association had "no president, no secretary, no auditor, no editor, no membership list and handled no funds."[56] But by 1949 the need for greater administrative continuity had become apparent, and at the seventh congress (New Zealand), the constitution was amended to create a permanent secretariat with an executive secretary. The secretariat was charged primarily with distributing Pacific scientific information, storing the records of the association, and providing assistance to institutions and individuals in carrying out the resolutions of the congresses.

Because PSA's focus was on the prosperity and problems of a particular geographic region, its congresses differed markedly in their organization from the meetings of typical national associations for the advancement of science. Individual contributions were organized not into sections by scientific speciality but into thematic symposia that were often interdisciplinary. Standing committees of scientists, sanctioned by the constitution to organize cooperative research, also reflected the problem-oriented, interdisciplinary nature of the association's interests.[57] Both the structure and the focus of these standing committees have been in constant flux because of changes in Pacific problems and because of the regular turnover of host countries charged with determining the symposia of the next congress. Such a system would seem chaotic in the short run, but in the long run it seems to have contributed substantially to the organization's adaptiveness.[58]

The First Pan-Pacific Science Conference was a product of two independent movements, backed by the energies of two quite different personalities. For over thirty years, Alexander Hume Ford was untiring in his promotion of a Hawaii-centered Pacific brotherhood of nations, eagerly latching onto any approach toward that end, science included. Herbert Gregory and his associates of the NRC Committee on Pacific Investigations saw the Pacific as a vast arena for scientific research. In spite of expeditions from Cook to *Challenger,* knowledge of the Pacific was still fragmentary. Moreover, there was an urgency in this research: human problems required solutions, and surveys of Pacific ethnography and natural history were needed before the data were lost for all time. The union of Ford's internationalism and Gregory's scientism created a durable organization in the 1920s, one that would pride itself on solid achievements and a progressive outlook, while on the other side of the world Europeans were mourning "the decline of the West."

Notes

The need for a historical study of the early Pacific Science Association was first suggested to me by Anne Pedersen, chairman of PSA's Committee on Scientific Communication and Education, and I thank her for opening up a new world to me. I am exceedingly grateful to the trustees of the Bernice P. Bishop Museum for permission to quote from the Herbert E. Gregory Papers, and to Cynthia Timberlake and her staff at the Bishop Museum library for their enthusiasm in making those and other papers available for my use. I am also very much indebted to Brenda Bishop, general secretary of the Pacific Science Association, for generously supplying me with materials from the PSA Archives. Finally, I am especially thankful that Roy MacLeod, in a late night conversation at his home in Sussex, convinced me that I should postpone other urgent research projects in order to take up Pacific science history.

1. A. P. Elkin, *Pacific Science Association: Its History and Role in International Cooperation,* Bernice P. Bishop Museum (hereafter BPBM) Special Publication 48 (Honolulu: Bishop Museum Press, 1961). See also Secretariat of the Pacific Science Council, *Report on the Pacific Science Association,* BPBM Special Publication 41 (Honolulu: Bishop Museum, 1951).

2. Brigitte Schroeder-Gudehus, "Science, Technology and Foreign Policy," in Ina Spiegel-Rösing and Derek de Solla Price, eds., *Science, Technology and Society: A Cross-Disciplinary Perspective* (London: Sage Publications, 1977), 473–506. Perhaps the earliest international scientific congress with an oceanic orientation was the Maritime Conference held in Brussels in 1853, at which ten nations drew up a plan of oceanographic data collection. See Matthew Fontaine Maury, *The Physical Geography of the Sea and Its Meteorology,* ed. John Leighly (Cambridge, Mass.: Harvard University Press, 1963), xi, 5.

3. Arthur Koestler, *The Call Girls* (New York: Dell Publishing, 1973).

4. Although sociologists of science have often stressed the significance of informal communication networks, there has not been as much sociological analysis of scientific meetings, especially at the international level, as one might like. But see William D. Garvey et al., "Research Studies in Patterns of Scientific Communication: II. The Role of the National Meeting in Scientific and Technical Communication," *Information Storage and Retrieval* 8 (1972): 159–169; Bertita E. Compton, "A Look at Conventions and What They Accomplish," *American Psychologist* 21 (1966): 176–183; A. J. Meadows, *Communication in Science* (London: Butterworths, 1974): 121–125; and John Ziman, *The Force of Knowledge* (Cambridge: Cambridge University Press, 1976), 110–112. Of course, the more such meetings an individual attends, the less significant each meeting may

seem, until one approaches the nadir described by John Ziman in *Puzzles, Problems and Enigmas: Occasional Pieces on the Human Aspects of Science* (Cambridge: Cambridge University Press, 1981), 267.

5. See Diana Crane, "Transnational Networks in Basic Science," *International Organization* 25 (1971): 585–601.

6. Constitution of the Pacific Science Association, Article 2b, in *Report on PSA,* 22.

7. Brigitte Schroeder-Gudehus, "Challenge to Transnational Loyalties: International Scientific Organizations after the First World War," *Science Studies* 3 (1973): 93–118, esp. 93; J. Rotblat, *Scientists in the Quest for Peace: A History of the Pugwash Conferences* (Cambridge, Mass.: MIT Press, 1972).

8. Daniel J. Kevles, " 'Into Hostile Political Camps': The Reorganization of International Science in World War I," *Isis* 62 (1971): 47–60; Paul Forman, "Scientific Internationalism and the Weimar Physicists: The Ideology and Its Manipulation in Germany after World War I," *Isis* 64 (1973): 150–180; A. G. Cock, "Chauvinism and Internationalism in Science: The International Research Council, 1919–1926," *Notes and Records of the Royal Society of London* 37 (1983): 249–288.

9. Herbert E. Gregory, "Historical Sketch and Acknowledgments," in *Proceedings of the First Pan-Pacific Scientific Conference,* BPBM Special Publication 7 (Honolulu: Bishop Museum, 1921), iii; idem, "The Pacific Science Congress," *Scientific Monthly* 19 (1924): 271–280. In a luncheon address before the Pan-Pacific Club in 1924, Gregory placed the beginnings of Pacific science enthusiasm even earlier: "for some reason or other, back in 1908, 1909, 1910, and 1911, there was running through all of the scientific societies of the world this problem of the Pacific—they were blocked by certain things—they wanted to know more about the plants in Tahiti, or something about the land shells in Moorea, or race migration to Samoa" (typescript, 7 April 1924, p. 4, Gregory Papers, BPBM).

10. W. M. Davis, "The Exploration of the Pacific," *Proceedings of the National Academy of Sciences* 2 (1916): 391–394.

11. H. Morse Stephens, "The Conflict of European Nations in the Pacific Ocean," in Stephens and Herbert E. Bolton, eds., *The Pacific Ocean in History: Papers and Addresses* (New York: Macmillan, 1917), 23–33. Stephens's four "chapters" in Pacific Ocean history were: (1) the Spanish Lake, ca. 1500–1700; (2) European competition, 1700–1800; (3) Spanish and American control of the west coast of America, the rise of Japan, 1800–1900; and (4) opening of the Panama Canal.

12. R. A. Daly, "Problems of the Pacific Islands," *American Journal of Science,* 4th ser., vol. 41 (1916): 153–186.

13. William E. Ritter, "Problems of Population of the North Pacific Area as Dependent upon the Biology, the Oceanography, and the Meteorology of the Area," *Science* 50 (8 August 1919): 119–125; Ritter, "The Problem of the Pacific," *Scripps Institution for Biological Research Bulletin,* no. 8 (1919), 8 pp. A report of the meeting appeared in *Science* 49 (23 May 1919): 483–487.

It should be remembered that in 1919 Japan was one of the five dominant powers at the Paris Peace Conference and a rising power in Asia with Germany's former Pacific islands mandated to her control. Japan's economy and population were growing rapidly, exacerbating the need for sources of raw materials and destinations for emigrants. A rapid buildup of the Japanese navy was also underway.

14. George Basalla, "The Spread of Western Science," *Science* 56 (1967): 611–622; I. Bernard Cohen, "Science in America: The Nineteenth Century," in Arthur M. Schlesinger, Jr., and Morton White, eds., *Paths of American Thought* (Boston: Houghton-Mifflin, 1963), 167–189.

15. Paul F. Hooper, *Elusive Destiny: The Internationalist Movement in Modern Hawaii* (Honolulu: University Press of Hawaii, 1980), chap. 3. In the mid-1880s tourists to Hawaii already numbered between 500 and 750 per year; by 1923 the recorded number was 12,021 (Edward Joesting, *Hawaii: An Uncommon History* [New York: Norton, 1972], 261–262).

16. Merze Tate, "Hawaii's Program of Primacy in Polynesia," *Oregon Historical Quarterly* 61 (1960): 377–407.

17. Valerie Noble, *Hawaiian Prophet: Alexander Hume Ford* (Smithtown, N.Y.: Exposition Press, 1980).

18. A. H. Ford, "The Pan-Pacific Union: Its Aims and Ambitions Briefly Told," *Mid-Pacific Magazine* (February 1918): 119–122. Ford's interest in organizations for international cooperation was apparently first aroused while working for the *Daily News Record* in Chicago in the 1890s. At that time he came in contact with William E. Curtiss, who later became first director of the Bureau of American Republics, predecessor to the Pan-American Union. See Paul F. Hooper, "A History of Internationalism in Hawaii between 1900 and 1940" (Ph.D. diss., University of Hawaii, 1972), 46–47.

19. BPBM, Charter of the Pan-Pacific Union, 1917, Pacific Science Association Archives (hereafter PSAA).

20. Ford, "The Pan-Pacific Union," 119, 122.

21. Hooper, *Elusive Destiny,* 66.

22. Some Pan-Pacific Union papers are presently held in Governor McCarthy —Miscellaneous Papers, Hawaii State Archives; and allegedly in the University of Hawaii Archives, although these could not be located at this writing. Ford's conference organizing experiences began at least as early as 1890, when he was involved in a midwest conference on irrigation (*Bulletin of the Pan-Pacific Union,* n.s., no. 6 [April 1920]: 10). And as early as 1911 the Hands-Around-the-Pacific Club had resolved to work toward convening a world peace congress in Hawaii (Hooper, *Elusive Destiny,* 68–69).

23. William Alanson Bryan Papers, University of Hawaii Archives.

24. William T. Brigham, "Shall We Explore the Pacific Islands Now?" title listed in *Proceedings, American Association of Museums* 1 (1907): 12; text printed separately, copy in BPBM Pamphlets, 7 pp. Brigham advocated "a survey of the mid-ocean groups; their topography, ethnology, marine zoology. While this applies primarily to the Polynesian and Micronesian region proper it perhaps more strongly attaches to the Solomon islands, the Bismarck Archipelago and New Guinea for in this region must be traces of the eastward bound immigration, if that theory be correct, and it seems to be a fact that Polynesian settlements are all along that line" (ibid., 3). Ethnology was thus uppermost in his mind. Earlier in the year, in his director's report for 1906 (submitted 11 January 1907),

Brigham described plans for a "comprehensive exploration of the whole Pacific region," which he claimed to have conceived forty years earlier. The program would require $450,000 per year, would take fifteen years, and would be published in one hundred quarto volumes (*Occasional Papers of the Bernice P. Bishop Museum* 2, no. 5: 5–8).

25. *Pacific Scientific Institution,* Charter of Incorporation and By-Laws, Special Series No. 1 (1907): 16 pp.; William A. Bryan, *The Pacific Scientific Institution: An Address,* Special Series No. 2 (1908): 16 pp.; "Monumental Scientific Work to Be Undertaken—Pacific Scientific Institution Fully Organized—Will Make Scientific Survey of the Pacific," *Pacific Commercial Advertiser* (14 December 1907): 1, 3.

26. Brigham expressed his exasperation and dislike for Bryan. See Brigham to James Edge-Partington, Honolulu, 30 December 1907, Edge-Partington–Brigham Scrapbook, BPBM.

27. Bryan, *Pacific Scientific Institution,* 8.

28. The Bryan Papers, University of Hawaii Archives, contain a five-page typescript, "Syllabus of a Proposed Pacific Exploring Expedition," which outlines a "James J. Hill Pacific Exploring Expedition" utilizing a yacht of between five hundred and one thousand tons and the Bishop Museum as a base. But by 1912 funding had not been found, and Bryan's energies were being expended elsewhere; see Bryan, *A Marine Biological Laboratory for Hawaii* (Honolulu: Hawaiian Gazette, 1912), 29 pp. (copy in BPBM Pamphlets). Bryan continued his professorship at the College (later University) of Hawaii until his wife died in 1919. He also became active in the local Democratic party and had a reasonable expectation of being named territorial governor by Woodrow Wilson in 1914, an expectation that was dashed at the last moment (see H. Brett Melendy, "The Controversial Appointment of Lucius Pinkham, Hawaii's First Democratic Governor," *Hawaiian Journal of History* 17 (1983): 185–208, esp. 196, 198). When his wife died Bryan returned to the mainland. He became director of the Los Angeles County Museum in 1921, retiring in 1940.

29. Hooper (*Elusive Destiny,* 98) suggests that Ford's Pan-Pacific Research Council may have been "inspired" by Bryan's earlier plans. See also Hooper, "History of Internationalism," 268.

30. A. H. Ford, "The Pan-Pacific Union and Its Activities," *Mid-Pacific Magazine* 14 (1917): 217–232. According to its charter, PPU hoped "to call in conference delegates from and representatives of all Pacific peoples for the purpose of discussing and furthering the interests common to Pacific nations" (ibid., 219).

31. Gregory, "Historical Sketch," iv.

32. "Call for the First Pan-Pacific Science Congress," *Bulletin of the Pan-Pacific Union,* n.s., no. 7 (May 1920): 7.

33. Trent, like Bryan, had been a Democratic hopeful in the gubernatorial nominations of 1914. See Melendy, "Lucius Pinkham," 193.

34. "Report of Secretary of the Pan-Pacific Union," *Bulletin of the Pan-Pacific Union,* n.s., no. 7 (May 1920): 14–16.

35. Gregory to J. Allen Thomson, 27 May 1924, *PSAA,* Chester R. Longwell, "Memorial to Herbert Ernest Gregory (1869–1952)," in *Proceedings of the Geological Society of America,* Annual Report for 1953, 115–124.

36. Edna Hope Gregory to Roland W. Force, 2 December 1966, PSAA.

37. Gregory was in Honolulu from at least 1 May until about 1 September 1919 when he left for teaching and museum responsibilities on the mainland (BPBM Minutes, Book 5, 28 August 1919).

38. H. E. Gregory, "Pan-Pacific Science Conference," printed announcement, 3 pp., 20 March 1920, Governor McCarthy—Miscellaneous Papers, File 1, Hawaii State Archives.

39. Ford to C. J. McCarthy, Washington, D.C., 31 January 1920, Governor McCarthy—Miscellaneous Papers, File 1; Noble, *Hawaiian Prophet,* 89.

40. Ford to McCarthy, Washington, D.C., 10 May 1920, Governor McCarthy—Miscellaneous Papers, File 1.

41. Governor McCarthy—Miscellaneous Papers, File 2.

42. Paul F. Hooper, "History of Internationalism," 144–146. Ford described the council's goals in "The Pan-Pacific Research Council," *Bulletin of the Pan-Pacific Union,* no. 17 (March 1921): 9–11; and the oceanographic possibilities were discussed by Frank R. Lillie, director of the Woods Hole Oceanographic Institution, in "Woods Hole of the Pacific," *Mid-Pacific Magazine* 34 (July 1927): 3–8. See also Peggy Robb and Louise Vicars, "Manoa's 'Puuhonua': The Castle Home, 1900–1941," *Hawaiian Journal of History* 16 (1982): 171–183, esp. 180–181.

43. Ford to Gregory, Honolulu, 20 March 1925, PSAA.

44. See Noble, *Hawaiian Prophet,* 96; Hooper, "History of Internationalism," 122; and [Ford], "A Personal Correction," *Bulletin of the Pan-Pacific Union,* no. 70 (November 1925): 16.

45. The breakdown of the 103 participants by country was: Hawaii (46), United States (36), Australia (7), Philippines (4), Japan (4), New Zealand (3), Canda (1), United Kingdom (1), and China (1) (see Delegates, *Proceedings of the First Pan-Pacific Scientific Conference,* 22–26). Other sources inexplicably list total attendance as 93 or 101.

46. Ibid., 5, 11, 153–158.

47. *Report on the Pacific Science Association,* 64–115, gives the text of all resolutions of the first seven congresses.

48. Gregory, "Pacific Science Congress," 280.

49. Henry S. Washington, "Pele to the Pan-Pacifics," *Pan-Pacifics to Hawaii* (1921): 4 pp., read at the Pan-Pacific Science Conference, 20 August 1920. Printed copy in Gregory Papers, BPBM. "Okolehao" refers to a local alcoholic beverage made from sugarcane; Achatinellidae is a family of land snails endemic to the Hawaiian Islands; "papa hee nalus" are surfers; "pahoehoe" and "aa" are the names for the ropy and clinker forms of lava respectively; "kamaaina" is the Hawaiian name for a long-time resident of the islands.

50. Elkin, *Pacific Science Association,* 21–25.

51. *Proceedings of the First Pan-Pacific Scientific Conference,* 895–937, esp. 899, 904, 918, 935.

52. Ibid., 902, 919.

53. Ibid., 915–916.

54. Elkin, *Pacific Science Association,* 31–32, 35.

55. Constitution of the Pacific Science Association, Article 2b, in *Report of the Pacific Science Association*, 22.

56. Elkin, *Pacific Science Association*, 51.

57. Ibid., 28.

58. In a future paper I hope to examine in detail these changes in scientific focus, as an index to the altering perceptions of Pacific problems in the twentieth century. Such an analysis would, it is hoped, generate insights into such areas as the stimulus of the Depression upon the social sciences; the scientific impact of World War II; the role of science in the rise of autonomous island nations; and the significance of non-Western, nonexploitative approaches in Pacific science.

9

Wilbert Chapman and the Revolution in U.S. Pacific Ocean Science and Policy, 1945–1951

HARRY N. SCHEIBER

*B*OTH the ocean sciences and the technology of marine fisheries have undergone profound changes since the end of World War II.[1] Of key importance to these changes was a cluster of interrelated scientific projects in the Pacific inaugurated between 1945 and 1951 by U.S. federal and state agencies and by an international tuna commission. These projects produced two effects of enduring importance. First, they generated an enormous body of new data on the marine resources and environments of the Pacific basin system. This research in turn led to the development of vast fisheries resources, especially skipjack and yellowfin tuna, and also produced a series of dramatic discoveries and consequent theoretical advances in geophysics and seafloor studies. More generally, these postwar advances stimulated support of oceanography in the United States and laid the groundwork for important contributions of the new ocean sciences to international law in the mid-1950s and after.[2]

Second, these projects contributed to a methodological revolution that transformed ocean science. By applying new instrumentation, financial resources, ships, and scientific personnel on a scale formerly unknown, the Pacific projects were able to treat ocean environments as complex biotic communities instead of as segmented processes or as small geographic units of the deep-sea world. The result was not only larger-scale research but also a significant reunification of physical and chemical oceanography with marine biology, resulting in an ecologically oriented "new oceanography." "To understand at least one ocean as a whole" was an ideal and a visionary hope in 1945, understood and shared by only a few scientists; within six years it seemed to be an objective well within the reach of modern ocean science.[3]

The career of Wilbert McLeod Chapman (1910–1970)—American ichthyologist, scientific entrepreneur, and self-designated "biopolitician"—was of fundamental importance to the development of the new oceanography and related policy initiatives.[4] As a publicist for new approaches to ocean research, but also as a promoter of the new projects, Chapman played a vital role in the transformation of marine science as well as in the institutional innovations of the postwar years. Hence this chapter will not only examine the history and consequences of these postwar scientific initiatives, but will also consider the contributions of Chapman to Pacific science and ocean policy in the postwar years.

American Pacific Research before 1945

Despite a rich tradition of American high-seas research in Pacific waters, from the Wilkes Expedition to the *Albatross* and *Carnegie* voyages in the early twentieth century, American Pacific research was languishing badly in the 1930s. Only one vessel capable of deepwater oceanographic study, the undersized but heroic *E. W. Scripps,* was operating in Pacific waters beyond the coastal region.[5] The scope of American marine biological research was narrowly limited to applied work on marine fisheries—that is, to the analysis of harvest statistics in relation to inputs of fishing effort—that would provide an empirical basis for commercial fisheries management. Both management programs and scientific research were largely confined, moreover, to three species: the Alaskan salmon, the halibut on the Pacific Northwest and British Columbia coasts, and the sardine (pilchard) of California. The basic-science tradition of deep-sea ichthyology that had been associated with David Starr Jordan and his students at Stanford University, and the more comprehensive marine biological studies associated with Charles A. Kofoid and others at the University of California, Berkeley, produced little important new work in the thirties. Few doctoral students with an interest in oceanography or biology were being turned out by the West Coast universities. The funds, vessels, and skilled personnel were all at levels far short of what was needed to reestablish American science as a factor of any importance in Pacific Ocean studies.[6]

World War II set in motion a transformation of this situation. First, the University of California's Scripps Institution of Oceanography became a base for elaborate projects in naval electronics technology, wave and currents research, and other studies in physical oceanography lavishly financed by the military and naval authorities. Second, the military authorities assigned a small group of five or six marine biologists to survey and develop fisheries resources in the South Pacific areas coming under U.S. military control as the Japanese were pushed back toward their home islands. Two of these scientists, Wilbert Chapman and Milner B. Schaefer, would emerge after 1945 as major figures in American Pacific research. Third, Congress took a new interest in the resources of the Pacific, ordering new scientific studies that—though necessarily superficial—proved to be of considerable influence in the immediate postwar period when a group of influential scientists and industry leaders campaigned for a major new commitment by the United States to sustained Pacific Ocean research.

In 1945 the ranks of ocean scientists concerned with the Pacific were thin indeed; the group numbered perhaps thirty at most in the West Coast universities, Hawaii, the state governments' marine fisheries management agencies, and the research wing of the federal fisheries agency in Alaska. Moreover, it was not a unified community of scientists. The physical and chemical oceanographers (strongest in the University of California, especially at Scripps Institution) had little contact with and manifested little interest in the work of the marine biologists and management agencies. In general, they viewed the work of the commercial fisheries specialists as unworthy of serious attention from basic scientists such as themselves.[7] For their part, marine biologists concerned with commercial fisheries seldom strayed far from the prevailing mode of statistical harvest-analysis studies. Although a few prominent marine biologists had begun to examine the ecological relationships between biological phenomena and the chemical and physical aspects of ocean environments, there was no real unity of ocean studies either conceptually or in the organization of the profession.[8]

In a mere five or six years all this had changed radically. New projects for Pacific research were under way with unprecedented scope, funding, and scale. These new projects, in turn, stimulated the expansion of doctoral programs and the recruitment of young scientists from the established disciplines into ocean-related studies. Oceanography was redefined, in effect, to embrace a unified ecological concept of physical, chemical, and biological studies centered on ocean environments and their populations. In sum, the "new oceanography"—which involved not only its conceptual transformation but also its emergence as part of Big Science in the organization and scale of sponsored research—had taken form and begun to flourish.

Wilbert Chapman as Scientist and Biopolitician

No individual had a greater influence than Wilbert McLeod Chapman on the development of the new oceanography in Pacific Ocean studies. To a large degree his role was that of publicist, promoter, and institution-builder; but he also remained close to his origins as an academic ichthyologist and commercial marine fisheries specialist, representing his fellow scientists eloquently with industry, government, and the public. Throughout an arduous campaign begun in 1945 for the development of U.S. Pacific research, Chapman demonstrated a sense of the rich possibilities offered by a unification of marine biology and physical-chemical oceanography, the essence of the new oceanography.[9]

Chapman was born in 1910 in Washington state, the son of a salmon packing-plant manager, and spent his youth in the heart of fishing country. Throughout his career, he would retain a strong sense of identity with the fisheries community. He studied at the University of Washington School of Fisheries, where he earned both the bachelor's degree and (in 1937) the doctorate, written under the direction of Dr. William F. Thompson, principal founder of modern commercial fisheries studies. Chapman early established himself, through work in state and federal fisheries ·agencies, as a promising commercial fisheries expert. He published papers on the sardine, oyster cultivation, trout, and salmon spawning runs. But he professed that his deepest interest was in ichthyology—a field of little interest to the management agencies. Chapman expanded the osteological study that comprised his dissertation to focus on the worldwide distribution and characteristics of the intertidal fish known as the blenny. Always enthusiastic for large projects, he began around 1942 to work on a checklist of fishes of the world, which he hoped to make a standard work in systematics.[10]

Rejected for military service because of blindness in one eye—otherwise, he was in fine health, energetic to an extent that became legendary—Chapman was appointed in 1942 curator of fishes at the California Academy of Sciences in San Francisco. He was determined, he wrote, "to make this [Academy] the principal repository of Pacific fisheries in the world, and the center of research upon them."[11] In 1943 he gained an opportunity to advance that dream while also contributing to the war effort when the military asked him to investigate tropical fisheries of the central and southern Pacific, in an area that embraced nearly all the major islands over which the Allies had taken control from Japan. Chapman's assignment was to survey resources that might provide Allied occupying troops with fresh protein.[12]

Chapman's work in the South Pacific was more extensive than any other Pacific survey by an American since the *Albatross* expeditions two and three decades earlier, and he made the most of his chance. In addition to finding the resources that the army and navy wanted, Chapman shipped back dozens of barrels of faunal specimens for the California Academy and National Museum collections. The academy thus emerged from the war with one of the world's most important collections in Pacific biology.[13]

The experience also left Chapman with a messianic zeal to advertise the scientific, geopolitical, and commercial importance of Pacific fisheries resources to the United States. He found a consuming passion in bringing to the attention of scientists, policymakers, and the public what he regarded as a vast and wholly unappreciated commercial fishery—especially for tuna—in Pacific waters. "Probably no food resource of equal quantity," he contended, "has been made available to our nation since the opening of the Middle West to agriculture." To awaken others to the possibilities of the "Pacific fisheries frontier," Chapman resorted to the traditional rhetoric of expansionism and imperialism: "We people in the West[ern United States] have not yet come to the point where we are through expanding," Chapman declared. The Pacific Ocean was "the Great Plains of the twentieth century."[14]

With the support of the director of the California Academy, oceanographer Robert C. Miller, Chapman embarked in 1945 on a protracted letter-writing campaign, gave public speeches, obtained appointment to several California industrial and governmental commissions, and otherwise involved himself wholly in the work of spreading his message about Pacific resources. His vision was comprehensive: he wanted an expansion of American ocean research in the Pacific region, with the scientific studies of several disciplines integrated and coordinated. He worked tirelessly as propagandist and lobbyist to obtain new commitments for funds, vessels, instrumentation, and equipment; and he also tried to build new political coalitions. These coalitions would bring together in the cause of scientific ocean research the commercial fisheries industries (fishing, packing, and marketing); fisheries scientists in the universities and in government resource agencies; and basic scientists in oceanography whose knowledge, laboratories, and cooperation were essential to the overall scientific vision Chapman was promoting. He also sought to overcome traditional divisions between federal and state scientific agencies, arguing for a new organizational structure in ocean science and fisheries management that reflected his efforts at "attempting to knit the industry into a [unified] coastwise power, . . . getting the USFWS [U.S. Fish and Wildlife Service, the federal agency] to work in harmony with the state agencies, getting the industry men to respect and work with the scientists, getting the scientists to work with the industry," and, withal, persuading all elements of the coalitions to recognize that both applied and basic ocean sciences research would be of importance to each and to their common interests.[15]

The New Programs, 1945–1951

Chapman's efforts centered first on tuna resources of the central and southern Pacific, but they soon came to embrace the problem of the California sardine, then facing depletion. Later, when serving as a high-ranking U.S. policy official, he grew interested in cooperative international tuna research in the eastern Pacific and problems of research and management in the salmon regions of the North Pacific. These projects were important both individually and as part of the overall postwar U.S. Pacific Ocean research effort.

The Farrington Bill and POFI

In 1945 Joseph Farrington, the congressional delegate from the Territory of Hawaii, introduced a bill to establish a federal tropical-fisheries research center in Hawaii. The bill proposed an appropriation of over $1 million, a sum that dwarfed previous U.S. expenditures for Pacific fisheries research.[16] Here was a genuine departure from the myopic and penurious approach that had prevailed, an initiative that could not have failed to arouse Wilbert Chapman's enthusiastic interest. Moreover, the bill was a nice complement to Chapman's attempt, then under way, to interest the U.S. government in concluding "bait treaties" with Great Britain, France, and the Netherlands so that the American tuna fleet might establish distant-water fresh-bait fishing in the South Pacific.[17] Both projects, Chapman believed, were vitally important for another reason: the famous Truman Fisheries Proclamation of September 1945 had stated that the U.S. government regarded it "proper" for nations to establish conservation zones on the high seas in fishing areas where their nationals had established themselves and where conservation measures were indicated.[18] To Chapman, this proclamation meant that the United States must aggressively conduct research on fisheries resources, establish its fishing industry in Pacific deepwater areas, and thereby establish its formal claims (under the Truman Proclamation) to such resources and potentially, at least, to their exclusive control by the American fishing fleet.[19]

In promoting the Farrington Bill, Chapman resisted the conventional scientific wisdom, which held that rich commercial fisheries were to be found only in cold-water areas over the continental shelf. Chapman contended that once adequate scientific surveys had been conducted, they would find latent tuna in great abundance in warm waters far out at sea. It was vital to find these resources, to identify the separate tuna species in order to chart their migrations and availability, and to embark on "the years of intensive research necessary to establish the scientific foundation for the rational development and regulation of a high seas fishery."[20]

When the bill failed to pass in 1946, Chapman led a determined political campaign for its reintroduction. He rewrote the measure, working on the draft with two friends—Milner B. Schaefer and Oscar Elton Sette of the U.S. Fisheries and Wildlife Service

(USFWS)—who (with Chapman himself) were among only about a half dozen American fisheries biologists with significant field experience in the tropical Pacific. They revised the bill to reduce its Hawaii orientation, substituting a clear charter for extensive fisheries research throughout the entire tropical Pacific. Chapman lobbied with industry leaders, West Coast state officials, and other politicians influential in ocean fishing districts, arguing that a project on tropical tuna would establish a precedent for extensive federal funding of ocean research and so redound eventually to the benefit of all marine fisheries.[21]

In 1947 the revised bill passed, creating the Pacific Oceanic Fishery Investigations (POFI) under the aegis of the USFWS, with a base in Hawaii. The bill provided for the outfitting of three oceangoing research vessels, a new laboratory in Honolulu, the translation of Japanese scientific literature on Pacific tuna and other fisheries, and full-scale programs that would cost over a million dollars per year for research on both marine biology and fishing technology in tropical waters.[22] POFI was a triumph for Chapman and his colleagues, signaling a radical change in federal ocean research policy. In fact, it also marked the beginning of a movement that over the next several years would afford oceanography full membership in the American scientific establishment as a discipline heavily supported with government funding both for equipment and diversified, large-scale research operations.

The Farrington Bill campaign gave Chapman a reputation, unique at the time, as a well-credentialed fisheries scientist who was also willing to devote himself to political lobbying, working hand in hand with industry representatives. He found this role frustrating at times, and he complained that many of the leaders of the West Coast fishing industry showed "about as much vision in regard to the future of their supply of raw material as a nearsighted bat."[23] With respect to his scientific colleagues, however, Chapman could become equally impatient: he found it continually necessary to remind them that industry had a legitimate concern to promote applied research. Contending that support for basic science would follow, he insisted on the need to "wise the boys up on where the money comes from" when the scientists scorned too close an industry connection.[24]

Chapman's closest friend, Milner Schaefer, was assigned by USFWS to take charge of the biological and oceanographic section of the newly organized POFI project in Hawaii. Oscar Sette, an older man with a long record of excellent Pacific fisheries research, was given charge of the entire POFI operation. The merger of physical-chemical oceanography with biology, something Chapman had been promoting consistently, was apparent from the start in Schaefer's research design for POFI. Among the first subjects of investigation were the vertical distribution of tuna in relation to temperature, the influence of meteorological and temperature variations on migration and availability, and the importance of upwelling in relation to the equatorial countercurrent.[25] Moreover, one of the three POFI vessels was equipped to collect eggs, larvae, and juvenile tuna as well as for systematic plankton gathering. The others were assigned to sample oceanographic sections across the equatorial currents to determine salinity, oxygen content, and nutrient chemical composition, employing the newly developed bathythermographic techniques of data collection. Identifying and translating captured Japanese scientific literature on Pacific fisheries, mostly unpublished, was another high priority of the project.[26]

The POFI organization had separate sections on technology and on exploratory fishing, assigned to pursue applied issues not only in fish harvesting but also in preservation, processing, and marketing. There was strong rivalry between Schaefer's biological and oceanographic section and the applied sections, which was finally resolved in favor of Schaefer.[27]

The California Sardine Investigations

A second major investigation in Pacific waters to which Chapman lent his efforts in 1946–1948 was a large-scale study of the depletion of the California sardine, or pilchard, in the waters off the California coast. Many scientists suspected an impending catastrophe from overfishing and lack of stringent regulation, as the harvests dropped from a peak of nearly 800,000 tons in the 1936–1937 season to only half that level in 1945–1946, then to 130,000 tons in 1947–1948.[28]

This sardine crisis, threatening California's leading fishery with disaster, gave Chapman another opportunity to promote his vision of industry-government-science cooperation, where oceanographic studies complemented basic fisheries research. He obtained the political support of some key industry leaders, the state fisheries agency, the University of California, and the West Coast-based USFWS scientists. By 1948 they had successfully designed and obtained funding for a cooperative interagency program that linked Scripps, the California state marine laboratory (which had long been in favor of closely regulating sardine fishing levels), USFWS (which in past years had been generally indifferent to regulation), and the California Academy of Sciences. Both state and federal funds were provided on an unprecedented scale. Of critical importance, Congress authorized the U.S. Navy to turn over to the University of California three vessels equipped with sonar and other newly developed gear that would permit state-of-the-art oceanographic research. Scientific studies were placed under the newly created Marine Research Committee (MRC), authorized to administer the state-appropriated funds raised by a special tax on sardine harvests. MRC was composed of nine persons, five of whom represented the industry, and four the scientific agencies and institutions doing the research.

The MRC strategy for the project paralleled what Schaefer was then instituting in POFI's investigations of tropical tuna: the integration of biological studies with traditional oceanography in a broad-ranging attack on ecosystemic problems. Research commenced in 1948 and the new program soon emerged as a milestone in the history of marine-biological inquiry. Within a few years the sardine study had broadened to include an intensive network of stations at sea for measuring chemical and physical properties; plankton and larval studies across a broad expanse of offshore coastal and deep waters; and extensive data collection on upwelling and horizontal currents. The ideal, in sum, was interdisciplinary research. As Roger Revelle, one of the scientists deeply involved in designing the project, wrote in 1947, "The sardines cannot be treated as isolated organisms living in a vacuum." Hence, Revelle said, MRC would seek

> to make dynamic analyses where possible of the processes of the sea, that is, the cause and effect relationships which affected sardine production. . . . The investigation must be an integrated one in which proper weight is given not only to the currents and other aspects of the physical environment but also to the entire organic assemblage including the plants and animals which form the food

chain of the sardines, their competitors for the food supply, and the predators, including man.

The premise on which the design rested was that "far more productive results [would be] obtained by complete analysis of all the factors which exist in a particular situation than by a statistical treatment of a few factors in many situations."[29]

This approach actually reflected well the northern European ecological research pioneered forty years earlier by Johan Hjort of Norway and others—a tradition that had been of relatively little importance in American marine biology in the interwar period but that now flourished in the hands of Schaefer and the MRC group. The holistic approach to marine systems that had become dominant in limnology—and had inspired Raymond Lindeman's work of the 1940s—now was being applied to the vaster and more obtuse communities and systems of the Pacific Ocean.[30]

Quite apart from its magnificent scientific achievements (which, ironically, greatly advanced the techniques of oceanographic science by the integration of chemical, physical, and biological studies, but did practically nothing to save the disappearing sardine stocks), MRC was important as a symbol of science in politics. Thus Chapman nurtured the agency as a crucial segment of his larger plan to "knit the industry into a coastwise power" and carry ocean sciences to a new level of importance. He was keenly aware that "about twelve farsighted industry men" had made the plan possible; if they could be satisfied by some early applied results, Chapman wrote, then full-scale industry support for basic oceans research would soon follow: "Within five years we will have more money and support for basic ocean study than has been dreamed of."[31]

Moreover, Chapman believed that MRC would provide a solid institutional model for industry-science-government cooperation in the future, and thus help eliminate historic conflicts within and among the groups interested in ocean research and fisheries. The threat of the sardine's depletion, Chapman declared, might well establish the necessary momentum, through MRC, for a fundamental recasting of political and organizational relationships: "I think for this reason," he said, "that one day we will look back and be grateful that the sardine missed San Francisco and Monterey Bay in 1946."[32] And in fact, though the sardine depletion continued until the industry had been virtually eliminated in California, the advancement of basic science that Chapman foresaw came to rich fruition with MRC as it did with the POFI project in Hawaii.

The Inter-American Tropical Tuna Commission

By 1949, POFI and MRC scientists had linked forces to cooperate in studying the currents, temperatures, and chemistry of ocean waters from the California coastline to the central Pacific. The web of systematic ocean research, on a new scale, applying new instrumentation developed during World War II was then further extended to include the waters off Central and South America. This rich fishing ground was the site of American tuna fishing efforts in what was the fastest growing—and, by the mid-1950s, the most valuable—U.S. commercial fishery. The extension of research activity commenced when the United States concluded a treaty with Costa Rica, later joined by other nations, for the establishment of the Inter-American Tropical Tuna Commission for systematic oceanographic and biological investigations of the eastern Pacific tuna.[33]

Again, Chapman played a key role. As a result of the spectacular successes of his other campaigns for Pacific research, he had become a trusted adviser of the fishing industry as well as an institution builder for science. His scientific accomplishments continued to be recognized: he was awarded a Guggenheim Fellowship in 1947 for his studies of the blenny; and shortly thereafter his alma mater, the University of Washington School of Fisheries, called him to succeed his mentor William F. Thompson as director. However, Chapman's tenure at the university was brief, for in 1948 the U.S. State Department, responding to political pressure from the fishing industry, named him to a newly created post as special assistant to the under secretary, with top-level responsibilities in fisheries policy planning. This made Chapman one of the two highest-ranking officers concerned with fisheries matters in the federal government. From his new office, Chapman did the planning and diplomatic groundwork for the treaty with Costa Rica and other nations off whose shores the U.S. tuna fleet was reaping a rich harvest.[34]

Milner Schaefer was appointed to direct the new Tuna Commission. Schaefer—Chapman's candidate for the job—was a man known for both his scientific genius and his hard-nosed unwillingness to have the United States "downtrodden by the downtrodden nations"![35] This was a vital consideration to Chapman because he hoped that the new commission would become an instrument for establishing the legitimacy of American commercial fishing vessels' claims to work Latin American waters. That is, the treaty would effectively serve as a hedge against any future efforts by Costa Rica or other nations to exclude American vessels or to make unilateral judgments on any tuna-depletion claims that might become a rationale for subjecting American nationals to their regulation.[36] From his State Department post, moreover, Chapman was influential in obtaining appropriations sufficient to launch the new commission on an ambitious research program.

Schaefer instituted a program of research by the Tuna Commission on the same kind of ambitious ecosystemic design as the POFI project. "Fisheries problems," he believed,

> are not entirely biological problems. . . . They are more likely to be problems of the dynamics of the ocean in its larger sense, that is the physical and chemical interchange in the ocean and the biological interchange as . . . part of the larger oceanic circulation. There is a circulation of life in the ocean along with a circulation of matter, and the dynamics of that situation are the center of interest of fishing research in its broadest sense.[37]

In common with the POFI project, Schaefer's new investigations of eastern Pacific tuna were dedicated to intensive research on an ecosystem that was in a "normal" state, rather than in crisis from some natural anomoly or overfishing as was the case of the sardine fishery being studied by MRC. The commission's tuna research began, Schaefer wrote, "at a stage in the development of the fishery when serious overfishing had not yet occurred," a context unlike the MRC sardine research projects.[38] The Tuna Commission studied both skipjack and yellowfin tuna in the tropical waters off the Latin American coast, and its plankton collections and oceanographic observations extended south by more than a thousand miles the network of ocean stations already in place off the California coast.[39] Linked with its basic oceanographic and biological research was an ambitious project monitoring the

American fleet's fishing effort and yields. This became the basis for a regulatory regime beginning in the mid-1950s.[40]

The Tuna Commission's studies also led to Schaefer's development of important new theoretical models of tuna population dynamics, work that had a major impact in the field of biostatistics.[41] Within five years, then, the commission's research had become a showcase of modern oceanographic scholarship in the new ecological mode, emerging in a close relationship to new applications of mathematical modeling. By the mid-1950s, POFI had paid important commercial dividends by its discovery of new tuna resources in the east-central Pacific, and also by pioneering research on Pacific currents, on upwelling in relation to fishery nutrition, and (as a windfall) on the mapping of the ocean floor. The two programs, then, were of prime importance both commercially and in their contributions to science.[42]

The Tripartite Treaty and the North Pacific Fisheries

As a result of the series of U.S. research initiatives, the number of scientific vessels flying the American flag in deepwater Pacific regions had increased by 1951 from one to nine. The resultant new research opportunities were bringing a new generation of young doctoral students into a scientific field undergoing a basic transformation. Funding rose from the 1947 amount of ten times the prewar level to perhaps twenty times the prewar level by 1951. The dedication of ocean scientists on the West Coast and in Hawaii had combined to produce a remarkable, large-scale, well-coordinated scientific enterprise.

An area of the Pacific not yet covered in 1951 by any of the three new research programs was the North Pacific coldwater region, which included the rich Alaskan salmon fishery. For the United States, this area posed major political problems: a renascent Japanese fishing industry might well enter those waters and make a shambles of the strict regulatory regime imposed by the federal government since the 1930s on American salmon fishermen. Similarly, a Japanese incursion could easily undermine the effectiveness of the international controls imposed by the United States and Canada restricting the fishing for halibut on the continental shelf and also in the Fraser River salmon fishery.[43]

Chapman therefore made it a priority to work toward bringing the Japanese—who in the prewar years had operated their distant-water fisheries in a highly exploitative manner, with few concessions to conservation or rational management—into a treaty with the United States and Canada that would limit any Japanese fishing in the eastern Pacific's salmon or halibut waters. From Chapman's efforts within the State Department and in international diplomatic talks came two agreements. The first, concluded while Japan was still under the Allied Occupation, was an exchange of letters in February 1951 (the Dulles-Yoshida Letters) in which the Japanese agreed to refrain from fishing in the eastern portion of North Pacific waters until a permanent treaty had been negotiated. The second was the 1952 International Convention for High Seas Fisheries of the Pacific Ocean, a tripartite agreement involving Canada, Japan, and the United States. The convention committed the three nations to such cooperative scientific studies as were "necessary to secure the maximum sustained productivity of fisheries" in the North Pacific. Japan yielded to American demands, pressed hard by Chapman, that it abstain for ten years from fishing salmon or other species considered at maximum yield —namely, halibut and herring—in the area east of the 175th meridian (which marked the mid-Pacific). Periodically a tripartite commission would study the condition of fisheries populations; so long as the stock was considered to be at maximum yield, under existing conservation programs, Japan would continue to be excluded.[44]

Thus the "abstention principle" entered into international law and shortly became a keystone of U.S. policy with respect to Law of the Sea.[45] Chapman recognized that the 1952 convention was an interim agreement only, subject to periodic reappraisal after ten years; but his more enduring achievement was to see embedded in the agreement a functional role for fisheries scientists, applying the new oceanography to determine the condition of ocean fisheries. The agreement itself was a political milestone, and it lent great importance to the new techniques and ecological orientation of oceanography in international resource management.[46]

Since the 1952 agreement, fisheries issues have continued to play a central part in the geopolitics of the Pacific, following the pattern of conflict and its resolution first delineated in the U.S.-Japanese-Canadian agreements. That is, Japan has resisted, though without enduring success, the extension of national jurisdiction over offshore resources, while the other Pacific rim and island nations generally have opposed Japan's claims to an unrestricted ocean. The states opposed to Japan have regularly invoked fisheries science and the goal of rational management to legitimate their policies of extended limits and, most recently, the institution of two hundred–mile economic zones provided for by the Law of the Sea convention under UN auspices.

Conclusion

Chapman put his individual stamp on all the American projects for Pacific research from 1945 to 1952 by insisting on the participation of industry representatives in decision-making that affected either the design of scientific research or any management plans. California's MRC was actually supervised by a board with a majority of members representing the industry. Although MRC scientists in fact managed to exert a controlling influence, to have their way they needed the industry votes. When POFI was established, Chapman pressed federal authorities to create an industry advisory board; USFWS at first resisted but finally accepted Chapman's view. Subsequent events in POFI's history showed that the industry advisers had a major influence on basic decisions, including the determination to pursue investigations initially in the eastern and central Pacific rather than in the South Pacific region that had so intrigued Chapman himself since the war's end. In writing the legislation to implement both the Tuna Commission and the U.S.-Japanese-Canadian tripartite treaties, Chapman included the creation of industry advisory groups; thus he created institutional mechanisms that reflected his hopes for an alliance of science, government, and industry. He sought "regulations [that would be] deliberately framed . . . not only to protect the fishery resource but to protect the [commercial] fishery itself," contending that "it is of no use whatever to have the ocean full of fish if there is not an industry available which has the economic strength to get the product from the sea to the consumer's table."[47]

Given the legendary individualism and fragmentation of the fishing industry, it is hardly surprising that such mechanisms merely institutionalized interest-group conflicts. In this respect, at least, the outcome fell far short of Chapman's hopes and plans and was but a dim shadow of his enormous successes on the scientific front.[48]

Until his death in 1970, Wilbert Chapman continued to champion the causes of fisheries research, oceanographic studies, and the development of new commercial marine fisheries, but he did so in the private sector—from 1951 to 1960 in the employ of the American Tunaboat Association, and thereafter, until his death, as research and policy adviser to the Van Camp Sea Food Company. Chapman also continued to be a prominent counsellor to governmental agencies at the state, national, and international levels, and he played a major role as spokesman for American distant-water fishing interests in the Law of the Sea conferences from 1955 to 1970.[49]

Chapman's success in shaping the responses of American science, public policy, and diplomacy to the challenges of Pacific Ocean studies stands as an intriguing example of the influence that American society will occasionally accord its scientists. Until 1951 Chapman had remained what Donald Fleming has termed an "influential" in science, with ties primarily to the scientific community itself, though as a biopolitician he had also reached out beyond his circle of colleagues to build new political coalitions and establish an independent base of influence on policy.[50] In the 1950s and 1960s, having given up ichthyology and associated himself with the private sector, Chapman could no longer play his role as influential in quite the same way; now he was more the scientific statesman, enjoying enhanced prestige from his State Department service, now somewhat distanced from the world of academic science yet in vital respects still its champion. His continuing influence in the ongoing debate on fisheries policies was founded on the central role he had played in scientific policy and institution building during the postwar years, when the Pacific Ocean research enterprise was first launched.

Notes

This research was sponsored in part by the National Oceanic and Atmospheric Administration (NOAA), the National Sea Grant College Program, and the Department of Commerce, under grant number NA80AA-D-00121, through the California Sea Grant College Program, and in part by the California State Resources Agency, project number R/MA-13 and R/MA-25, through the Center for the Study of Law and Society, University of California, Berkeley. The U.S. government is authorized to produce and distribute reprints of this chapter for governmental purposes. Additional support was given by the Boalt Hall School of Law, University of California, Berkeley.

I gratefully acknowledge the expert and dedicated research assistance of three Sea Grant trainees: Berta Schweinberger, Victoria Saker, and Barbara Leibhardt. Part of the research on the California sardine investigation was done in collaboration with Arthur F. McEvoy, whose book *The Fisherman's Problem: Ecology and Law in the California Fisheries, 1850–1980* (Cambridge, Cambridge University Press, 1986) incorporates some of the joint research from the Sea Grant project.

Thanks are also owed to Donald Bevan, Vernon Carstensen, Biliana Cicin-Sain, Deborah Day, John Dwyer, Roger Hahn, Susan B. Scheiber, and Jane L. Scheiber. The archivists and librarians of Scripps Institution of Oceanography, the University of Washington, the California Academy of Sciences, the Hawaii State Archives, and the U.S. National Archives all have extended invaluable help.

1. See, inter alia, Edward Miles et al., *The Management of Marine Regions: The North Pacific: An Analysis of Issues Relating to Fisheries, Marine Transportation, Marine Scientific Research, and Multiple Use Conditions and Conflicts* (Berkeley and Los Angeles: University of California Press, 1982); and Biliana Cicin-Sain, "Managing the Ocean Commons: U.S. Marine Programs in the Seventies and Eighties," *Marine Technology Society Journal* 16 (1982): 6.

2. As yet there is no study of U.S. Pacific ocean research in this era comparable to the fine studies of Susan Schlee on Atlantic Ocean research. The themes in this study are treated in a detailed way in Harry N. Scheiber, "Pacific Ocean Resources, Science, and Law of the Sea: Wilbert M. Chapman and the Pacific Fisheries, 1945–70," *Ecology Law Quarterly* 13 (1986): 381–534. I also have in progress a book on this theme.

The main sources for the themes of this study are the Papers of Wilbert Chapman, in the Manuscripts Collection, University of Washington Library (hereafter cited as UW Library); the Archives of the Scripps Institution of Oceanography, University of California at La Jolla (SIO Archives); the U.S. Fish and Wildlife Service (USFWS) Records, National Archives, Washington, D.C. (National Archives); the California Academy of Sciences Archives, San Francisco (CAS Archives); the Hawaii State Archives (Hawaii Archives); and published congressional and administrative documents.

3. The quotation is from remarks of Columbus Iselin, director of the Woods Hole Oceanographic Institution, in the transcript of the conference on "The Position of SIO in the University, the State and the Nation" (La Jolla, March 1951), 73, SIO Archives.

4. A fine introduction and overview of Chapman's life is provided by his friends Donald L. McKernan and William T. Burke, in *An Inventory-Guide to the Wilbert Mcleod Chapman Papers, 1939–1970* (Seattle: University of Washington Libraries, 1977), "Introduction," i.

5. See Elizabeth N. Shor, *Scripps Institution of Oceanography: Probing the Oceans, 1936–1976* (San Diego: Tofua Press, 1978).

6. Lionel Walford, *Fishery Resources of the United States* (Washington: U.S.

Department of the Interior, [1945]); Chapman, "Looking beyond Today," *Pacific Fisherman* (July 1946): 61; J. L. McHugh, "Trends in Fishery Research," in Norman Benson, ed., *A Century of Fisheries in North America*, Special Publication No. 7 (Washington: American Fisheries Society, 1970); Carl L. Hubbs, "History of Ichthyology in the U.S. after 1850, "*Copeia* 1 (1964): 42–60; Arthur F. McEvoy, "Law, Public Policy, and Industrialization in the California Fisheries, 1900–1925," *Business History Review* 57 (1983): 494.

7. Chapman to Robert Miller, [June 1943], Miller Papers, CAS Archives; House Committee on Merchant Marine and Fisheries, *Development of the High Seas Fishing Industry: Hearings, May 12, 1947*, 80th Cong., 1st sess., 1949, Chapman testimony, 3–11; Chapman to Carl Hubbs, 13 August, 29 October 1947, Hubbs Papers, SIO Archives. The federal government also carried on a small, two-person research effort based in Palo Alto and concerned with study of tropical tuna.

8. Chapman to Hubbs, 30 April 1948, Hubbs Papers.

9. Biographical data on Chapman can be found in McKernan and Burke, *Inventory-Guide;* John L. Kask, "Introduction," in Brian J. Rothschild, ed., *World Fisheries Policy: Multidisciplinary Views* (Seattle: University of Washington Press, 1972), v–xi; Chapman's biographical summary and application for Guggenheim Fellowship (1946), Chapman Papers, CAS Archives; and Chapman to Miller Freeman, 12 May 1948, Chapman Papers, UW Library.

10. Appointment file, Chapman Collection, Miller Papers, CAS Archives.

11. Chapman to Richard Eakin, 23 June 1943, Chapman Papers, CAS Archives.

12. This episode is recounted in Chapman's book, *Fishing in Troubled Waters* (Philadelphia: Lippincott, 1949).

13. Chapman to Miller, 24 May 1944, Miller Papers.

14. Quotations from testimony cited in House Committee, *Development of the High Seas Fishing Industry;* Frank J. Taylor, "A Million Miles of Fishing," *Collier's* 117 (18 May 1946): 90, 93; and Chapman, "The Wealth of the Ocean," *Scientific Monthly* 64 (1947): 192. See also Chapman to John Heimburger, 25 September 1945 (circular letter copied to approximately one hundred others), Chapman Papers, UW Library.

15. Chapman to Montgomery Phister, [1947] and 19 September 1947, Chapman Papers, UW Library; Chapman to Hubbs, correspondence, 1945–1947, Hubbs Papers.

16. Taking federal, state, and territorial expenditures into account, U.S. governmental research on Pacific oceanography and marine biology, excluding navy hydrographic work, probably totaled no more than $180,000 per year in the 1930s.

17. Chapman to Miller, 4 April 1945, Miller Papers; Chapman, "Tuna in the Mandated Island," *Far Eastern Survey* 15 (9 October 1946): 317–319; Chapman, "On the Tuna Resources of the Central Pacific," in *Transactions, 12th North American Wildlife Conference* (Washington, 1947), 356–363.

18. See Ann L. Hollick, *U.S. Foreign Policy and the Law of the Sea* (Princeton, N.J.: Princeton University Press, 1981), 18–60.

19. Chapman to Farrington, 7 November 1945, Farrington files, Hawaii

Archives; Chapman to Ira Gabrielson, 9 November 1945, Chapman Papers, UW Library.

20. Chapman to Farrington, 7 November 1945, Farrington files; see also, Chapman, Address to AAAS Pacific Division meeting, June 1946, Chapman Papers, UW Library (excerpt reprinted in *Pacific Fisherman* [September 1946]: 52).

21. Chapman correspondence with Edward Allen and Montgomery Phister, 1947, Chapman Papers, UW Library.

22. 16 *United States Code* 758 (1982); M. Schaefer, "The Federal Programme with Relation to the Future Development of Pacific Fisheries," *Proceedings of the 7th Pacific Science Congress,* vol. 4 (1949): 634–638.

23. Chapman to Phister, 6 March 1947, Chapman Papers, UW Library.

24. Chapman to Hubbs, 29 October 1947, Hubbs Papers.

25. M. Schaefer, "Presentation of Proposed [POFI] Program . . . 1950," 7 October 1949, USFWS Papers, National Archives. Upwelling was a problem studied by Harald Sverdrup and others at SIO in the late 1930s off the California coast, with increasing concern for impact on nutriments distribution. See Harald Sverdrup, "On the Process of Upwelling," *Journal of Marine Research* 1 (1938): 155–164. For a later overview, see O. E. Sette, "Consideration of Midocean Fish Production as Related to Oceanic Circulatory System," *Journal of Marine Research* 14 (1955): 398–414.

26. O. E. Sette, *Progress in Pacific Oceanic Fishery Investigations, 1950–53* U.S. Department of Interior, Special Scientific Report: Fisheries No. 116 (Washington, Government Printing Office, 1954).

27. This account is based on archival correspondence of POFI officials, 1949–1952, National Archives. See also Scheiber, "Pacific Ocean Resources," 414–416.

28. See Arthur F. McEvoy and Harry N. Scheiber, "Scientists, Entrepreneurs, and the Policy Process: A Study of the Post-1945 California Sardine Depletion," *Journal of Economic History* 44 (June 1984): 393–406, for extensive documentation of material not otherwise annotated in this section.

29. Revelle to Colonel I. M. Isaacs, 29 November 1947, SIO Directors' Files, SIO Archives.

30. On Hjort and the northern European tradition generally, see E. S. Russell, *The Overfishing Problem* (Cambridge: Cambridge University Press, 1942); and J. R. Dymond, "European Studies of the Populations of Marine Fisheries," *Bulletin of the Bingham Oceanographical Collections* (Yale University), vol. 11 (1948): 50–80. See also Hans-Joachim Elster, "History of Limnology," *Mitteilungen der Internationalen Vereinigung für Theoretische und Angewandte Limnologie* 20 (June 1947): 7–30, for essential background on the connection to limnology. The more conventional view, represented by Donald Worster *(Nature's Economy: The Roots of Ecology* [San Francisco: Sierra Club, 1977], 294–306), does not make this connection. In my forthcoming book I offer an extended argument on that connection, stressing the continuity of northern European marine biological studies in an ecological mode and the contributions of both that tradition and of limnology to the new oceanography of the late 1940s. See Scheiber, "Pacific Ocean Resources," 424–426.

31. Chapman to Hubbs, 13 August 1947, Subject Files, SIO Archives.

32. Chapman to Allen, 29 January 1947, Chapman Papers, UW Library.

33. Schaefer, "Management of the American Pacific Tuna Fishery," in Benson, *Fisheries in North America,* 237–248.

34. The trade journal *Pacific Fisherman* covered the campaign for the new fisheries post in the State Department and Chapman's appointment, November 1947 to March 1948. The other highest-ranking fisheries officer was the director of the USFWS.

35. Chapman to Phister, 1 November 1949, Chapman Papers, UW Library.

36. As of 1949, American flag vessels comprised nearly the entire fishery in Latin American waters. The United States saw the Tuna Commission as a means by which to guarantee that U.S. nationals would continue to share in that fishery even if a collaborative research agency found management necessary. Chapman sought thereby "to spike any claim by Latin America that our tuna fishermen were depleting either tuna or bait fish" in Latin American offshore waters (Phister to Donald Loker, 19 September 1955 [copy], Chapman Papers, UW Library).

37. M. Schaefer, in transcript of conference on "The Position of SIO," p. 72.

38. M. Schaefer, *Scientific Investigation of the Tropical Tuna Resources of the Eastern Pacific* (United Nations Doc. A/CONF.10/L.11, prepared for 1955 Rome Conference, mimeo), 201. Lionel A. Walford had developed that point earlier in his "The Case for Studying Normal Patterns in Fish Biology," *Journal of Marine Research* 7 (1948): 506–510.

39. Map of stations, in Schaefer, *Scientific Investigation,* 108. For a similar map of stations of the MRC sardine program, over an ocean area of 760,000 square miles, see Scheiber, "Pacific Ocean Resources," 422.

40. Schaefer, *Scientific Investigation,* 213–220. See also Michael Orbach, *Hunters, Seamen, and Entrepreneurs: The Tuna Seinermen of San Diego* (Berkeley and Los Angeles: University of California Press, 1977).

41. M. Schaefer, "Some Considerations of Population Dynamics and Economics in Relation to the Management of the Commercial Marine Fisheries," *Journal of the Fisheries Research Board of Canada* 14 (1957): 669–681; Kask, "Introduction," for an essay on Shaefer's and Chapman's contributions.

42. See O. E. Sette, "Midocean Fish Production"; Schaefer, "Pacific Tuna Fishery," 237–242; and, on the fortuitous discovery of the Cromwell Current, Robert C. Cowen, *Frontiers of the Sea: The Story of Oceanographic Exploration* (Garden City, N.Y.: Doubleday, 1969), 165–166.

43. Chapman sounded an earlier clarion call himself, in "Whither the Fisheries under the Treaty with Japan?" *Pacific Fisherman* (January 1948): 33. See also Hollick, *U.S. Foreign Policy,* 95–102.

44. Miles et al., *Management of Marine Regions,* 55–57; Douglas Johnston, *The International Law of Fisheries* (New Haven, Conn.: Yale University Press, 1965), 273–277. Chapman's diplomatic activities with regard to Japan figure prominently in Bernard C. Cohen, *The Political Process and Foreign Policy: The Making of the Japanese Peace Settlement* (Princeton, N.J.: Princeton University Press, 1957).

45. William C. Herrington, *Comments on the Principle of Abstention,* UN Doc. A/CONF.L.19, prepared for the 1955 Rome Conference, mimeo. As Hollick makes clear *(U.S. Foreign Policy),* William Herrington not only was Chap-

man's successor in the State Department fisheries post in 1951, but also had a major role in developing the concept of abstention and negotiating it into the tripartite treaty.

46. Richard Van Cleve, "The Economic and Scientific Basis of the Principle of Abstention," in UN Conference on Law of the Sea, *Official Records*, vol. 1: *Preparatory Documents* (Geneva, 1958): 47–62.

47. Chapman, "The North," November 1950 address at University of Washington, Seattle, School of Fisheries building dedication ceremonies (copy in Chapman Papers, UW Library).

48. The 1976 Magnuson Fisheries Management and Conservation Act has had similar effects. See Margaret Dewar, *Industry in Trouble: The Federal Government and the New England Fisheries* (Philadelphia: Temple University Press, 1983); Marc L. Miller and John Van Maanen, "The Emerging Organization of Fisheries in the United States," *Coastal Zone Management Journal* 10 (1983): 369–378.

49. See Scheiber, "Pacific Ocean Resources," 516–532; also, Arthur McEvoy, *The Fisherman's Problem: Ecology and Law in the California Fisheries, 1850–1980* (Cambridge: Cambridge University Press, 1986).

50. Donald Fleming, "Roots of the New Conservation Movement," *Perspectives in American History* 6 (1971): 40–41 and passim. Chapman decidedly did not conform to the classification "politico-scientist" postulated by Fleming: an activist who sought to "stir up a lay constituency" in causes generally critical of the established political, economic, and scientific order, along the lines of Fleming's portrayal of Barry Commoner (ibid., 40–52). Chapman was a reformer, but not a publicist against the industry or in any sense against the scientific community. In fact, his outlook and overall career are comparable to, say, Gifford Pinchot's, including the strain that suggests faith in what has been called "the gospel of efficiency" more than to those of Barry Commoner. Cf. Samuel P. Hays, *Conservation and the Gospel of Efficiency: The Progressive Conservation Movement, 1890–1920* (Cambridge, Mass.: Harvard University Press, 1959).

10

Soviet Science in the Pacific:
The Case of Marine Biology

ROBERT H. RANDOLPH
JOHN E. BARDACH

SOVIET scientists today play a major role in the study of the Pacific Ocean, as did the scientists of prerevolutionary Russia before them. No discussion of the history of science in the Pacific, therefore, would be complete without some attention to the Russian and Soviet experience in Pacific Ocean research. In this chapter we propose to illuminate some peculiarities of that experience, focusing on a particular branch of study—marine biology—which has always enjoyed high priority in Soviet research on the Pacific and which today has wide-ranging implications for resource use, economic and political relations, and other aspects of Soviet activity in the Pacific region. Of particular interest are (1) the unique pattern of institutional development that has taken place under the influence of broader trends in Soviet science, economy, and politics, and (2) the dynamic relationship between Soviet research on living resources in the Pacific and Soviet policies regarding their exploitation or husbandry.

Although the Soviet Union is sometimes thought of as primarily a European and hence Atlantic power, the actual Soviet presence in the Pacific Ocean has often been greater than that in the Atlantic. Russian navigators first ventured upon Pacific waters in 1645, when Russia's access to the Atlantic was blocked by Swedes in the north and Turks in the south.[1] Russian explorers from the seventeenth century onward left their names on Pacific straits, bays, and coasts, while Russian traders, trappers, and naval commanders carried Russia's flag to Alaska, California, and even Hawaii, where one can still see Russian forts and chapels. Soviet authors in recent years have continued to proclaim the importance of the Pacific Ocean, observing that it constitutes fully half of the world's total ocean area, "washes the coast of the most important countries," and contains "incalculable material resources," yielding for instance about 60 percent of the world's total fish catch.[2] Soviet concern for the Pacific is reinforced by the continuing national priority on development of Siberia and the Soviet Far East, exemplified by the construction of the Baikal-Amur Mainline Railway (BAM), which is intended to open up vast previously inaccessible areas north of the older Trans-Siberian Railway.[3]

Scientific investigation has been an integral part of Russian and Soviet activity in the Pacific since the time of the earliest explorers, and has been strengthened in recent decades by the growth of local

Figure 13. The Soviet Far East. (Drawn by April Kam)

scientific capabilities in the Soviet Far East.[4] The increasing importance attached to Pacific science in the Soviet era is illustrated by the rising level of Soviet involvement in the Pacific Science Association (PSA), the leading nongovernmental international scientific body in the Pacific. Soviet scientists took part in PSA activities as early as 1926, although their involvement was relatively modest until the 1950s. Currently their role has become much more intense, with numerous Soviet scientists having served as chairmen and members of PSA committees and with the late Academician Aleksandr Vasil'evich Sidorenko, then vice-president of the Academy of Sciences of the USSR (AN SSSR), also having served as president of the PSA.[5] The Soviet Union rightly took pride in hosting PSA's fourteenth congress (1979) in Khabarovsk, the first held on Soviet soil, and the results of the congress were considered important enough to be presented at a special session of the Presidium of the AN SSSR.[6] Equally telling is the fact that in 1976 nearly half of all voyages undertaken by research vessels of the Soviet academies of sciences were in the Pacific and Far East seas—almost three times as many as in any other single ocean area.[7]

Soviet concern for marine biology itself also has a rich heritage. Research in this field by Russian scientists began as early as the eighteenth century with the work of Georg Wilhelm Steller (1709–1746), Stepan Petrovich Krasheninnikov (1713–1755), and others. In the 1870s, one of the world's first marine biology stations was established at Sevastopol' in the Crimea to explore the unique biota of the Black Sea.[8] Today marine biology is recognized as having ever-increasing practical significance. As one Soviet author put it, "Solving problems of marine biology is necessary for successful solution of the most important practical tasks facing mankind, namely, preservation of an environment favorable for mankind and the rational use and expansion of biological resources."[9]

This general concern for marine biology has long applied to the Pacific in particular. The work of Krasheninnikov and Steller took place largely in the Pacific and adjoining seas, and other expeditionary research continued throughout the prerevolutionary period. The idea of creating a permanent marine biology research station on the Pacific was raised in the late nineteenth century by such figures as Fedor Fedorovich Busse, an admiral of the Imperial Russian Navy, and N. A. Pal'chevskii, vice-president of the Society for the Study of the Amur Region.[10] That such concern continues today is illustrated by the fact that Academician Sidorenko's presentation on the fourteenth Pacific science congress to the Presidium of the AN SSSR opened with a consideration of biological research in the Pacific,[11] and by the strong biological emphasis in the work of the Far East Science Center in Vladivostok and Nakhodka.

Institutional Beginnings, 1923–1928

Despite this early interest and activity, institutional development and large-scale research began only in the Soviet era.[12] In January 1923, barely five years after the Bolshevik October Revolution and less than a year after Soviet control had been extended to the Far Eastern region around Vladivostok, authorities in the area began organizing marine affairs by placing them under a newly created agency whose official name—the Far East Administration of Fisheries, Hunting of Marine Wild Animals, and State Industry —was mercifully abbreviated to "Dal'ryba" (Far-Fish). Scientific work was delegated to a Dal'ryba subdivision known as Dal'-nauchrybbiuro (Far East Fishery Research Bureau). Lacking its own laboratories, this body drew its scientific personnel from the newly formed Far East State University. It undertook studies of salmon, crab, and other marine species from six observation posts around the shores of Peter the Great Bay near Vladivostok.

In the summer of 1924 a similar institution—the Sadgorod Biological Station—was established on the shore of the Amur Gulf through the joint efforts of the Far East State University and the Primor'e (Maritime) Branch of the State Geographical Society. The latter, interestingly, had been formed on the basis of the prerevolutionary Society for the Study of the Amur Region, and so the new Sadgorod station represented a fulfillment of the vision proclaimed by the society's vice-president twenty-five years before.

Although both Dal'nauchrybbiuro and the Sadgorod station performed useful work, chiefly inventories of local marine fauna, the Far East authorities began to see that a single institution under fully qualified scientific leadership would be even more beneficial. In 1925, therefore, a distinguished Leningrad hydrobiologist, Professor Konstantin Mikhailovich Deriugin was invited to undertake the leadership of a new institution under Dal'ryba that would replace both of the earlier ones. Such a task, under Soviet conditions at the time, represented something of a challenge. On the eve of Deriugin's scheduled departure for Vladivostok with a small team of colleagues, for example, no funds for the trip had yet arrived from the Far Eastern authorities. Deriugin's reputation as an enthusiastic and resourceful scientific entrepreneur, however, had been well earned; faced with this pecuniary obstacle, Duriugin personally borrowed the necessary funds, and the little team set off as planned.

Deriugin's new institution, the Pacific Fisheries Research Station (Tikhookeanskaia nauchno-promyslovaia stantsiia, or TONS), began operation in refurbished buildings on Cape Basargin, not far from Vladivostok. Despite the earlier efforts of Dal'-nauchrybbiuro and the Sadgorod station, most recent authors consider Deriugin's new station to be the first significant marine biology institution in the Soviet Far East. Over the next few years, Deriugin's research team conducted valuable studies of local marine life, publishing their results in the station's *Izvestiia* (News), which is still published today.

Another major institution—the State Hydrological Institute (Gosudarstvennyi gidrologicheskii institut, or GGI)—became involved in Pacific marine biology in 1926, the year after TONS was founded. This involvement, initially on an expeditionary basis with yearly voyages into the Japan Sea, extended into the Sea of Okhotsk in 1928 and into the Bering Sea and the Sea of Chukotsk soon after.

The "Great Break" and Its Aftermath, 1928–1940

In 1928 the Soviet Union began a period of political, social, and economic transformation generally referred to as the "Great Break," coinciding with Joseph Stalin's consolidation of power, the collectivization of agriculture, and the imposition of political control—in the form of central planning—on the national economy and other areas of institutional activity, including science.[13] The effects on Pacific marine biology were complex and impossible to trace in detail from information available in the West, but the general patterns are clear.

The new push for socialist economic development resulted in rapidly expanding demands on the Far Eastern fisheries industry. The industry's state-planned production target for 1930, for example, was two-and-a-half times the previous year's actual catch. The only way to meet such targets was to shift fishing activities from coastal waters to more productive offshore areas, but to do this required new information and thus expanded research.

To begin addressing this need, several institutional changes were made. First, the Pacific Fisheries Research Station (TONS) was transformed in 1929 into an institute, the Pacific Fisheries Research Institute (Tikhookeanskii nauchnyi institut rybnogo khoziaistva, or TIRKh), with several departments and with its quarters relocated from Cape Basargin to the center of Vladivostok. This move away from the shore effectively symbolizes the change taking place in the institution's research focus, a shift from local waters to the more distant open ocean.

At this time, the State Hydrological Institute (GGI) also took action to support intensified offshore research, proposing the establishment of a base on the Kamchatka peninsula. This proposal was accepted by the planning authorities, and in 1931 GGI's Kamchatka Marine Station (Kamchatskaia morskaia stantsiia, or KMS) came into being at Avachinsk Inlet, near Petropavlovsk-kamchatskii. KMS set to work, operating partly through cooperative agreements with TIRKh and the Far East Geophysical Institute. KMS and TIRKh even drafted a five-year plan for joint work over the period 1933–1937, although this plan apparently was never implemented. The importance of GGI's intended role in these years is suggested by its claim to exercise overall leadership of hydrological and hydrobiological work in the Far East, even though the work was carried out on the ships of TIRKh. Significantly, the head of GGI's Marine Branch at this time was none other than K. M. Deriugin, founder and still director of TONS-TIRKh.

Although the principal emphasis was now on offshore research, specialized needs for investigations in coastal waters continued concerning local fish and also seaweed as a raw material for the iodine and agar-agar industries. To study seaweed, the Algobiological Station of TIRKh was established in 1930 on Petrov Island, and for fisheries research the Experimental Fishery Station was created on Putiatin Island in 1931.

Also in 1931, TIRKh was called upon to intensify its relations with industry; it attempted to comply by concluding an agreement with the Far East State Fisheries Trust, Dal'gosrybtrest. By the terms of this agreement, the trust would make available for TIRKh's use its entire fishing fleet and one line at the local cannery for one day of every ten in exchange for the labor of eight TIRKh workers the rest of the time. The arrangement proved unsuccessful because scientific experiments had to be sacrificed to the fulfillment of highly demanding production plans. The discredited arrangement was cancelled in 1932.

In the summers of 1932 and 1933, GGI and TIRKh conducted joint expeditions on a scale unprecedented at that time.[14] Six ships performed simultaneous hydrological, hydrobiological, and ichthyological research on the Japan, Okhotsk, Bering, and Chukotsk seas, intended to clarify whether trawling was a viable high-yield approach to fishing in those seas. The negative results led to the dissolution in 1934 of the Trawling Trust, which since 1929 had been optimistically assembling a substantial trawling fleet.

During the years 1932–1936, institutions involved in Far East marine biology experienced rapid growth. In the summer of 1932, for instance, TIRKh observation posts on Sakhalin Island and the Kamchatka peninsula were upgraded to the status of departments. Two years later, TIRKh itself was expanded by the addition of an Oceanography Sector, with laboratories of hydrology, hydrochemistry, and marine geology. In token of its expanded character, the institute was renamed the Pacific Research Institute of Fisheries and Oceanography (Tikhookeanskii nauchno-issledovatel'skii institut rybnogo khoziaistva i okeanografii, or TINRO), under which name it remains active today. Also in 1934, the Algobiological Station on Petrov Island was reorganized into the Fishery-Biological Station (Prombiostantsiia).[15] At first the station merely added research on crabs to the seaweed work it had begun earlier, but it gradually expanded its scope to include a broad range of both descriptive and experimental work, carried out by expeditions as well as in the laboratory. Recent commentary on the history of the Prombiostantsiia has argued that it was developing into a type of biological research station entirely new to the Soviet Far East—a truly comprehensive marine biology institute.

Besides the institutions mentioned so far, several others—including Moscow and Leningrad state universities and the zoological, botanical, oceanological, and other institutes of the AN

SSSR—took part in Pacific marine biological research during these early years. One final institution with its own local facilities should be mentioned: the Marine Hydrobiology Laboratory (Laboratoriia morskoi gidrobiologii) of the Far East Branch of the Academy of Sciences (Dal'nevostochnyi filial Akademii nauk SSSR, or DVF AN SSSR). Development of this laboratory was evidently a high-priority undertaking for the academy's new Far East Branch, judging from the fact that it was created in 1933, barely a year after the founding of the Far East Branch itself. An interesting sidelight on the workings of Far Eastern science, specifically the interplay of institutional arrangements and scientists' career paths, is offered by the background of the sector's first laboratory director, Konstantin Abramovich Brodskii. Brodskii received his postgraduate training at the Zoological Institute of the USSR Academy of Sciences (Zoologicheskii institut AN SSSR, or ZIN). Then by an agreement with TINRO he worked for a number of years at the Algobiological Station on Petrov Island, until invited by the Academy's Far East Branch to organize its new laboratory. This mobile scholar was thus involved, in various ways, with most of the key institutions in the field.[16]

Abruptly in 1936 the rapid institutional development of Pacific marine biology was interrupted by a series of major reorganizations.[17] First, GGI's Kamchatka Marine Station (KMS) was closed. Its hydrological research functions passed to a Marine Observatory that had been created there in 1933, while its hydrobiological activities were taken over by the Kamchatka Department of TINRO. Significantly, at about the same time, GGI's Marine Branch was liquidated. Starting in 1936, the role GGI had played as TINRO's principal research partner was assumed by ZIN, which had been sending its own expeditions into the area since 1934, using as a base the Prombiostantsiia on Petrov Island. However, in 1936 the Prombiostantsiia too was abruptly closed, and in 1939 the same fate befell Brodskii's Marine Hydrobiology Laboratory.

Available Soviet sources offer little direct evidence for the reasons behind this sudden institutional destruction. One Soviet author suggests that the 1936 closing of KMS occurred in connection with a reorganization of the USSR Hydrometeorological Service (Gidrometeorologicheskaia sluzhba SSSR, or "Gidrometsluzhba"), parent body of the GGI; however, available information on the history of the Gidrometsluzhba and of GGI casts little if any light on the events in question.[18] The 1939 closure of Brodskii's laboratory can be more definitely linked to broader institutional developments, in this case the disbanding of the entire DVF AN SSSR in 1939, but subsequent Soviet writings have said only that this took place "under the influence of the war danger created in the Far East by the imperialists"—by no means a complete explanation.[19] Equally unsatisfactory is the reason given for liquidation of GGI's Marine Branch, said to have occurred because, during World War II, a "broadening of the content and an increase of the volume of work" of the GGI Marine Branch led to creation of the State Oceanographic Institute "on the basis of" the Marine Branch —an especially peculiar explanation, given that the Marine Branch appears to have been closed sometime between 1936 and 1938, at least three years before Soviet entry into World War II.[20] As to the closure of the Prombiostantsiia, available sources provide no explanation for this whatever.

It should be noted, of course, that the late 1930s were a traumatic time for Soviet science, as for all of Soviet society. These years, for instance, marked the beginning of virulent Lysenkoism —the period of political interference in Soviet biology associated with the notorious Trofim Denisovich Lysenko (1898–1976).[21] Lysenko's pseudoscientific notions about inheritance of acquired traits by plants and animals promised agricultural breakthroughs and thus captured the imagination of the Soviet leadership. The upshot was suppression of those ideas, institutions, and individuals of whom Lysenko and his associates disapproved—including the entire field of modern genetics and other offensive practices such as the use of mathematics in biological research. Also, 1936 was the height of the great Stalin purges, which went on until 1940 and had a great influence on science, causing the decimation of personnel and shifts in the leadership of many institutions. The universal dominance of Moscow also was an important factor in Soviet science. But it seems likely that Far Eastern marine biology may have been less vulnerable to events of the 1930s than some other branches of Soviet science. The field was, at that time and also later, very predominantly descriptive; after all, there was so much to be discovered and described. Therefore, one might expect that the ideological struggles that bedeviled other branches of Soviet science would have caused ripples there, at most. Nevertheless, in the absence of more complete information, one must assume that events in marine biology were at least indirectly affected by these broader developments.

It is interesting to note what evidence we have about the fate of individuals involved in Pacific marine biology at the time. For example, K. A. Brodskii, director of the Marine Hydrobiology Laboratory of the DVF AN SSSR, survived its demise in 1939 and moved to ZIN, where he continued his earlier research on *Calanoida* and published major books on this and related subjects over the next forty years. In the 1970s, presumably at the age of more than sixty, Brodskii also tackled new topics, publishing on theoretical questions of animal systematics and phylogeny and—of all things—the riverine fauna of the Tien-Shan Mountains.[22]

K. M. Deriugin, who lost part of his institutional base when the GGI Marine Branch closed in 1936, retained his directorship of TINRO and even succeeded in counteracting some of the effects of the turmoil at GGI. With the endorsement of the director of ZIN, Deriugin persuaded the president of the Academy of Sciences to resume under ZIN auspices a former GGI publication series presenting research results on the Far Eastern seas.[23] Deriugin died in 1938, but judging from a laudatory necrology published at the time, the publication over the next dozen years of his remaining manuscripts, and subsequent admiring biographical treatment, there is no reason to believe that his death was from other than natural causes.[24]

The fate of other scientists is more difficult to determine. For example, A. Ia. Kurharskii, director of the TINRO Prombiostantsiia, seems to have disappeared from history when the station was closed in 1936. Since his only recorded transgression was to be less helpful than he might have been to the ZIN researchers who used his station as a base of operations in 1934,[25] one can only guess what may have become of him.

War and Reconstruction, 1941–1964

World War II disrupted work in Soviet marine biology, although perhaps less in the Far East than elsewhere. Some senior scientists working near combat zones in other parts of the Soviet Union were relocated to safer areas but were able to continue their research. For example, Aleksandr Mikhailovich D'iakonov, the leading Soviet specialist on *Echinodermata* (starfish, sea urchins, etc.), was evacuated in 1942 at age fifty-five from the Zoological Museum of the AN SSSR in Leningrad to Alma Ata in Soviet Central Asia; there he continued his analysis and writing and succeeded in publishing, in 1945, a major work on the relationship between Pacific and Arctic fauna based on evidence from his specialty.[26] Many younger scientists, however, were called to arms, and a sadly diminished number returned. A. Ia. Taranets, a respected young ichthyologist, is one Far Eastern scholar specifically known to have died in battle.[27]

After the war, several years were needed before the scope and effort of the prewar era could be restored. In 1945–1949, for instance, major efforts by TINRO scientists, working in collaboration with colleagues from the Zoology Institute of Moscow State University, focused on the Amur River area—an immediately accessible area where research could be conducted with minimal material support.[28] Other researchers resumed work on data gathered previously, even as far back as the GGI/TINRO expeditions of 1932–1935; the last major volume of findings from these expeditions was published as late as 1950.[29]

By 1947, TINRO was able to resume expeditionary research, beginning with a three-year series of voyages, in collaboration with ZIN, to Sakhalin and the Kurile Islands (newly acquired from Japan). In 1949 the Institute of Oceanology of the AN SSSR began a long and very productive series of expeditionary voyages on the research vessel *Vitiaz'*, with initial attention primarily on the Kurile-Kamchatka Trench. By 1957–1958, expeditionary efforts had been expanded by the efforts of cytologists and then other biologists from Moscow and Leningrad, focusing on the Japan Sea.[30]

The Modern Era, 1965–Present

In the early postwar period, as we have seen, numerous Soviet institutions became involved in Pacific marine biology research. Because most of these institutions were based far from the Pacific, however, they had to conduct their investigations on an expeditionary basis, which—as in the prewar era—was not entirely satisfactory, particularly for experimental aspects of the work. Thus in the mid-1960s proposals began to surface for creation of a new, broadly defined, institute of marine biology in the Soviet Far East.[31] At first it was suggested that an even broader institute for the study of the sea might be established, with a marine biology section, but this proposal foundered. Then, a group of Leningrad biologists proposed the organization of a special marine biology institute for Pacific Ocean research. This suggestion found support in the Primor'e Regional Committee of the Communist Party of the Soviet Union (CPSU) and the Siberian Department of the AN SSSR, and in 1966 the Presidium of the AN SSSR decreed the creation of a Section on Marine Biology within the Far East Branch of the Siberian Department. To implement the tasks of this section, the Institute of Marine Biology was established in January 1970 as one of the initial eight institutes in the academy's new Far East Science Center (Dal'nevostochnyi nauchnyi tsentr, or DVNTs), under the methodological guidance of the academy's Section on General Biology.

The institute's founder, and still its director as of 1986, was Aleksei Viktorovich Zhirmunskii, one of the more eminent figures in Soviet marine biology in general and Pacific marine biology in particular.[32] Zhirmunskii's stature, and indirectly that of his institute, is suggested by the fact that as a corresponding member of the AN SSSR, he is the only marine biologist currently honored with either full or corresponding membership in the academy.[33]

The main research focus of the Institute of Marine Biology was, at least initially, on experimental work and the region of the continental shelf.[34] The institute began publishing its findings in its *Nauchnye soobshchenie* (Scientific Communications) in 1971, adding a periodical *Sbornik rabot* (Collection of Works) in 1974 and the broader monthly journal *Biologiia moria* (Marine Biology) in 1975. The international stature of this last publication is attested by the fact that it is translated into English in its entirety under the title *Soviet Journal of Marine Biology*. The importance of the new institute is also suggested by the fact that it was chosen to host the USSR's first "all-union" (nationwide) conference on marine biology, held in September 1977.[35]

Throughout the postwar period, Soviet marine biology in the Pacific (and elsewhere) has greatly expanded its range of activity. Expeditions are going farther, into tropical and Antarctic waters, and deeper, to depths of two thousand meters and below.[36] Here, as in other advanced nations, enhanced ocean research marked the 1960s; new creatures were studied and new questions raised—about the feed base for various species, about every phase of a creature's life cycle, about many interrelated aspects of marine ecosystems. New research methods and tools began to be used—satellites to study ocean currents and their effects on fish stocks, radiation techniques to study coral growth, submersibles for direct observation of organisms in their natural habitat.[37] New institutes have been created to study marine problems from the standpoint of highly specialized new disciplines (e.g., biochemistry) and even from a social-science point of view (e.g., the new Institute of Ocean Economics in Vladivostok).[38] Joint research has been conducted with institutions in other countries, including the United States. Research results have been embodied in broad survey volumes, atlases, and an immense number of monographs and articles.[39]

Critical Issues: Man's Relation to the Biosphere

By official mandate, the main thrust of Soviet work in marine biology, in the Pacific as elsewhere, has been toward the development and exploitation of marine biological resources for use by man. When the need for broader study of marine plants and animals was proclaimed at the twenty-fifth congress of the CPSU in 1976, explicit emphasis was placed on research that might increase fisheries production. Research findings are used as a source of recommendations for both long-term and operational plans of the fishing industry. Some research is directed toward improving methods for extraction and processing of living marine resources, including utilization of previously unexploited species. Such efforts have met with considerable success, especially in the Pacific and adjacent seas, making it the leading fish-producing region of the USSR. Some authors are optimistic that this process can continue, claiming that a total catch twice the volume achieved today is entirely possible.[40]

At the same time, however, increasing attention is being given to the problem of human influences on the marine biosphere, and on the possibility that there may be significant limits to the growth of production. At the 1977 all-union conference on marine biology, various presentations made clear that the greatest influences on fluctuations in the available stocks of fish and other living marine resources are human, such as fishing, pollution, and physical disruption.[41] Such concerns had been voiced earlier, even officially, for instance at the twenty-fourth congress of the CPSU in 1970. Then it was noted that as a result of intensified production, the ecological balance in the marine environment is disturbed, and that possibilities for environmental protection should be studied.[42] Scientists commenting on the problem went even further, arguing that there was a genuine danger of depleting marine resources and that limits to fisheries were not far off.[43] Recent arguments have gone further still:

> Resources of some commercial types [of marine creatures] are already exhausted. Thus in 100 years about 2 million head of whales have been caught, which has led to their complete destruction in the northern hemisphere and a sharp exhaustion of reserves in the southern. . . . The opening up of new regions of production, and also of frontal zones with increased biological productivity and new objectives (including exploitation of antarctic zooplankton—krill, earlier the food base for whales) can only postpone somewhat the time of complete exhaustion of commercial resources.[44]

Soviet authors generally recognize two approaches for dealing with these problems. The first approach is to regulate extractive activities (e.g., fishing), based on comprehensive knowledge of the biological systems involved and the effects different rates and patterns of extraction will have. The focus here is on population dynamics as influenced by anthropogenic factors (fishing, pollution, etc.). Methods of research often include mathematical modeling as a basis for short- and long-term forecasting. Academician Sidorenko, for instance, in his 1979 report on the fourteenth Pacific science congress, began the discussion by describing, as an example of the practical significance of marine biological research in the region, a mathematical model of tropical plankton communities and its ability to forecast their development. Such efforts draw on the findings of nonbiological research as well, such as the studies being conducted by the Pacific Oceanological Institute of the DVNTs on anthropogenic pollution of the oceans. The vision suggested by this approach is of a changeover from unregulated hunting of marine creatures to a planned marine economy based on comprehensive knowledge, wise policies, and international agreements.[45] Proponents of the approach suggest that it may even have the potential to rebuild currently depleted resources; as one author puts it, "on such a basis, it might be possible in the future to restore the whale industry too."[46]

Some specific steps are already being taken in the Soviet Union to preserve the marine environment. Under Soviet law, legal protection is provided for bodies of water, including the oceans.[47] While only protecting a very small portion of the sea, it is nevertheless of note that the Soviet Union's first marine park was created in March 1978 near Vladivostok, in Peter the Great Bay, under the management of the Institute of Marine Biology of DVNTs. This Far East State Marine Park, which includes 63,000 hectares of water and 1,360 hectares of land, is intended to protect and restore the natural environment and genetic stock of a biologically rich but threatened coastal site, and to serve as a focus for research and educational activities. Iurii Dmitrievich Chugunov, a staff member of the park, wrote in 1979 that "the very fact of the creation of the first marine park in the USSR has a definite psychological and pedagogical influence on the education of Soviet people about the new communist relation to the protection of nature."[48] A presentation about the marine park project reportedly gave rise to "great interest" at the 1977 all-union conference on marine biology. More recently, it is said that other marine parks are foreseen by the scientists of the Institute of Marine Biology, first on the Moneron and southern Kurile islands, where undersea life is especially rich, and also in areas of the Japan Sea adjacent to existing terrestrial parks.[49]

The second main approach advocated in the USSR toward solving the marine biological resource problem is human intervention to increase the biological productivity of the ocean. Proponents of this approach have likened it to agriculture and animal husbandry as methods of enhancing the productivity of the land; it would be an extension of current land-based and near-shore activities in aquaculture. According to one recent discussion by Andrei Sergeevich Monin,[50] the principal requirement for such an effort in the open ocean would be to increase the growth of phytoplankton, the starting point in the ocean food chain. This in turn might well be achieved, Monin suggests, through use of applied fertilizer, per-

Figure 14. Pacific Ocean Bioorganic Chemistry Institute, Peter the Great Bay, photographed by S. Kozlov. (Tass from Sovfoto)

haps in the form of floating slow-release granules. Initial experiments could be conducted in semi-enclosed bodies of water, or in midocean areas isolated by the circular Gulfstream or Kuroshio currents. Other projects might include modification of the flow of water through the Bering and other oceanic straits, or the creation of artificial upwellings to bring nutrient-rich deep-ocean water to the surface by placing atomic reactors on the seabed as a concentrated heat source. These are schemes born of technological optimism quite disregarding the gigantic inputs necessary, and even Monin acknowledges that some of them might not work (noting for instance that natural thermal releases from the seabed typically do not break through stable water strata above). He also admits that "today we still do not know how to evaluate all consequences of such measures." Nevertheless, he concludes that such ideas may deserve renewed attention sometime in the future.

Although some of the schemes just mentioned may seem far-fetched, more modest versions of ocean resource cultivation are already known, in the form of mariculture. In some areas of the Soviet Far East, mariculture development efforts began at the end of the 1960s.[51] As of the late 1970s, both TINRO and the Institute of Marine Biology had substantial research teams focusing on possibilities for breeding seaweed and several types of fish, and on the underlying biological study of the species and ecosystems involved.[52] As in Japan, a prime proponent of such efforts, mariculture is viewed in the Soviet Union as an important link joining basic and applied research in marine biology, and as a vitally important focus for further research.[53] Recent evaluations suggest that the Primor'e area, southern Sakhalin, and the southern Kurile Islands should be especially suitable for temperate ocean mariculture. It was reported in 1982 that TINRO has a base on Popov Island which is intended to grow into a large scientific and production complex for mariculture, and that the cost-benefit assessment of a general scheme for the development and location of mariculture enterprises in Primor'e was nearing completion. By 1984 a major experimental base employing two hundred persons had been established at the coastal settlement of Glazkovka. Long-range prospects are considered good, although in the short term mariculture development is admitted to face both psychological

Figure 15. Workers on a Far Eastern marine farm prepare equipment for pecten (scallop) breeding. Photo by S. Kozlov. (Tass from Sovfoto)

Figure 16. Sea pecten (scallop) farming under way in the Soviet Far East. Photo by S. Kozlov. (Tass from Sovfoto)

obstacles, such as the tendency of fishermen to think in terms of just finding a better place to fish, and the numerous practical problems that hinder innovation throughout the Soviet economy, including shortages of labor, housing, and mechanization equipment, compounded by bureaucratic bottlenecks.[54]

As a final illustration of the various trends discussed here, it is interesting to consider the position taken by Soviet marine biologists regarding a particular marine resource that has been especially controversial in recent years: whales.

Although some Western observers have seen the Soviet attitude toward whales as being primarily destructive,[55] Soviet marine biologists have been aware at least since the 1930s that whale stocks are declining and that some varieties of whales are gravely endangered. In 1934, for example, cetacean specialist Boris Aleksandrovich Zenkovich warned that "the character of the migration of gray whales allows for their easy catch and threatens the complete extinction of this most interesting species. Their surviving remnants require immediate international protection." Such warnings alas had little effect; recent Soviet reviews of long-term data have shown that the gray whales in the Sea of Okhotsk, once numerous, had declined to a mere four individuals by 1964 and to one lone survivor a decade later.[56]

Despite this sad history, some Soviet scientists in recent years have urged increased harvesting of the few types of whales still in plentiful supply, on the (not very tenable) grounds that their consumption of food competes with other commercially important marine species.[57] Others, however, have taken an entirely different attitude, specifically discussing the dangers of depletion and threatened extinction, and proposing a series of steps leading to a more rational, sustainable utilization of whales as a renewable natural resource. The first step, it is suggested, would be increased selectivity in harvesting, culling individuals that are old or have low reproductive potential, to minimize the effect on the reproductive potential of the population as a whole. The second step would be a kind of "herding," with year-round monitoring of selected families of—one would assume—small, nonmigratory species, by fast, long-range boats, aircraft, and/or satellites. This step could also include efforts to encourage the use of optimal migration routes and feeding and breeding grounds; to protect the whale herds from disturbance by other ships, military maneuvers, and ocean mining; to intensify reproduction, for instance by hormone injections; and to conduct genetic selection, possibly including aerial transportation of selected breeding stock to desired locations. The third step would be true whale farming, in captive or semi-captive conditions, possibly using the lagoons of coral islands.[58]

Such proposals make exciting reading, but they are close to science fiction for biological and economic, let alone technical, reasons. They are born of the Marxist tendency to be doctrinarily over-optimistic when it comes to assessing possibilities of man mastering nature. Although these proposals involve animal breeding, we could trace no connection with the aberrant theories of Lysenko which, if true, would make it easier to "change the nature of the whale," as it were, making it more amenable to what is proposed. Lysenko's dominance over Soviet official plant and animal breeding endeavors ended with the ouster of his patron, Nikita Khrushchev, in 1964; the whale-breeding proposals were proferred in the late 1970s and early 1980s.

Whatever the prospects might be for implementing such proposals in the future, the issue of Soviet policy toward whaling has been resolved along other lines, at least for the time being. The Soviet Union has announced that it will cease commercial whaling as of 1987—officially because of declining whale stocks, but presumably also partly because of U.S. sanctions imposed in 1985 in response to alleged Soviet violation of whaling quotas set by the International Whaling Commission. Although the cessation is claimed to be temporary, the chances of resumption are small given the climate of world opinion (to which the Soviet leadership under Mikhail Gorbachev appears to be more sensitive than in earlier periods), as well as the uncertain economic viability of the aging Soviet whaling fleet.[59]

Conclusions

In some respects, the Soviet experience in Pacific marine biology has been comparable to that of other nations. The USSR now shares with the United States, and to some extent Japan, preeminence in the marine biological sciences of all oceans, prominently including the Pacific. There is, naturally, more emphasis on the north temperate than the tropical seas, but there is also much research activity in the southern oceans where Soviet fishing vessels and those of their socialist allies are very active.

Soviet scientists have recognized, as have those of other nations, that there is an ever-increasing need to ascertain quantitative ecologic relations among various trophic levels and the physical, chemical, and anthropogenic effects on them. They have also become engaged, prominently, in oceanographic model-making and in ascertaining interactions of climate, the oceans, and their living denizens.

Soviet scientists are also in the process of probing into the real limits of biological production that can be attained *economically;* in the early years of Soviet fishing science, those limits were seen as more extended than now appears the case—this notwithstanding the fact that Soviet fisheries are less influenced by market forces than those of capitalist nations.

Again like other nations (except Japan), the Soviet Union has faced serious problems of distance and bases. Early efforts to overcome these problems had mixed success, but the situation is improving rapidly at present with several Far Eastern laboratories well established and with large research platforms available in the form of both research vessels and fishing vessels that also do research.

On the other hand, marine biology in the Soviet Far East has faced some challenges unknown in most other countries. Especially during the period of the Great Break in 1929–1932, research institutions found themselves pushed and pulled by the dictates of socialist social experimentation. The abortive attempt to mesh science and production through a mechanical sharing of personnel and equipment between the Pacific Fisheries Research Institute and the Far East State Fisheries Trust in 1930–1932 is a case in point. It should be noted, however, that the underlying concern here is not unique to the Soviet Union. Data from the production phase are important to marine biology, and it is not only the Soviet Union that seeks to find and implement the best mode of interaction between research and production. Experimentation with this interaction can be seen in all nations active in fisheries and marine biological research.

Far more serious and more unique to the Soviet experience are instances of destructive political interference such as the Lysenko era and the Stalin purges. Although the available evidence is incomplete, it seems probable that some of the Soviet institutions and individuals in Pacific marine biology that disappeared during the late 1930s may have been victims of these broader forces.

Conditions of the Stalin era are mercifully long past. Nevertheless, Soviet science in the Pacific continues to be affected by political factors, especially with regard to the international arena. Soviet discussions of the Pacific Science Association, for instance, do not confine themselves to the strictly scientific considerations that we have mentioned so far. Instead, Soviet commentators have also viewed the association as a potential mechanism for addressing social issues in the Pacific region, issues related to the "colonial or semicolonial" status of many of the Pacific Island nations and to the many acute problems perceived to exist in connection with the use of resources, population growth and relocation, economics, history, culture, education, and other matters not purely scientific in the usual Western sense.[60]

When Soviet commentators have occasion to characterize the reception that Soviet scientific activities receive from other countries in the region, they sometimes appear to deceive themselves. Academician Nikolai Alekseevich Shilo, head of the DVNTs, has for example claimed that the "humane goals" pursued by Soviet research vessels have "made them popular in many developing countries of the Pacific Ocean basin,"[61] leaving unmentioned the fact that some Pacific countries have explicitly declared their waters off-limits to such vessels. Soviet authors tacitly acknowledge the existence of such restrictions when they argue that "oceanologists must be assured freedom of scientific research on all water areas of the world ocean and, even more, active cooperation of littoral countries [in] carrying out such research in the zones of national interests along their shores."[62] That some countries might be wary of permitting Soviet research vessels into their waters, however, is not surprising, given the strong hints that such vessels may sometimes have more than purely scientific missions. It is known that the distinction between ocean sciences data that serve fisheries and those that can serve for strategic planning is tenuous indeed (e.g., data on underwater sound propagation are pertinent to animal communication and fishfinding, but also to the detection of submarines).[63] One wonders whether it is purely coincidental that of the five sites selected for study in a recent worldwide oceanographic research program conducted by the Soviet Union and several of its East European allies,[64] two are off the east coast of the United States, one off the coast of Japan, and one in the strategically important Iceland Straits.

In this connection, it is also interesting to note that in February 1985 the Pacific Science Association passed a Soviet-introduced resolution calling upon member states to render appropriate assistance to research vessels of other member nations. Whether or not this will have an influence on implementation of certain articles of the Convention on the Law of the Sea (UNCLOS III), which stipulated that permission to conduct research within any nation's Exclusive Economic Zone must be applied for, remains to be seen.

Notes

Russian-language sources are indicated here by author and short title only. Complete citations are given in the list of Russian-language references following these notes.

AN *Vestnik*	Akademiia nauk SSSR, *Vestnik*
DVFAN *Vestnik*	Akademiia nauk SSSR, Dal'nevostochnyi filial, *Vestnik*
Issledovaniia	Akademiia nauk SSSR, *Issledovaniia dal'nevostochnykh morei SSSR*

1. George V. Lantzeff and Richard A. Pierce, *Eastward to Empire: Exploration and Conquest on the Russian Open Frontier, to 1750* (Montreal: McGill-

Queen's University Press, 1973), 158. As a result of Russian activities in the Pacific in these early years, Soviet archives offer important sources for the study of Pacific history in general. See for instance *Avstraliia i Okeaniia,* especially the chapter by L. A. Shur. Portions of this chapter (translated by Ella W. Wiswell and prepared for publication by Robert Langdon) have been published as "Russian Sources for the Writing of Pacific History," *Journal of Pacific History* 17, no. 4 (October 1982): 218–221.

2. Suziumov, "50-letie," 103.

3. For a general discussion of Soviet interest in the Pacific, see Stephen Uhalley, Jr., "The Soviet Far East: Growing Participation in the Pacific," *American Universities Field Staff Reports,* East Asia Series 24, no. 1 (1977).

4. See, for example, G. Marchuk, *Science and Siberia* (Moscow: Novosti, 1983); Pushkar', *Tikhookeanskii forpost;* and Shilo, "Nauka Dal'nego Vostoka."

5. On early Soviet involvement in PSA, see A. P. Elkin, *Pacific Science Association: Its History and Role in International Cooperation* (Honolulu: Bishop Museum Press, 1961), 44. As of 1983, Soviet scientists were chairing three of the sixteen scientific committees of the Pacific Science Association; see Pacific Science Association, *Information Bulletin* 35, nos. 1–2 (April 1983): 11–12. The extent of their interest in Pacific marine questions seemingly remote from domestic Soviet concerns is suggested by the presence of two Soviet members on PSA's scientific committee on coral reefs; see PSA, *Information Bulletin* 35, no. 6 (December 1983): 62. This last is not quite so peculiar as it might appear, incidentally, since geological structures of coral-reef origin do exist in the Soviet Union, far from any ocean.

6. Geodekian and Evgrafov, "XIV Tikhookeanskii nauchnyi kongress."

7. Kravchenko, "V Otdelenii okeanologii."

8. "Zadachi zhurnala." Steller was one of many foreign scientists who came to Russia in the eighteenth century and whose investigations are rightly claimed as part of the Russian-Soviet scientific heritage.

9. Ibid., 5.

10. Pushkar', *Tikhookeanskii forpost,* 91.

11. Geodekian and Evgrafov, "XIV Tikhookeanskii nauchnyi kongress."

12. Except as indicated, material in this section and the next is drawn chiefly from Zasel'skii, "O pervykh Sovetskikh morskikh biologicheskikh stantsiiakh" and idem, "Morskie biologicheskie stantsii." These extraordinary works are based largely on materials in Soviet archives to which non-Soviet scholars would be unlikely to obtain comparable access.

13. See Sheila Fitzpatrick, ed., *Cultural Revolution in Russia, 1928–1931* (Bloomington: Indiana University Press, 1978).

14. On these expeditions, see for example Brodskii, "Sektor morskoi gidrobiologii"; Deriugin, "Dal'nevostochnye moria"; Gomoiunov, "Rybokhoziaistvennye issledovaniia"; L. A. Zenkevitch [i.e., Lev Aleksandrovich Zenkevich], *Biology of the Seas of the USSR* (New York: Interscience Publishers, 1963), 676–678, esp. 678.

15. Zasel'skii, "Morskie biologicheskie stantsii."

16. For Brodskii's own account of the founding of the Marine Hydrobiological Laboratory, see Brodskii, "Sektor morskoi gidrobiologii."

17. On the closing of KMS, see Ratmanov, "Gidrometeorologicheskoe izuche-

nie"; on GGI's Marine Branch, see Deriugin, "Predislovie"; for ZIN's role, see Lindberg, "Kratkii polevoi otchet"; on the fate of the Prombiostantsiia and the Marine Hydrobiology Laboratory, see Zhirmunskii, "Organizatsiia instituta."

18. For the explanation of the KMS closing, see Zasel'skii, "Morskie biologicheskie stantsii"; on the history of the Gidrometsluzhba, see, e.g., Fedorov, "Sovetskaia gidrometeorologicheskaia sluzhba"; *Gosudarstvennyi ordena trudovogo krasnogo znameni gidrologicheskii institut;* Korzun, "Gidrometeorologicheskaia sluzhba SSSR"; Moshenichenko, "Iz istorii"; Ratmanov, "Gidrometeorologicheskoe izuchenie."

19. Akademiia nauk SSSR, Dal'nevostochnyi filial, Vladivostok, *Nauka na Dal'nem Vostoke,* 5.

20. *Gosudarstvennyi ordena trudovogo krasnogo znameni gidrologicheskii institut,* 5.

21. See, e.g., David Joravsky, *The Lysenko Affair* (Cambridge, Mass.: Harvard University Press, 1970); and Zhores A. Medvedev, *The Rise and Fall of T. D. Lysenko* (New York: Columbia University Press, 1969).

22. For Brodskii's continued work on *Calanoida* and related topics, see Brodskii, *Fauna veslonogikh rachkov,* and idem, *Calanoida of the Far Eastern Seas and Polar Basins of the USSR,* trans. from Russian by A. Mercado (Jerusalem: Israel Program for Scientific Translations, 1967); Brodskii and Vyshkvartseva, eds., *Ekologiia morskogo planktona;* Brodskii and Vyshkvartseva, *Morskoi plankton.* For an example of his earlier work in this area, see Brodskii, "K biologii." His later work on broader topics is exemplified by idem, *Teoreticheskie voprosy,* and idem, *Gornyi potok,* also available in English as *Mountain Torrent of the Tien Shan: A Faunistic-Ecology Essay,* trans. V. V. Golosov (The Hague: Junk, 1980).

23. Deriugin, "Predislovie."

24. For the necrology, see Gur'ianova, "Pamiati." Several of Deriugin's posthumously published works are cited in Pravdin, *Konstantin Mikhailovich Deriugin.* Pravdin's book is a highly appreciative biography of Deriugin, by a colleague who accompanied him on his 1925 journey from Leningrad to Vladivostok.

25. Lindberg, "Kratkii polevoi otchet."

26. Lindberg, "Aleksandr Mikhailovich D'iakonov."

27. Schmidt, *Ryby Tikhogo okeana,* 4.

28. "Tikhookeanskii nauchno-issledovatel'skii institut."

29. *Issledovaniia* 2 (1950).

30. Zenkevitch, *Biology of the Seas,* 679, 680; Suziumov, "50-letie"; Zhirmunskii, "Organizatsiia instituta."

31. Zhirmunskii, "Organizatsiia instituta."

32. "Sozdanie instituta."

33. *World of Learning, 1986* (London: European Publications, 1985), 1220 and passim.

34. Zhirmunskii, "Organizatsiia instituta."

35. Zolotarev, "Pervaia vsesoiuznaia konferentsiia."

36. "Tikhookeanskii nauchno-issledovatel'skii institut."

37. Pushkar', *Tikhookeanskii forpost,* 91–112; Zolotarev, "Pervaia vsesoiuznaia konferentsiia." It should be noted that the ecological concerns of Soviet sci-

entists today are not entirely new. On the contrary, until the early 1930s Soviet scholars were in the forefront of ecological science, as Douglas R. Weiner has documented in "The History of the Conservation Movement in Russia and the USSR from Its Origin to the Stalin Period" (Ph.D. dissertation, Columbia University, 1983) and in "Community Ecology in Stalin's Russia: 'Socialist' and 'Bourgeois' Science" (*Isis* 75 [1984]: 684–696). Indeed it is interesting to note that the suppression of ecological concerns that accompanied the Stalinist drive for accelerated economic development was decidedly incomplete, at least among marine biologists. For example, the academy's Zoological Institute in 1938 published a detailed study of the biology of the Japan Sea, with an explicit focus on biocenoses (ecological communities) as a unit of analysis. See Akademiia nauk SSSR, Zoologicheskii institut, Gidrobiologicheskaia ekspeditsiia Zoologicheskogo instituta Akademii nauk SSSR v 1934 godu na Iaponskoe more, *Trudy.*

38. See AN *Vestnik*, 1973, no. 3:146; 1974, no. 6:125; and 1984, no. 2:139.

39. On cooperative research, see Robert H. Randolph and John E. Bardach, "Soviet-American Scientific Cooperation in the Pacific," in J. J. Stephan and V. P. Chichkanov, eds., *Soviet-American Horizons on the Pacific* (Honolulu: University of Hawaii Press, 1986; Moscow: Nauka, forthcoming); and Geodekian and Evgrafov, "XIV Tikhookeanskii nauchnyi kongress." Two important survey volumes are *Tikhii okean;* and P. A. Moiseev, ed., *Soviet Fisheries Investigations in the Northeast Pacific* (Jerusalem: Israel Program for Scientific Translations, 1968). A major atlas is Akademiia nauk SSSR, Zoologicheskii institut, *Atlas of the Invertibrates of the Far Eastern Seas of the USSR*, ed. E. N. Pavlovskii (Jerusalem: Israel Program for Scientific Translations, 1966).

40. "60 let"; P. A. Moiseev, "Fisheries Investigations and Basic Ideas on Fisheries Management in the USSR," in Pacific Science Association, XIII Pacific Science Congress, *Record of Proceedings*, vol. 1, *Abstracts of Papers* (Vancouver, B.C., Canada, 1975), 61; "Tikhookeanskii nauchno-issledovatel'skii institut"; Frantsei, "Delikates"; Shuntov, "Zamechaniia"; Moiseev, "Mirovoe rybolovstvo."

41. Sidorenko, "Prirodnye resursy."

42. Meleshkin et al., "Metodologicheskie osnovy."

43. Meleshkin, et al., "Metodologicheskie osnovy," 58.

44. Monin, "Perspektivy issledovaniia," 121. The reality and gravity of the problem of overfishing are widely acknowledged among Soviet marine biologists. For example, P. A. Moiseev, deputy director of the All-Union Research Institute of Fisheries and Oceanography (VNIRO), has published world statistics on this issue, and has in veiled terms hinted at some of the implications, juxtaposing a comment on the decline in use of very large fishing vessels in "some capitalist countries" against an account of the massive increases in the size of Soviet fishing equipment over the past half-century (trawling gear, for example, having increased in size 1000-fold in some cases). See Moiseev, "Mirovoe rybolovstvo."

45. "Tikhookeanskii nauchno-issledovatel'skii institut"; Geodekian and Evgrafov, "XIV Tikhookeanskii nauchnyi kongress"; *Kompleksnye issledovaniia;* Monin, "Perspektivy issledovaniia." See also Gauze, "Problema optimal'nogo ulova"; Bol'shakov and Iablokov, "Priroda na zavtra."

46. Monin, "Perspektivy issledovaniia," 121.

47. See Belichenko and Volkov, *Pravovaia okhrana vod.*

48. Chugunov, "Pervyi morskoi zapovednik," 79.

49. Pushkar', *Tikhookeanskii forpost,* 112.

50. Monin, "Perspektivy issledovaniia," 122. On the other hand, there are some Soviet scholars who admit that large-scale ocean fertility enhancement is unrealistic, insisting only that it would be possible on a smaller scale in some more-or-less detached areas; see Zenkevich and Bogorov, "Biologicheskie resursy."

51. Pushkar', *Tikhookeanskii forpost,* 104.

52. On TINRO's work, see "Tikhookeanskii nauchno-issledovatel'skii institut." For examples of each institution's mariculture research, see Krasnov and Moiseev, "V Iapono-Sovetskii simpozium." See also Moiseev, "Perspektivy razvitiia."

53. "60 let."

54. Pushkar', *Tikhookeanskii forpost,* 106; Markovtsev, "Morskoi 'ogorod.' "

55. E.g., Uhalley, "The Soviet Far East," 1.

56. Zenkovich, "Materialy," 25 (quotation); Berzin, "O rasprostranenii." On the overall problem of extinction of whale populations and the imperative need for international regulation, see also Zenkevich and Bogorov, "Biologicheskie resursy."

57. Sobolevskii, "Morskie mlekopitaiushchie."

58. Iablokov and Berzin, "Perspektivy razvitiia."

59. *New York Times,* 20 July 1985.

60. Suziumov, "50-letie."

61. Shilo, "Nauka Dal'nego Vostoka."

62. Monin, "Perspektivy issledovaniia."

63. John E. Bardach, "Ocean Exploitation," *Encyclopedia Britannica,* 1985.

64. Sarkisian, "Krupnomasshtabnye."

Russian-Language References

Akademiia nauk SSSR, Dal'nevostochnyi filial, Vladivostok [Academy of Sciences of the USSR, Far Eastern Branch, Vladivostok]. *Nauka na Dal'nem Vostoke (k 40-letiiu Velikoi Oktiabr'skoi sotsialisticheskoi revoliutsii i 35-letiiu sovetskoi vlasti na Dal'nem Vostoke)* [Science in the Far East (On the 40th Anniversary of the Great October Socialist Revolution and the 35th Anniversary of Soviet Power in the Far East)]. Vladivostok: 1957.

Akademiia nauk SSSR, Institut okeanologii. *Tikhii okean* [The Pacific Ocean]. 10 vols. Moscow, 1966–1972.

Akademiia nauk SSSR, Zoologicheskii institut, Gidrobiologicheskaia ekspeditsiia Zoologicheskogo instituta Akademii nauk SSSR v 1934 godu na Iaponskoe more [Academy of Sciences of the USSR, Zoological Institute, Hydrobiological Expedition of the Zoological Institute of the Academy of Sciences of the USSR in 1934 on the Japan Sea]. *Trudy* [Works], vol. 1. Moscow: 1938.

Avstraliia i Okeaniia: Istoriia i sovremennost' [Australia and Oceania: History and the Present]. Moscow: Nauka, 1970.

Belichenko, Iurii Petrovich, and Viktor Ivanovich Volkov. *Pravovaia okhrana vod* [The Legal Protection of Waters]. Moscow: Iurid. lit., 1980.

Berzin, Al'fred Antonovich. "O rasprostranenii i chislennosti zapreshchennykh k promyslu kitov v Tikhom okeane" [On the Distribution and Number of Whales Protected from Hunting in the Pacific Ocean]. *Biologiia moria,* 1978, no. 4:22–29.

Bol'shakov, V., and A. Iablokov. "Priroda na zavtra: Ratsional'no ispol'zovat' zhivoe bogatstvo" [Nature Tomorrow: To Utilize Living Riches Rationally]. *Pravda,* 10 November 1984.

Brodskii, Konstantin Abramovich. *Fauna veslonogikh rachkov (Calanoida) i zoogeograficheskoe raionirovanie severnoi chasti Tikhogo okeana i sopredel'nykh vod* [Oar-Legged Crayfish (Calanoida) and the Zoogeographic Regionalization of the Northern Part of the Pacific Ocean and Contiguous Waters]. Moscow: Izd-vo AN SSSR, 1957.

———. *Gornyi potok Tian'-Shania: Ekol.-faunist. ocherk* [Mountain Torrent of the Tien Shan: An Ecological-Faunistic Essay]. Leningrad: Nauka, Leningr. otd-nie, 1976. (Also available in English as *Mountain Torrent of the Tien Shan: A Faunistic-Ecology Essay,* trans. V. V. Golosov. The Hague: Junk, 1980.)

———. "K biologii i sistematike veslonogogo raka (Calanus cristatus Kr.)" [On the Biology and Systematics of the Oar-Legged Crayfish (Calanus cristatus Kr.)]. DVFAN *Vestnik,* 1938, no. 29 (2): 147–171.

———. "Sektor morskoi gidrobiologii v DVFAN" [The Marine Hydrobiology Sector of the Far Eastern Branch of the Academy of Sciences]. DVFAN *Vestnik,* 1934, no. 1 (8): 51–53.

———, ed. *Teoreticheskie voprosy sistematiki i filogenii zhivotnykh (Sb. statei)* [Theoretical Questions of the Systematics and Philogeny of Animals (A Collection of Articles)]. AN SSSR, Zoologicheskii institut. *Trudy 53.* Leningrad: Nauka, Leningr. otd-nie, 1974.

Brodskii, Konstantin Abramovich, and N. V. Vyshkvartseva. *Morskoi plankton: Sistematika i faunistika: Sbornik nauch. rabot* [Marine Plankton: Systematics and Faunistics: A Collection of Scientific Works]. Leningrad: Zool. in-t, 1977.

Brodskii, Konstantin Abramovich, and N. V. Vyshkvartseva, eds. *Ekologiia morskogo planktona: Sbornik nauch. rabot* [Ecology of Marine Plankton: Collection of Scientific Works]. Leningrad: Zool. in-t, 1977.

Chugunov, Iurii Dmitrievich. "Pervyi morskoi zapovednik v Sovetskom Soiuze" [The First Marine Park in the Soviet Union]. *Biologiia moria,* 1979, no. 4:74–79.

Deriugin, Konstantin Mikhailovich. "Dal'nevostochnye moria i ikh bogatstva" [The Far Eastern Seas and Their Riches]. *Nauka i zhizn',* 1939, no. 2:43–46.

———. "Predislovie" [Foreword]. *Issledovaniia* 1 (1941): 3.

Fedorov, Evgenii Konstantinovich. "Sovetskaia gidrometeorologicheskaia sluzhba k 50-letiiu Velikoi Oktiabr'skoi sotsialisticheskoi revoliutsii" [The Soviet Hydrometeorological Service on the 50th Anniversary of the Great October Socialist Revolution]. In E. K. Fedorov, ed., *Meteorologiia i gidrologiia za 50 let Sovetskoi vlasti: Sbornik statei* [Meteorology and Hydrology during 50 Years of Soviet Power: A Collection of Articles]. Leningrad: Gidromet. izd-vo, 1967.

Frantsei, O. "Delikates, rozhdennyi mikrovzryvom [A Delicacy, Born of a Microburst]. *Pravda*, 13 November 1984.

Gauze, G. F. "Problema optimal'nogo ulova" [The Optimal Catch Problem]. *Zoologicheskii zhurnal* 17, no. 3 (1938): 419–426.

Geodekian, A. A., and I. D. Evgrafov. "XIV Tikhookeanskii nauchnyi kongress" [The XIV Pacific Science Congress]. AN *Vestnik,* 1980, no. 1:83–92.

Gomoiunov, A. "Rybokhoziaistvennye issledovaniia na Dal'nem Vostoke" [Fisheries Research in the Far East]. DVFAN *Vestnik,* 1932, no. 1–2:104–105.

Gosudarstvennyi ordena trudovogo krasnogo znameni gidrologicheskii institut [The State "Order of the Red Banner of Labor" Hydrological Institute]. Leningrad: Gidrometeorologicheskoe izd-vo, 1969.

Gur'ianova, E. "Pamiati K. M. Deriugina, Issledovatel' dal'nevostochnykh morei: Nekrolog" [Recollections of K. M. Deriugin, Investigator of the Far Eastern Seas: A Necrology]. *Issledovaniia* 1 (1941): 5–9.

Iablokov, Aleksei Vladimirovich, and Al'fred Antonovich Berzin. "Perspektivy razvitiia issledovaniia kitoobraznykh" [Prospects for Development of Research on Cetaceans]. *Biologiia moria,* 1978, no. 5:3–13.

Kompleksnye issledovaniia problemy antropogennogo zagriazneniia okeana [Comprehensive Investigations of the Problem of Anthropogenic Pollution of the Ocean]. Vladivostok: DVNTs, 1981.

Korzun, Valentin Ignat'evich. "Gidrometeorologicheskaia sluzhba SSSR za 50 let" [The Hydrometeorological Service of the USSR during 50 Years]. *Meteorologiia i gidrologiia,* 1967, no. 11:3–12.

Krasnov, E. V., and Petr Alekseevich Moiseev. "V Iapono-Sovetskii simpozium po marikul'ture Tikhogo okeana" [At the Japanese-Soviet Symposium on Pacific Ocean Mariculture]. *Biologiia moria,* 1977, no. 3:83–86.

Kravchenko, D. V. "V Otdelenii okeanologii, fiziki atmosfery i geografii" [In the Department of Oceanology, Atmospheric Physics and Geography]. AN *Vestnik,* 1977, no. 8:65–68.

Lindberg, Georgii Ustinovich. "Aleksandr Mikhailovich D'iakonov, 17 I 1886–1 IV 1956" [Aleksandr Mikhailovich D'iakonov, 17 January 1886–1 April 1956]. *Issledovaniia* 5 (1958): 381–385.

———. "Kratkii polevoi otchet o gidrobiologicheskoi ekspeditsii ZIN AN v raione o. Petrova v Iaponskom more" [A Short Field Account about the Hydrobiological Expedition of the Zoological Institute of the Academy of Sciences in the Region of Petrov Island in the Japan Sea]. DVFAN *Vestnik,* 1935, no. 12:93–98.

Markovtsev, V. "Morskoi 'ogorod' " [Marine "Garden"]. *Sel'skaia zhizn',* 4 December 1984.

Meleshkin, Mikhail Timofeevich, et al. "Metodologicheskie osnovy ekonomiki mirovogo okeana" [Methodological Foundations of the Economics of the World Ocean]. AN *Vestnik,* 1974, no. 12:58–66.

Moiseev, Petr Alekseevich. "Mirovoe rybolovstvo, ego razvitie" [World Fishing, Its Development]. *Biologiia moria,* 1983, no. 3:3–12.

———. "Perspektivy razvitiia morskoi akvakul'tury v SSSR" [Prospects for Development of Marine Aquaculture in the USSR]. In *Biologicheskie resursy Mirovogo okeana,* S. A. Studenetskii, ed., 201–208. Moscow: Nauka, 1979.

Monin, Andrei Sergeevich. "Perspektivy issledovaniia i ispol'zovaniia mirovogo okeana" [Prospects for Investigation and Use of the World Ocean]. AN *Vestnik,* 1980, no. 5:118–126.

Moshenichenko, Ivan Elizarovich. "Iz istorii gidrometeorologicheskogo obsluzhivaniia morskogo flota i rybnoi promyshlennosti na Dal'nem Vostoke" [From the History of the Hydrometeorological Service of the Ocean Fleet and Fish Industry in the Far East]. *Meteorologiia i gidrologiia,* 1967, no. 8:103–107.

Pravdin, I. F. *Konstantin Mikhailovich Deriugin, 1878–1938* [Konstantin Mikhailovich Deriugin, 1878–1938]. Petrozavodsk: Gos. izd-vo Karel'skoi ASSR, 1957.

Pushkar', Arnol'd Ignat'evich. *Tikhookeanskii forpost nauki* [Pacific Outpost of Science]. 2d ed. Khabarovsk: Khabarovskoe knizhnoe izd-vo, 1982.

Ratmanov, G. E. "Gidrometeorologicheskoe izuchenie morei Soiuza SSR za 20 let" [Hydrometeorological Study of the Seas of the USSR during 20 Years]. Leningrad, Gosudarstvennyi gidrologicheskii institut. *Sbornik,* no. 1. Leningrad: Gidrometeorologicheskoe izd-vo, 1938.

Sarkisian, Artem Sarkisovich. "Krupnomasshtabnye okeanograficheskie eksperimenty" [Large-Scale Oceanographic Experiments]. AN *Vestnik,* 1983, no. 10:83–89.

Schmidt [Shmidt], Petr Iul'evich. *Ryby Tikhogo okeana: Ocherk sovremennykh teorii i vozzrenii na rasprostranenie i razvitie fauny ryb Tikhogo okeana* [Fish of the Pacific Ocean: A Sketch of Contemporary Theories and Views on the Diffusion and Development of the Fish Fauna of the Pacific Ocean]. Moscow: Pishchepromizdat, 1948.

"60 [shestdesiat'] let sovetskoi morskoi biologii" [60 Years of Soviet Marine Biology]. *Biologiia moria,* 1977, no. 5:4–5

Shilo, Nikolai Alekseevich. "Nauka Dal'nego Vostoka—Narodnomu khoziaistvu" [The Science of the Far East—For the National Economy]. AN *Vestnik,* 1984, no. 1:68–79.

Shuntov, V. P. "Zamechaniia o nekotorykh stat'iakh sbornika 'Ratsional'noe prirodopol'zovanie v usloviiakh dal'nego vostoka (Zadachi i napravleniia)' " [Notes on Some Articles in the Collection "Rational Use of Nature under Conditions of the Far East (Tasks and Directions)"]. *Biologiia moria,* 1983, no. 3:74–78.

Sidorenko, Aleksandr Vasil'evich. "Prirodnye resursy Tikhogo okeana—na blago chelovechestva" [The Natural Resources of the Pacific Ocean—For the Welfare of Mankind]. In *Tikhii okean—liudiam* [The Pacific Ocean—For People], R. B. Mamaeva, comp., 3–5. Moscow: Znanie, 1983.

Sobolevskii, E. I. "Morskie mlekopitaiushchie Okhotskogo moria, ikh raspredelenie, chislennost' i rol' kak potrebitelei drugikh zhivotnykh" [Marine Mammals of the Sea of Okhotsk, Their Distribution, Number and Role as Consumers of Other Animals]. *Biologiia moria*, 1983, no. 5:13–20.

"Sozdanie instituta biologiia moria" [Creation of the Institute of Marine Biology]. AN *Vestnik*, 1970, no. 10:143.

Suziumov, Evgenii Matveevich. "50-letie Tikhookeanskoi nauchnoi assotsiatsii" [The 50th Anniversary of the Pacific Science Association]. AN *Vestnik*, 1970, no. 8:103–108.

"Tikhookeanskii nauchno-issledovatel'skii institut rybnogo khoziaistva i okeanografii (TINRO)" [The Pacific Scientific-Research Institute of Fisheries and Oceanography (TINRO)]. *Biologiia moria*, 1978, no. 1:86–92.

"Zadachi zhurnala 'Biologiia moria' " [The Tasks of the Journal "Marine Biology"]. *Biologiia moria*, 1975, no. 1:5–6.

Zasel'skii, V. I. "Morskie biologicheskie stantsii na Dal'nem Vostoke v 1931–1941 gg." [Marine Biological Stations in the Far East in 1931–1941]. *Biologiia moria*, 1982, no. 4:63–66.

―――. "O pervykh Sovetskikh morskikh biologicheskikh stantsiiakh na Dal'nem Vostoke (1923–1931 gg.)" [On the First Soviet Marine Biological Stations in the Far East (1923–1931)]. *Biologiia moria*, 1982, no. 1:62–67.

Zenkevich, Lev Aleksandrovich, and Veniamin Grigor'evich Bogorov. "Biologicheskie resursy mirovogo okeana" [Biological Resources of the World Ocean]. In *Okean i chelovechestvo: Besedy po aktual'nym problemam nauki* [The Ocean and Mankind: Conversations about Urgent Problems of Science], 42–49. Moscow: Znanie, 1968.

Zenkovich, Boris Aleksandrovich. "Materialy k poznaniiu kitoobraznykh DV morei" [Materials on the Study of the Large Cetaceans of the Far Eastern Seas]. DVFAN *Vestnik*, 1934, no. 10:9–27.

Zhirmunskii, Aleksei Viktorovich. "Organizatsiia instituta biologii moria i osnovnye rezul'taty nauchnykh rabot za 1969 i 1970 gody" [Organization of the Institute of Marine Biology and the Basic Results of (Its) Scientific Work during 1969 and 1970]. AN SSSR, Dal'nevostochnyi nauchnyi tsentr, Institut biologii moria. *Nauchnye soobshcheniia*, 1971, no. 2:9–15.

Zolotarev, V. N. "Pervaia vsesoiuznaia konferentsiia po morskoi biologii" [The First All-Union Conference on Marine Biology]. *Biologiia moria*, 1978, no. 5:91–93.

Contributors

John E. Bardach, former director of the Hawaii Institute of Marine Biology, has represented the U.S. National Academy of Sciences on the Council of the Pacific Science Association (PSA) and is director of the PSA's Institute of Pacific Science, Honolulu, Hawaii. He is also adjunct professor in the departments of geography and oceanography at the University of Hawaii, and adjunct research associate at the East-West Center in Honolulu.

Barry W. Butcher was educated at the University of Melbourne, Australia, majoring in the history and philosophy of science. He has interests in both the history of Australian science and the sociology of knowledge. He is writing a doctoral thesis on "The Reception and Impact of Darwinism in Australia, 1860–1914," and he teaches in the social studies of science at Deakin University, Geelong, Victoria, Australia.

David G. Frodin was educated in botany at universities in the United States and Great Britain, completing his Ph.D. at Cambridge with a study on the umbrella-tree genus *Schefflera*. For fifteen years he was with the University of Papua New Guinea in Port Moresby, where he taught in botany, ecology, and general biology. During this time he also became interested in the history of botany in New Guinea. He is the author or coauthor of two books and many articles, among them the reference *Guide to Stan-*

dard Floras of the World (1984). In 1986 he became a research associate at the Academy of Natural Sciences of Philadelphia, Pennsylvania, and in March 1987 became collections manager in botany at the same institution.

Alan Frost was educated at the universities of Queensland and Rochester, New York, taking his doctorate in English literature. He is the author of *Convicts and Empire: A Naval Question, 1776–1811* (1980) and *Arthur Phillip, 1738–1814: His Voyaging* (1987). He teaches Australian history at La Trobe University, Melbourne.

Miranda Hughes was educated at the University of Melbourne, taking her degree in history and philosophy of science. Her Ph.D. thesis concerns the development of the social sciences at the beginning of the nineteenth century in Paris. She currently teaches history and philosophy of science at Melbourne.

Roy MacLeod is professor of history at the University of Sydney, where he teaches imperial history, military history, and the history of science. He has held university appointments at Cambridge, Sussex, and London, and visiting positions in Paris and Amsterdam, in Washington, D.C., and at Harvard. He is the author of many articles and has written and edited several books, including, as coeditor (with G. Lemaine et al.) *Perspectives on the Emergence of New Disciplines* (1976); (with W. H. Brock) *Natural Knowledge in Social Context: The Journals of Thomas Archer Hirst, FRS* (1979); (with P. Collins) *The Parliament of Science* (1981); and (with M. Lewis) *Disease, Medicine and Empire* (1988). He has also edited and contributed to *The Commonwealth of Science* (1988) and *Government and Expertise in Nineteenth-Century Britain* (1988). He is coeditor of the journal *Social Studies of Science*. His current work includes studies of Australian science and European scientific endeavor in the Pacific and Antarctic regions.

Isabel Ollivier was educated in French and English literature at the universities of Canterbury and Auckland, New Zealand. For some years she has been transcribing and translating shipboard journals from French voyages in New Zealand for a series on *Early Eyewitness Accounts of Maori Life,* published by the Alexander Turnbull Library, Wellington. She is preparing a doctoral thesis at the University of Paris VII on French accounts of New Zealand.

Robert H. Randolph was educated at Yale and Stanford, taking his degrees in Soviet and East European history. He has conducted research at the Institute for the Future (Middletown, Connecticut, and Menlo Park, California); at the International Institute for Applied Systems Analysis (Laxenburg, Austria), where he was a member of a Soviet-led team concerned with science and technology policy; and at the East-West Center (Honolulu, Hawaii), where he was assistant director of the Resource Systems Institute. Dr. Randolph has written on science and technology in the Soviet Union and in the Pacific basin, on international scientific cooperation, and on technology assessment. He is currently assistant director of the National Council for Soviet and East European Research in Washington, D.C.

Philip F. Rehbock was educated at Stanford University and received his doctorate in history of science from Johns Hopkins. He is the author of *The Philosophical Naturalists: Themes in Early Nineteenth-Century British Biology* (1983) and articles on the history of biology and oceanography. He served as editor of the *Hawaiian Journal of History* and is currently editing the *Challenger* letters of Joseph Matkin, under the auspices of Scripps Institution of Oceanography, La Jolla, California. He also edits the *Pacific Circle Newsletter.* He teaches in the history and general science departments at the University of Hawaii in Honolulu.

Harry N. Scheiber is professor of law in the Jurisprudence and Social Policy Program of the School of Law, University of California, Berkeley. He has published extensively on environmental law and policy.

O. H. K. Spate read English and Geography at Cambridge, and after service at the University of Rangoon and the London School of Economics, became Foundation Professor of Geography at the Australian National University. He is a Visiting Fellow in the Australian National University's Research School of Pacific Studies, of which he was director in 1967–1972. He has written a standard geography of India and Pakistan and many papers on historical and geographical themes, especially concerning South and Southeast Asia and the Pacific. He has recently completed a three-volume history of *The Pacific since Magellan*.

Index

Vaillant, M., 47
Vancouver, Captain George, 13, 14, 21, 39
Van Diemen's Land. See Tasmanians
van Steenis, Cornelis, 120
Vaughn, T. Wayland, 198
Venus, transit of, 17, 33
Veron, Pierre, 31
Vitiaz (ship), 255
Vogt, Carl, 146
Voltaire, 15
von Hansemann, Adolph, 107, 115
von Mueller, Ferdinand, 103, 104, 130 n. 33, 131 n. 44, 142, 155 n. 7
Voyage aux îles de Mangareva (Oceanie). See Lesson, Pierre-Adolphe
Voyage des découvertes aux terres Australes. See Péron, François
Voyage of the Beagle. See Darwin, Charles
Voyage round the World, 1748. See Anson, George
Voyage round the World, 1777. See Forster, George
Voyages and Adventures of Captain Robert Boyle. See Chetwood, William

Wafer, Lionel, 14
Wager (ship), 16
Wales, William: The Original Astronomical Observations, 19
Wallace, Alfred Russel, 91–94, 97, 98, 100, 104; The Geographical Distribution of Animals, 92, 93 (illus.); The Malay Archipelago, 91
Wallis, Helen, 18
Wallis, Samuel, 17, 30, 31, 33
Walpole, Horace, 17
Warburg, Otto, 126 n. 5
Washington, Henry S., 209
Watts, W. W., 165
Weber, Max, 113
Wesley, John, 19
Wharton, William, 165, 167, 169, 183–184 n. 25, 185 n. 34, 186 n. 40
White, Cyril Tenison, 109
Whitlam, Gough, 7
Wilkes, Charles. See Wilkes Expedition
Wilkes Expedition, 3, 23, 161, 224
Willey, Arthur, 134 n. 72
Williams, Francis Edgar, 132 n. 53, 133 n. 57
Woman of Pleasure, 18
Woods-Jones, Frederick, 178
Woolls, William, 157 n. 40
Woolnough, W. G., 187 n. 40
Worcester, Dean C., 137 n. 98
World Encompassed by Sir Francis Drake, The, 13

Young, Robert, 140

Zelée (ship), 97
Zenkovich, Aleksandrovich, 262
Zhirmunskii, Aleksei Viktorovich, 256
Zipelius, Alexander, 96, 97, 128 n. 18
Zollinger, Heinrich, 97, 129 n. 26

Production Notes

This book was designed by Roger Eggers.
Composition and paging were done on the
Quadex Composing System and typesetting on
the Compugraphic 8400 by the design and
production staff of University of Hawaii Press.

The text typeface is Sabon and the display
typefaces are Sabon and Galliard.

Offset presswork and binding were done by
Vail-Ballou Press, Inc. Text paper is Writers
RR Offset, basis 50.